CYBER 2021

The Sixth International Conference on Cyber-Technologies and Cyber-Systems

October 3 - 7, 2021

Barcelona, Spain

CYBER 2021 Editors

Steve Chan, Decision Engineering Analysis Laboratory, USA

Joshua A. Sipper, Cyber Warfare Studies, Air Force Cyber College, USA

Printed from e-media with permission by:

Curran Associates, Inc.
57 Morehouse Lane
Red Hook, NY 12571

Some format issues inherent in the e-media version may also appear in this print version.

International Academy, Research, and Industry Association (IARIA)
412 Derby Way
Wilmington, DE 19810

Phone: (408) 893-6407
Fax: (408) 527-6351

petre@iaria.org

Additional copies of this publication are available from:

Curran Associates, Inc.
57 Morehouse Lane
Red Hook, NY 12571 USA
Phone: 845-758-0400
Fax: 845-758-2633
Email: curran@proceedings.com
Web: www.proceedings.com

Table of Contents

CYBER 2021

Forward

The Sixth International Conference on Cyber-Technologies and Cyber-Systems (CYBER 2021) continued a series of events covering many aspects related to cyber-systems and cyber-technologies considering their challenges and potential solutions. It was also intended to illustrate appropriate current academic and industry cyber-system projects, prototypes, and deployed products and services.

The increased size and complexity of the communications and networking infrastructures are making it difficult to investigate resiliency, security, safety, and crimes. Mobility, anonymity, counterfeiting, are characteristics that add more complexity in Internet of Things and Cloud-based solutions. Cyber-physical systems exhibit a strong link between the computational and physical elements. Techniques for cyber resilience, cyber security, protecting the cyber infrastructure, cyber forensic and cybercrimes have been developed and deployed. Some new solutions are nature-inspired and social-inspired, leading to self-secure and self-defending systems. Despite the achievements, security and privacy, disaster management, social forensics, and anomalies/crimes detection remain challenges within cyber-systems.

We take here the opportunity to warmly thank all the members of the CYBER 2021 technical program committee, as well as all the reviewers. The creation of such a high-quality conference program would not have been possible without their involvement. We also kindly thank all the authors who dedicated much of their time and effort to contribute to CYBER 2021. We truly believe that, thanks to all these efforts, the final conference program consisted of top-quality contributions. We also thank the members of the CYBER 2021 organizing committee for their help in handling the logistics of this event.

CYBER 2021 Chairs

CYBER 2021 General Chair
Steve Chan, Decision Engineering Analysis Laboratory, USA

CYBER 2021 Steering Committee
Carla Merkle Westphall, UFSC, Brazil
Barbara Re, University of Camerino, Italy
Rainer Falk, Siemens AG, Corporate Technology, Germany
Soultana Ellinidou, Cybersecurity Research Center | University Libre de Bruxelles (ULB), Belgium
Anne Coull, University of New South Wales, Australia
Patrik Österberg, Mid Sweden University, Sundsvall, Sweden
Daniel Kästner, AbsInt GmbH, Germany
Steffen Fries, Siemens, Germany

CYBER 2021 Publicity Chairs
Lorena Parra, Universitat Politecnica de Valencia, Spain
José Miguel Jiménez, Universitat Politecnica de Valencia, Spain

CYBER 2021
Committee

CYBER 2021 General Chair
Steve Chan, Decision Engineering Analysis Laboratory, USA

CYBER 2021 Steering Committee
Carla Merkle Westphall, UFSC, Brazil
Barbara Re, University of Camerino, Italy
Rainer Falk, Siemens AG, Corporate Technology, Germany
Soultana Ellinidou, Cybersecurity Research Center | University Libre de Bruxelles (ULB), Belgium
Anne Coull, University of New South Wales, Australia
Patrik Österberg, Mid Sweden University, Sundsvall, Sweden
Daniel Kästner, AbsInt GmbH, Germany
Steffen Fries, Siemens, Germany

CYBER 2021 Publicity Chairs
Lorena Parra, Universitat Politecnica de Valencia, Spain
José Miguel Jiménez, Universitat Politecnica de Valencia, Spain

CYBER 2021 Technical Program Committee
Aysajan Abidin, imec-COSIC KU Leuven, Belgium
Shakil Ahmed, Iowa State University, USA
Cuneyt Gurcan Akcora, University of Manitoba, Canada
Khalid Alemerien, Tafila Technical University, Jordan
Usman Ali, University of Connecticut, USA
Mohammed S Alshehri, University of Arkansas, Fayetteville, USA
Marios Anagnostopoulos, Critical Infrastructure Security and Resilience group - Norwegian University of Science & Technology, Norway
Alina Andronache, University of West of Scotland, UK
Abdullahi Arabo, University of the West of England, UK
A. Taufiq Asyhari, Coventry University, UK
Morgan Barbier, ENSICAEN, France
Sébastien Bardin, Université Paris-Saclay | CEA LIST, France
Samuel Bate, EY, UK
Vincent Beroulle, Univ. Grenoble Alpes, France
Khurram Bhatti, Information Technology University (ITU), Lahore, Pakistan
Davidson R. Boccardo, Clavis Information Security, Brazil
Ravi Borgaonkar, SINTEF Digital / University of Stavanger, Norway
Enrico Cambiaso, Consiglio Nazionale delle Ricerche (CNR), Italy
Nicola Capodieci, University of Modena and Reggio Emilia (UNIMORE), Italy
Pedro Castillejo Parrilla, Technical University of Madrid (UPM), Spain
Steve Chan, Decision Engineering Analysis Laboratory, USA
Christophe Charrier, Normandie Universite, France
Bo Chen, Michigan Technological University, USA
Mingwu Chen, Langara College, Canada
Lu Cheng, ArizonaState University, USA

Ioannis Chrysakis, FORTH-ICS, Greece / Ghent University, Belgium
Giovanni Costa, ICAR-CNR, Italy
Domenico Cotroneo, University of Naples, Italy
Anne Coull, University of New South Wales, Australia
Heming Cui, University of Hong Kong, Hong Kong
Monireh Dabaghchian, Morgan State University, USA
Vincenzo De Angelis, University of Reggio Calabria, Italy
Lorenzo De Carli, Worcester Polytechnic Institute, USA
Noel De Palma, University Grenoble Alpes, France
Luigi De Simone, Università degli Studi di Napoli Federico II, Italy
Jerker Delsing, Lulea University of Technology, Sweden
Nicolás E. Díaz Ferreyra, University of Duisburg-Essen, Germany
Patrício Domingues, Polytechnic Institute of Leiria, Portugal
Paul Duplys, Robert Bosch GmbH, Germany
Soultana Ellinidou, Cybersecurity Research Center | University Libre de Bruxelles (ULB), Belgium
Rainer Falk, Siemens AG, Corporate Technology, Germany
Omair Faraj, Internet Interdisciplinary Institute (IN3) | UOC, Barcelona, Spain
Umer Farooq, Dhofar University, Slalalah, Oman
Yebo Feng, University of Oregon, USA
Eduardo B. Fernandez, Florida Atlantic University, USA
Steffen Fries, Siemens Corporate Technologies, Germany
Damjan Fujs, University of Ljubljana, Slovenia
Steven Furnell, University of Nottingham, UK
Gina Gallegos Garcia, Instituto Politécnico Nacional, Mexico
Kambiz Ghazinour, SUNY Canton, USA
Uwe Glässer, Simon Fraser University - SFU, Canada
Mehran Goli, The University of Bremen - Institute of Computer Science / German Research Centre for Artificial Intelligence (DFKI), Bremen, Germany
Chunhui Guo, San Diego State University, USA
Amir M. Hajisadeghi, AmirkabirUniversity of Technology, Iran
Arne Hamann, Robert Bosch GmbH, Germany
Zecheng He, Princeton University, USA
Ehsan Hesamifard, University of North Texas, USA
Gahangir Hossain, West Texas A&M University, Canyon, USA
Mehdi Hosseinzadeh, Washington University in St. Louis, USA
Zhen Huang, DePaul University, USA
Maria Francesca Idone, University of Reggio Calabria, Italy
Christos Iliou, Information Technologies Institute | CERTH, Greece / Bournemouth University, UK
Kevin Jones, University of Plymouth, UK
Georgios Kambourakis, University of the Aegean - Karlovassi, Samos, Greece
Sayar Karmakar, University of Florida, USA
Saffija Kasem-Madani, University of Bonn, Germany
Daniel Kästner, AbsInt GmbH, Germany
Basel Katt, Norwegian University of Science and Technology (NTNU), Norway
Mazaher Kianpour, Norwegian University of Science and Technology, Norway
Sotitios Kontogiannis, University of Ioannina, Greece
Maria Krommyda, Institute of Communication & Computer Systems (ICCS), Greece
Dragana S. Krstic, University of Nis, Serbia

Fatih Kurugollu, University of Derby, UK
Cecilia Labrini, University of Reggio Calabria, Italy
Ruggero Lanotte, University of Insubria, Italy
Petra Leimich, Edinburgh Napier University, Scotland, UK
Rafał Leszczyna, Gdansk University of Technology, Poland
Eirini Liotou, National and Kapodistrian University of Athens, Greece
Jing-Chiou Liou, Kean University - School of Computer Science and Technology, USA
Hao Liu, University of Cincinnati, USA
Xing Liu, Kwantlen Polytechnic University, Canada
Qinghua Lu, CSIRO, Australia
Yi Lu, Queensland University of Technology, Australia
Mahesh Nath Maddumala, Mercyhurst University, Erie, USA
Jorge Maestre Vidal, Universidad Complutense de Madrid, Spain
Louai Maghrabi, Dar Al-Hekma University, Jeddah, Saudi Arabia
Yasamin Mahmoodi, Tübingen University | FZI (Forschungszentrum Informatik), Germany
David Maimon, Georgia State University, USA
Timo Malderle, University of Bonn, Germany
Mahdi Manavi, Mirdamad Institute of Higher Education, Iran
Sayonnha Mandal, St. Ambrose University, USA
Sathiamoorthy Manoharan, University of Auckland, New Zealand
Michael Massoth, Hochschule Darmstadt - University of Applied Sciences / CRISP – Center for Research in Security and Privacy, Darmstadt, Germany
Vasileios Mavroeidis, University of Oslo, Finland
Golizheh Mehrooz, University of Southern Denmark, Denmark
Carla Merkle Westphall, UFSC, Brazil
Massimo Merro, University of Verona, Italy
Caroline Moeckel, Royal Holloway University, UK
Yasir F. Mohammed, University of Arkansas, USA
Lorenzo Musarella, University Mediterranea of Reggio Calabria, Italy
Maria Mushtaq, LIRMM | Univ. Montpellier | CNRS, Montpellier, France
Vasudevan Nagendra, Stony Brook University, USA
Roberto Nardone, University Mediterranea of Reggio Calabria, Italy
Klimis Ntalianis, University of West Attica, Greece
Jason Nurse, University of Kent, UK
Jordi Ortiz, University of Murcia, Spain
Patrik Österberg, Mid Sweden University, Sundsvall, Sweden
Richard E. Overill, King's College London, UK
Antonio Pecchia, University of Sannio, Italy
Eckhard Pfluegel, Kingston University, London, UK
Mila Dalla Preda, University of Verona, Italy
Paweł Rajba, Institute of Computer Science | University of Wrocław, Poland
Ramesh Rakesh, Hitachi India Private Limited, India
Danda B. Rawat, Howard University, USA
Barbara Re, University of Camerino, Italy
Antonio J. Reinoso, Alfonso X University, Spain
Leon Reznik, Rochester Institute of Technology, USA
Jan Richling, South Westphalia University of Applied Sciences, Germany
Giulio Rigoni, University of Florence / University of Perugia, Italy

Andres Robles Durazno, Edinburgh Napier University, UK
Antonia Russo,University Mediterranea of Reggio Calabria, Italy
Peter Y. A. Ryan, UniversityofLuxembourg, Luxembourg
Asanka P. Sayakkara, University of Colombo School of Computing (UCSC), Sri Lanka
Florence Sedes, Université Toulouse 3 Paul Sabatier, France
Abhijit Sen, Kwantlen Polytechnic University, Canada
Luisa Siniscalchi, AarhusUniversity, Denmark
Daniel Spiekermann, Polizeiakademie Niedersachsen, Germany
Srivathsan Srinivasagopalan, AT&T CyberSecurity (Alien Labs), USA
Ciza Thomas, Government of Kerala, India
Zisis Tsiatsikas, Atos Greece / University of the Aegean, Greece
Tobias Urban, Institute for Internet Security - Westphalian University of Applied Sciences, Gelsenkirchen, Germany
Eric MSP Veith, OFFIS e.V. - Institut für Informatik, Germany
Simon Vrhovec, University of Maribor, Slovenia
Stefanos Vrochidis, ITI-CERTH, Greece
James Wagner, University of New Orleans, USA
Khan Ferdous Wahid, Airbus Digital Trust Solutions, Germany
Ruoyu "Fish" Wang, Arizona State University, USA
Zhiyong Wang, Utrecht University, Netherlands
Zhen Xie, JD.com American Technologies Corporation, USA
Cong-Cong Xing, Nicholls State University, USA
Ping Yang, State University of New York at Binghamton, USA
Wuu Yang, National Chiao-Tung University, HsinChu, Taiwan
George O. M. Yee, Aptusinnova Inc. & Carleton University, Ottawa, Canada
Kailiang Ying, Google, USA
Yicheng Zhang, University of California, Irvine, USA
Piotr Zwierzykowski, Poznan University of Technology, Poland

Copyright Information

For your reference, this is the text governing the copyright release for material published by IARIA.

The copyright release is a transfer of publication rights, which allows IARIA and its partners to drive the dissemination of the published material. This allows IARIA to give articles increased visibility via distribution, inclusion in libraries, and arrangements for submission to indexes.

I, the undersigned, declare that the article is original, and that I represent the authors of this article in the copyright release matters. If this work has been done as work-for-hire, I have obtained all necessary clearances to execute a copyright release. I hereby irrevocably transfer exclusive copyright for this material to IARIA. I give IARIA permission or reproduce the work in any media format such as, but not limited to, print, digital, or electronic. I give IARIA permission to distribute the materials without restriction to any institutions or individuals. I give IARIA permission to submit the work for inclusion in article repositories as IARIA sees fit.

I, the undersigned, declare that to the best of my knowledge, the article is does not contain libelous or otherwise unlawful contents or invading the right of privacy or infringing on a proprietary right.

Following the copyright release, any circulated version of the article must bear the copyright notice and any header and footer information that IARIA applies to the published article.

IARIA grants royalty-free permission to the authors to disseminate the work, under the above provisions, for any academic, commercial, or industrial use. IARIA grants royalty-free permission to any individuals or institutions to make the article available electronically, online, or in print.

IARIA acknowledges that rights to any algorithm, process, procedure, apparatus, or articles of manufacture remain with the authors and their employers.

I, the undersigned, understand that IARIA will not be liable, in contract, tort (including, without limitation, negligence), pre-contract or other representations (other than fraudulent misrepresentations) or otherwise in connection with the publication of my work.

Exception to the above is made for work-for-hire performed while employed by the government. In that case, copyright to the material remains with the said government. The rightful owners (authors and government entity) grant unlimited and unrestricted permission to IARIA, IARIA's contractors, and IARIA's partners to further distribute the work.

Enhancing Attack Resilience in the Presence of Manipulated IoT Devices within a Cyber Physical System

Rainer Falk, Steffen Fries
Corporate Technology
Siemens AG
Munich, Germany
e-mail: {rainer.falk|steffen.fries}@siemens.com

***Abstract*—Industrial cyber physical systems are exposed to attacks. Security standards define how such systems and the used devices can be protected against attacks (prevent). Despite all efforts to protect from attacks, it should always be assumed that attacks may happen. Security monitoring allows to detect successful attacks (detect), so that corresponding measures can be performed (react). This prevent-detect-react cycle is common approach in security of information technology and operation technology. This paper describes an additional approach for protecting cyber physical systems. The devices are designed in a way that makes it harder to use them for launching attacks on other devices. A device-internal hardware-based or isolated firewall limits the network traffic that the device software executed on the device can send or receive. Even if the device software contains a vulnerability allowing an attacker to compromise the device, the possible impact on other connected devices is limited, thereby enhancing the resilience of the cyber physical system in the presence of manipulated devices.**

Keywords–cyber security; cyber resilience; system integrity; cyber physical systems; industrial automation and control system; Internet of Things.

I. INTRODUCTION

Traditionally, IT security has been focusing on information security, protecting confidentiality, integrity, and availability of data at rest and data in transit, and sometimes also protecting data in use by confidential computation. In Cyber-Physical Systems (CPS), major protection goals are availability, meaning that automation systems stay productive, and system integrity, ensuring that it is operating as intended. Typical application domains are factory automation, process automation, building automation, railway signaling systems, intelligent traffic management, and power system management. Cyber security is covering different phases during operation as there are protect, detect, and react: Protecting against threats, detecting when an attack has occurred, and recovering from attacks.

When designing a security solution for a CPS or a device used within the CPS, the focus is on protecting the assets of the CPS or device, by preventing attacks against the relevant assets. However, this is not sufficient from a more holistic perspective: Also, the environment of a device or a CPS has to be protected from attacks originating from a manipulated CPS or one of its devices. In particular, Internet of Things (IoT) devices have been attacked with the objective to use them for launching attacks against *other* systems. Dao, Phan et al. described distributed denial of service (DDoS) attacks originating from manipulated IoT devices [1]. As (consumer) IoT devices have often also a weak security management, so that vulnerabilities are often not patched in time, making them an easy victim.

This paper presents an approach for protecting the network environment, i.e., other devices of a CPS and further connect devices, from attacks originating from a manipulated component of the CPS. The objective is to limit the impact of a manipulated CPS device on other devices of the CPS, enhancing resilience of the CPS. The intention is to keep the CPS in an operational state even if some devices of the CPS should have been successfully attacked and be manipulated. Devices have to be designed in a way that it is made hard to use them for attacks even if they should be hacked. After giving an overview on cyber physical systems and on industrial cyber security in Sections II and III, a new approach on protecting the network environment from manipulated devices of a CPS is described in Section IV. It is a concept to increase the resilience of a CPS when being under attack. Aspects to evaluate the new approach are discussed in Section V. Section VI concludes the paper.

II. CYBER PHYSICAL SYSTEMS

A cyber-physical system, e.g., an Industrial Automation and Control System (IACS), monitors and controls a technical system. Examples are process automation, machine control, energy automation, and cloud robotics. Automation control equipment with sensors (S) and actuators (A) is connected directly with automation components, or via remote input/output modules. The technical process is controlled by measuring its current state using the sensors, and by determining the corresponding actuator signals.

Figure 1 shows an example of an industrial automation and control system, comprising different control networks connected to a plant network and a cloud backend system. Separation of the network is typically used to realize distinct control networks with strict real-time requirements for the interaction between sensors and actuators of a production cell,

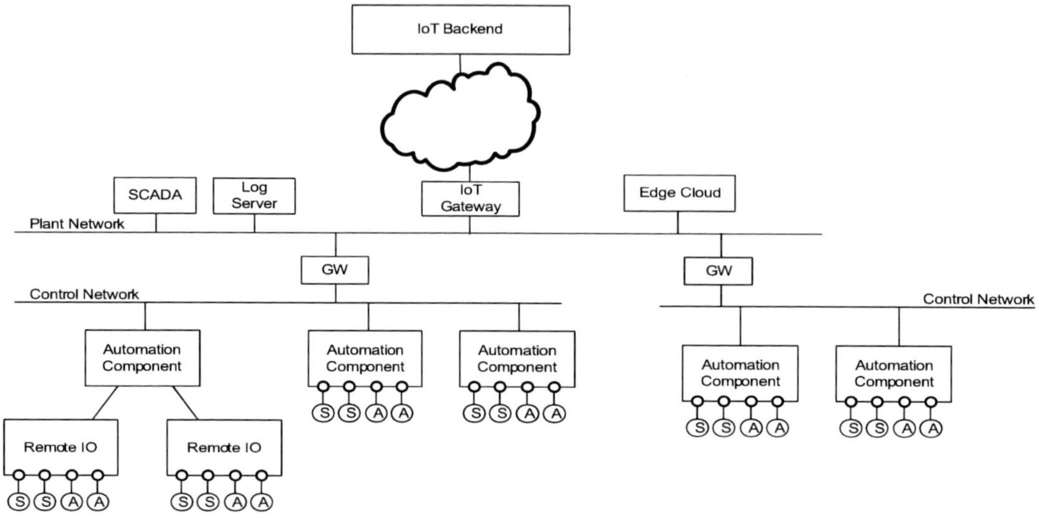

Figure 1. Example – Industrial Automation and Control System

or to enforce a specific security policy within a production cell. Such an industrial automation and control system is an example of a CPS and is utilized in various automation domains, including discrete automation (factory automation), process automation, railway automation, energy automation, and building automation.

Figure 2 shows the typical simplified structure of automation components. The functionality realized by an automation component is largely defined by the firmware/software and the configuration data stored in its flash memory.

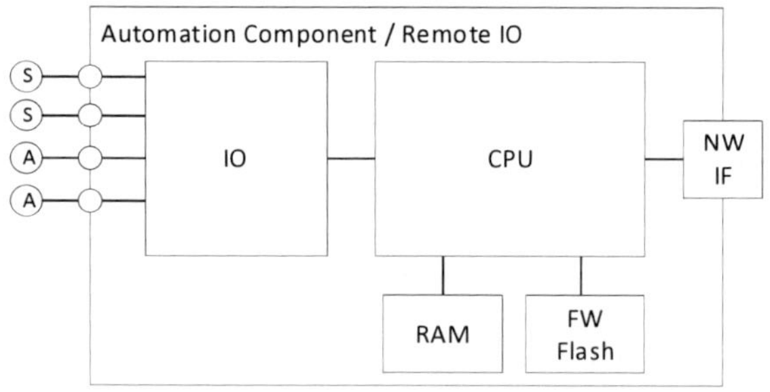

Figure 2. Automation Component

In practice, it has to be assumed that each software component may comprise vulnerabilities, independent of the effort spend to ensure high software quality. This is one reason why automation systems are usually organized in separate security zones. Network traffic can be filtered using network firewalls between different zones, limiting the impact of an impact in one security zone on other connected security zones. In addition, it is often not possible to fix known vulnerabilities immediately by installing a software update, as updates have to be tested thoroughly in a test system before being installed in an operational system, and as an installation is often possible only during a scheduled maintenance window. Also, the priorities of security objectives in different security zones are often different, too. In CPSs, the impact of a vulnerability in an OT system may not only affect data and data processing as in classical IT, but it may have an effect also on the physical world. For example, production equipment could be damaged, or the physical process may operate outside the designed physical boundaries, so that the produced goods may not have the expected quality or even that human health or life is endangered.

III. Industrial Cyber Security

Protecting IACSs against intentional attacks is increasingly demanded by operators to ensure a reliable operation, and also by regulation. This section gives an overview on industrial security, and on the main relevant industrial security standard IEC 62443 [11].

A. Industrial CPS Security Requirements

Industrial security is called also Operation Technology security (OT security), to distinguish it from general Information Technology (IT) security. Industrial systems have not only different security requirements compared to general IT systems, but come also with specific side conditions preventing the direct application of security concepts established in the IT domain in an OT environment. For example, availability and integrity of an automation system often have a higher priority than confidentiality. As an example, high availability requirements, different organization processes (e.g., yearly maintenance windows), and required certifications may prevent the immediate installations of updates.

The three basic security requirements are confidentiality, integrity, and availability ("CIA" requirements). However, in automation systems or industrial IT, the priorities are commonly just the other way around: Availability of the IACS has typically the highest priority, followed by integrity. Confidentiality is often no strong requirement for control communications, but may be needed to protect critical business know-how.

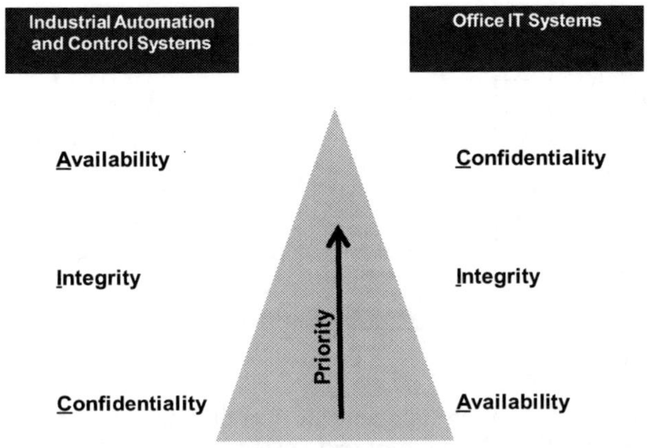

Figure 3. The CIA Pyramid [9]

Figure 3 shows that in common IT systems, the priority is "CIA". As shown graphically, the CIA pyramid is inverted (turned upside down) in many automation systems.

Specific requirements and side conditions of an IACS like high availability, planned configuration (engineering info), long life cycles, unattended operation, real-time operation, and communication, as well as safety requirements have to be considered when designing a cyber security solution. Often, an important aspect is that the applied security measures do not put availability and integrity of the automation system at risk. Depending on the considered industry (vertical), they may also be part of the critical infrastructure domain, for which security requirements are also imposed for instance by the European Network and Information Systems (NIS) directive [10] or country specific realizations of the directive. Further security requirements are provided by applying standards defining functional requirements, for instance defined in IEC 62443. The defined security requirements can be mapped to different automation domains, including energy automation, railway automation, building automation, process automation.

Security measures to address these requirements range from security processes, personal and physical security, device security, network security, and application security. No single security technology alone is adequate, but a combination of security measures addressing prevention, detection, and reaction to incidents is required ("defense in depth").

B. *Overview IEC 62443 Industrial Security Standard*

The international industrial security framework IEC 62443 [11] is a security requirements framework defined by the International Electrotechnical Commission (IEC). It addresses the need to design cybersecurity robustness and resilience into industrial automation and control systems, covering both organizational and technical aspects of security over the life cycle. Specific parts of this framework are applied successfully in different automation domains, including factory and process automation, railway automation, energy automation, and building automation. The standard specifies security for Industrial Automation and Control Systems (IACS) and covers both, organizational and technical aspects of security. Specifically addressed for the industrial domain is the setup of a security organization and the definition of security processes as part of an Information Security Management System (ISMS) based on already existing standards like ISO 27001 [12] or the NIST cyber security framework. Furthermore, technical security requirements are specified distinguishing different security levels for industrial automation and control systems, and also for the used components. The standard has been created to address the specific requirements of industrial automation and control systems.

Different parts of the IEC62443 standard are grouped into four clusters, covering:

– common definitions and metrics;
– requirements on setup of a security organization (ISMS related, similar to ISO 27001 [12]), as well as solution supplier and service provider processes;
– technical requirements and methodology for security on system-wide level, and
– requirements on the secure development lifecycle of system components, and security requirements to such components at a technical level.

The framework parts address different roles over different phases of the system lifecycle: The operator of an IACS operates the IACS that has been integrated by the system integrator, using components of product suppliers. In the set of corresponding documents, security requirements are defined, which target the solution operator and the integrator but also the product manufacturer.

According to the methodology described in IEC 62443 part 3-2, a complex automation system is structured into zones that are connected by and communicate through so-called "conduits" that map for example to the logical network protocol communication between two zones. Moreover, this document defines Security Levels (SL) that correspond with the strength of a potential adversary. To achieve a dedicated SL, the defined requirements have to be fulfilled.

Part 3-3 of IEC 62443 [14], addressing an overall automation system, is in particular relevant for the system integrator. It defines seven foundational requirements that group specific requirements of a certain category:

– FR 1 Identification and authentication control
– FR 2 Use control
– FR 3 System integrity
– FR 4 Data confidentiality
– FR 5 Restricted data flow
– FR 6 Timely response to events
– FR 7 Resource availability

For each of the foundational requirements, several concrete technical security requirements (SR) and requirement enhancements (RE) are defined. Related security requirements are defined for the components of an industrial automation and control system in IEC 62443 part 4-2 [15], addressing in particular component manufacturers.

IV. Protecting Network Environment from Manipulated IoT Devices

The security objective "resilience under attack" means that a CPS, e.g., an IACS or an industrial Internet of Things (IoT) environment, should stay operational even when some devices would be manipulated. Considering the manifold of devices used in real-world CPS, it has to be assumed that some of them will have vulnerabilities that can be used to install malware to attack other devices. Hence, it shall be avoided that a successfully hacked device can be used to launch attacks against other devices. This is a specific security objective: When designing the security architecture for a device, usually attacks against the device are investigated. Here, it shall be avoided that even if a device would be attacked successfully despite its designed-in protection means, the impact of this attack on the network environment is reduced.

The software execution environment executes the software (firmware) of the device that might have a vulnerability. A separated, e.g., a separate hardware based, on-device firewall limits the network communication that the executed software can perform. This enforcement is realized independently from the executed device software, so that it is still working even if the device software has been manipulated by an attacker. This independence is a necessary pre-requisite. In the described design, this independence is achieved by separate hardware-based component. However, the independence from the executed device software could be achieved also by using an isolated software execution environment, e.g., a separate processor or a separate trusted execution environment. Using a hardware-based realization has the advantage of limiting the impact on real-time communication properties as delay and jitter, and also on the energy consumption. It can be easily implemented if a dedicated hardware-based network interface is in use anyhow to support real-time communication protocols.

Possible filter criteria are source and destination network addresses, protocols, port numbers, transmit rate (frames/packets per second), or data volume. In an advanced form, the firewall may even verify on application level, whether certain control flows are aligned with either the typical (historical) behavior of the device or with an engineered process. The policy might be fixed, e.g., for embedded control devices with a fixed functionality, or configurable. Important is that the device software cannot modify the filter policy on its own.

The filter policy might be adapted automatically depending on the patch status of the device software, or depending on a cryptographically protected health check confirmation received from a device integrity monitoring service. This would allow to keep the system operational, although with potentially limited capabilities, thus keeping it resilient. Also, limiting specific functionalities as result of missing device integrity may stipulate the timely application of patches, to get the system back to normal operation with full functionality and performance.

Figure 4 shows an IoT Field Device with a central processing unit CPU executing device firmware/software stored in a flash of RAM memory.

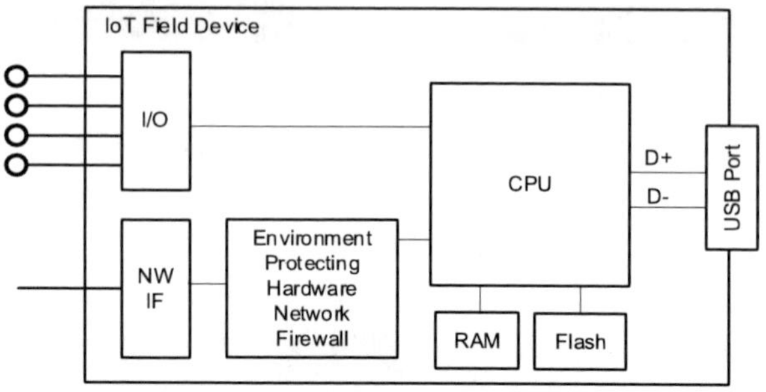

Figure 4. Attack-preventing IoT Device Architecture

The software can communicate over the network interface (NW IF) with other devices, e.g., using HTTPS or OPC UA over TCP/IP. Also, sensors and actuators can be connected via an input-output (I/O) interface. An USB interface allows to configure the device or to install a firmware update.

To enhance resilience, the device includes a hardware-based network firewall to protect the network environment from attacks originating from the IoT field device. It limits the type of network communication that can be performed by the device software executed on the CPU. This function is fixed, so that the device software cannot modify it, so that the filtering is performed with high level of trustworthiness. The hardware-based network firewall is still effective even if the device software should be manipulated.

The hardware-based firewall can be realized by an integrated circuit, e.g., an application-specific integrated circuit (ASIC), a field programmable gate array (FPGA), or a separate microcontroller or security controller, or it can be integrated with a hardware-based network interface. The filter policy might be adapted, depending on whether a cryptographically protected network access token (NAcT) is provided to the hardware firewall. The NAcT can be provided by a backend device integrity check service. The device software may provide a received NAcT token to the device hardware firewall, but cannot manipulate it. This allows the backend device integrity check service to temporarily activate a less restrictive policy if the device integrity has been verified successfully. A NAcT token can be protected by a cryptographic checksum, e.g., a digital signature (e.g., RSA, DSA, ECDSA) or a symmetric message authentication code (e.g., HMAC, AES-CBC-MAC). The NAcT token realizes an authenticated watchdog, as described by England, Aigner, Marochko, Mattoon, Spiger, and Thom [3]. However, here it is used for selecting a firewall policy, not for initiation a device recovery procedure. If an integrity monitoring system monitoring the integrity of control devices or a network-based intrusion detection system, realizing the device integrity check service, detects an ongoing attack in the IACS, it can limit reliably the network communications of devices, allowing to confine the attack.

A different approach compared to attack monitoring is to monitor write access to the flash memory, i.e., to check whether the device software (firmware) stored in the flash memory is updated regularly. The less restrictive, open filter policy stays activated only if the device firmware is updated regularly.

V. EVALUATION

While the original motivation for "plug and produce", as defined for Industry 4.0, is to increase flexibility in production and to reduce the time needed to reconfigure an automation environment for different manufacturing tasks or batches, this flexibility is also advantageous for increasing resilience under attack: Even if some of the devices are manipulated (attacked) and cannot be used for production until they are patched, the flexibility of the overall production system allows to reconfigure the IACS components, avoiding or at least limiting the interaction with affected devices. Therefore, production can continue, maybe with limitations, even when some devices should have been manipulated. When using the enhancement described in section IV, it depends on the specific IACS and on the specific attack scenario to what degree the IACS can stay operational under attack. For the evaluation, it has to be determined to what degree relevant risks of the IACS are reduced by introducing such protection measures.

The security of a CPS is evaluated in practice in various approaches and stages of the system's lifecycle:

- A Threat and Risk Analysis (TRA, also abbreviated as TARA) is typically conducted at the beginning of the product or system development, and updated after major design changes, or to address a changed threat landscape. In a TRA, possible attacks (threats) on the system are identified. The impact that would be caused by a successful attack and the probability that the attack happens are evaluated to determine the risk of the identified threats. The risk evaluation allows to prioritize the threats, focusing on the most relevant risks and to define corresponding security measures. Security measures can target to reduce the probability of an attack by preventing it, or by reducing the impact.
- Security checks can be performed during operation or during maintenance windows to determine key performance indicators (e.g., check compliance of device configurations) and to verified that the defined security measures are in fact in place.
- Security testing (penetration testing, also called pentesting for short) can be performed for a system that has been built, but that is currently not in operation. A pentest can usually not be performed on an operational automation and control system, as the pentest could endanger the reliable operation auf the system. Pentesting can be performed during a maintenance window when the physical system is in a safe state, or using a separate test system. Security testing can be performed also on a digital representation of a target system, e.g., a simulation in the easiest case. This digital representation is also called "digital twin". This allows to perform security checks and pentesting for systems that are not existing yet physically (design phase), or to perform pentesting of operational systems in the digital world without the risk of disturbing the regular operation of the real-world system.

As long as the technology proposed in the paper has not been proven in a real-world operational setting, it can be evaluated conceptually by analyzing the impact that the additional security measure would have on the identified residual risks as determined by a TRA. The general effect of the presented security measure is that the impact of a threat, i.e., a successful attack, on the physical world controlled by the CPS is reduced. Whatever attack is ongoing on the IT-based automation and control system, still the possible impact on the real, physical world is limited. While security measures often target the prevention of attacks, the proposed resilience measure reduces the impact and thereby the risk. The impact of a threat is reduced if the IACS in fact can stay operational, at least with limited functionality, in relevant attack scenarios.

However, TRAs for real-world CPS are not available publicly. Nevertheless, an illustrative example may be given by a chemical production plant performing a specific process like refinery, or a factory producing glue or cement. If the plant is attacked, the attack may target to destroy the production equipment by immediately stopping the process leading to physical hardening of the chemicals / consumables and thus to a permanent unavailability of the production equipment. In this case, trusted sensors could be used to detect a falsified sensor signal, and the physical-world firewall can be used to limit actions in the physical world. Both, the trusted sensors and the physical world firewall build a security overlay network, independent from the actual operational control network. Thereby, a physical damage of the production equipment can be avoided. If needed, a controlled shutdown of the production site can be performed.

As the evaluation in a real-world CPS requires significant effort, and as attack scenarios cannot be tested that could really have a (severe) impact on the physical world, a simulation-based approach or using specific test-beds are possible approaches, allowing to simulate or evaluate in a protected test-bed the effect on the physical world of certain attack scenarios with compromised components. The simulation would have to include not only the IT-based control function, but also the physical world impact of an attack. Using physical-world simulation and test beds to evaluate the impact of attacks have been described by Urbina, Giraldo et al. [24].

VI. CONCLUSION

A CPS comprises the operational cyber-technology and the physical world with which the system interacts. Both parts have to be covered by a security concept and solution. Traditional cyber security puts the focus on the cyber-part, i.e., automation and control systems. The security of the physical part, like machinery, is protected often by physical and organizational security measures, only. This paper presented a concept for a new approach that enhances the resilience of a CPS in the presence of attacked devices, by making it harder that a compromised device is used for attacking other devices of the CPS. This can be a useful element to ensure the availability of the automation system, as even under attack, the automation system has not to be shut down. It is complementary to other approaches for enhancing CPS resilience by protecting the physical-world interface [2].

REFERENCES

[1] N. N. Dao, T. V. Phan, Umar Sa'ad, Joongheon Kim, Thomas Bauschert, and Sungrae Cho, "Securing Heterogeneous IoT with Intelligent DDoS Attack Behavior Learning", arXiv: 1711.06041v3 [cs.NI] 7 Aug 2019, [Online]. Available from: https://arxiv.org/pdf/1711.06041.pdf [retrieved August, 2021]

[2] R. Falk and S. Fries, "Enhancing Resilience by Protecting the Physical-World Interface of Cyber-Physical Systems", The Fourth International Conference on Cyber-Technologies and Cyber-Systems CYBER 2019, pp. 6–11, September 22, 2019 to September 26, 2019 - Porto, Portugal, [Online]. Available from: https://www.thinkmind.org/index.php?view=article&articleid=cyber_2019_1_20_80033 [retrieved August, 2021]

[3] P. England, R. Aigner, A. Marochko, D. Mattoon, R. Spiger, and S. Thom, "Cyber resilient platforms", Microsoft Technical Report MSR-TR-2017-40, Sep. 2017, [Online]. Available from: https://www.microsoft.com/en-us/research/publication/cyber-resilient-platforms-overview/ [retrieved August, 2021]

[4] Electronic Communications Resilience&Response Group, "EC-RRG resilience guidelines for providers of critical national telecommunications infrastructure", version 0.7, March 2008, available from: https://assets.publishing.service.gov.uk/government/uploads/system/uploads/attachment_data/file/62281/telecoms-ecrrg-resilience-guidelines.pdf [retrieved August, 2021]

[5] D. Urbina, J. Giraldo, N. O. Tippenhauer, and A. Cardenas, "Attacking fieldbus communications in ICS: applications to the SWaT testbed", Singapore Cyber-Security Conference (SG-CRC), IOS press, pp. 75–89, 2016, [Online]. Available from: http://ebooks.iospress.nl/volumearticle/42054 [retrieved August, 2021]

[6] C. C. Davidson, T. R. Andel, M. Yampolskiy, J. T. McDonald, W. B. Glisson, and T. Thomas, "On SCADA PLC and fieldbus cyber security", 13th International Conference on Cyber Warfare and Security, National Defense University, Washington, DC, pp. 140–148, 2018

[7] D. Bodeau and R. Graubart, "Cyber resiliency design principles", MITRE Technical Report, January 2017, [Online]. Available from: https://www.mitre.org/sites/default/files/publications/PR%20170103%20Cyber%20Resiliency%20Design%20Principles%20MTR17001.pdf [retrieved August, 2021]

[8] A. Kott and I. Linkov (Eds.), "Cyber Resilience of Systems and Networks", Springer, 2019

[9] R. Falk and S. Fries, "Enhancing integrity protection for industrial cyber physical systems", The Second International Conference on Cyber-Technologies and Cyber-Systems, CYBER 2017, pp. 35–40, November 12 - 16, 2017, Barcelona, Spain, [Online]. Available from: http://www.thinkmind.org/index.php?view=article&articleid=cyber_2017_3_30_80031 [retrieved August, 2021]

[10] European Commission, "The directive on security of network and information systems (NIS Directive)", [Online]. Available from: https://ec.europa.eu/digital-single-market/en/network-and-information-security-nis-directive [retrieved August, 2021]

[11] IEC 62443, "Industrial automation and control system security" (formerly ISA99), [Online]. Available from: https://webstore.iec.ch/searchform&q=62443 [retrieved August, 2021]

[12] ISO/IEC 27001, "Information technology – security techniques – Information security management systems – requirements", October 2013, [Online]. Available from: https://www.iso.org/standard/54534.html [retrieved August, 2021]

[13] NIST, "Framework for Improving Critical Infrastructure Cybersecurity", Version 1.1, April 16, 2018, [Online]. Available from: https://nvlpubs.nist.gov/nistpubs/CSWP/NIST.CSWP.04162018.pdf [retrieved August, 2021]

[14] IEC 62443-3-3:2013, "Industrial communication networks – network and system security – Part 3-3: System security requirements and security levels", Edition 1.0, August 2013

[15] IEC 62443-4.2, "Industrial communication networks - security for industrial automation and control systems - Part 4-2: technical security requirements for IACS components", Feb. 2019

[16] P. Bock, J. P. Hauet, R. Françoise, and R. Foley, "Ukrainian power grids cyberattack - A forensic analysis based on ISA/IEC 62443", ISA InTech magazine, 2017, [Online]. Available from: https://www.isa.org/intech-home/2017/march-april/features/ukrainian-power-grids-cyberattack [retrieved August, 2021]

[17] ZVEI, "Orientation guideline for manufacturers on IEC 62443", "Orientierungsleitfaden für Hersteller zur IEC 62443" [German], ZVEI Whitepaper, 2017, [Online]. Available from: https://www.zvei.org/presse-medien/publikationen/orientierungsleitfaden-fuer-hersteller-zur-iec-62443/ [retrieved August, 2021]

[18] H. R. Ghaeini, M. Chan, R. Bahmani, F. Brasser, L. Garcia, J. Zhou, A. R. Sadeghi, N. O. Tippenhauer, and S. Zonouz, "PAtt: Physics-based Attestation of Control Systems", 22nd International Symposium on Research in Attacks, Intrusions and Defenses, USENIX, pp. 165–180, September 23-25, 2019, [Online]. Available from: https://www.usenix.org/system/files/raid2019-ghaeini.pdf [retrieved August, 2021]

[19] Plattform Industrie 4.0, "Industrie 4.0 Plug-and-produce for adaptable factories: example use case definition, models, and implementation", Plattform Industrie 4.0 working paper, June 2017, [Online]. Available from:https://www.zvei.org/fileadmin/user_upload/Presse_und_Medien/Publikationen/2017/Juni/Industrie_4.0_Plug_and_produce/Industrie-4.0-_Plug-and-Produce-zvei.pdf [retrieved August, 2021]

[20] T. Hupperich, H. Hosseini, and T. Holz, "Leveraging sensor fingerprinting for mobile device authentication", International Conference on Detection of Intrusions and Malware, and Vulnerability Assessment, LNCS 9721, Springer, pp. 377–396, 2016, [Online]. Available from: https://www.syssec.ruhr-uni-bochum.de/media/emma/veroeffentlichungen/2016/09/28/paper.pdf [retrieved August, 2021]

[21] H. Bojinov, D. Boneh, Y. Michalevsky, and G. Nakibly, "Mobile device identification via sensor fingerprinting", arXiv:1408.1416, 2016, [Online]. Available from: https://arxiv.org/abs/1408.1416 [retrieved August, 2021]

[22] P. Hao, "Wireless device authentication techniques using physical-layer device fingerprint", PhD thesis, University of Western Ontario, Electronic Thesis and Dissertation Repository, 3440, 2015, [Online]. Available from: https://ir.lib.uwo.ca/etd/3440 [retrieved August, 2021]

[23] R. Falk and M. Trommer, "Integrated Management of Network and Host Based Security Mechanisms", 3rd Australasian Conference on Information Security and Privacy, ACISP98, pp. 36-47, July 13-15, 1998, LNCS 1438, Springer, 1998

[24] D. Urbina, J. Giraldo, A. Cardenas, N. O. Tippenhauer, J. Valente, M. Faisal, J. Ruths, R. Candell, and H. Sandberg, "Limiting The Impact of Stealthy Attacks on Industrial Control Systems", ACM Conference on Computer and Communications Security (CCS), pp. 1092–1105, Vienna, Austria, 2016

The Risk of a Cyber Disaster

Estimating the Exceedance Probability Function of a Global Computer Virus

Vaughn H. Standley
National Defense University
Fort Lesley J. McNair
Washington D.C. 20319 USA
email: vaughn.standley@nnsa.doe.gov

Roxanne B. Everetts
National Defense University
Fort Lesley J. McNair
Washington D.C. 20319 USA
email: roxanne.everetts@ndu.edu

***Abstract*— Rigorous assessment of disaster risk requires an exceedance probability function relating the probability that 'S', a random variable representing the severity of the disaster, exceeds some threshold 's' above which destruction is expected. Calculating a valid exceedance probability function for disasters is not straightforward. The Power Law has served as a panacea for this difficulty, often erroneously. Here, an alternative approach is demonstrated using empirical data for interstate war, the coronavirus pandemic, and identity theft. The method relates the frequency distribution of severity S (deaths or failures per state) to the product of frequency distributions for vulnerability V (deaths or failures per case or combatant), exposure E (cases or combatants per capita), and population P (population per state). The probability density function for S, from which the exceedance probability function is derived, may then be computed using obtainable distributions for V, E, and P if data for S is not directly available. The method is used to estimate the risk of a global cyber disaster. Results suggest that the probability density functions for this situation follow log-gamma distributions. The fits can be used in stochastic decision formulae enabling authorities to optimally choose among alternative cyber preparedness or resilience measures to minimize overall risk.**

Keywords- catastrophe theory; military; power law; risk analysis.

I. Introduction

"What is cyber risk?" – "What are the costs and detrimental effects caused by cyber risk?" – "Where do we find data on cyber risk?" – "How can we model cyber risks?" These first four of ten key questions posed by The Geneva Association [1] suggest that as recently as 2016 very few of the technical fundamentals of cyber risk are understood. Fast forward five years; a global biological virus – not a digital virus – will help to answer these critical questions.

Malicious, replicating digital software is called a "computer virus" because it is characterized by rapid proliferation and high unpredictability, just like a biological virus. One phenomenon has real-life implications for the other. These implications ought to be studied and applied for common benefit, such as in decision formulae used to minimize risk. Informed by empirical data, these equations can help optimally choose long-term investments to mitigate cyber threats, be integrated into operational software to defend against cyber-attacks in real-time or be used by actuarial scientists to determine insurance premiums when cyber-defenses fail, among other applications.

Network epidemiology holds that the spread of disease can be modelled with network theory [2]. Social and commuter networks, modelled as nodes and segments in a matrix, approximate disease transmission. Similarly, in the case of a computer virus it is the internet cables, servers, and client computers that form the network. If the impacts of a virus across a network are great, sudden, and unforeseen, a disaster ensues. Catastrophe theory was developed to address the stochastic nature of these events so that logical investments into preparedness and resilience measures could be made.

In this study, we extend previous catastrophe theory that has been applied to interstate war [3] to the coronavirus pandemic to develop a method for characterizing the magnitude and uncertainty of the severity of a worst-case computer virus that spreads to Internet-connected computers. The results are expected to help inform the development and implementation of cyber preparedness and resilience measures.

Section II provides additional background on exceedance probabilities and why use of the Power Law is not valid. Section III describes a method to estimate the exceedance probability for a global computer virus. Section IV reports the results. Section V is a summary of conclusions.

II. Background

Probability distributions of severity embody the highly unpredictable nature of catastrophic phenomena. A Probability Density Function (PDF) quantifies the relative likelihood that the value of a random variable '*S*' representing severity is equal to some severity '*s*'. The complement (i.e., subtracted from one) of the integral of the PDF from zero to s is the exceedance probability function, $P(S>s)$. The exceedance function relates the probability that *S* exceeds a threshold s above which destruction is expected [4]. For example, to construct a building to survive earthquakes, the architect is concerned with the probability that the earthquake will be less than some specified Richter value, such as "9". Above this severity, destruction of the building cannot be reasonably avoided. We would write this exceedance probability as $P(S>9)$.

War is a man-made disaster that may be characterized by an exceedance probability. Beginning in 1960 with Lewis Fry Richardson's famous "The Statistics of Deadly Quarrels" [5] the Power Law has been widely used to model the exceedance probability of war. A phenomenon may be probabilistically distributed according to the Power Law if the logarithm of the exceedance probability plotted against the logarithm of severity s appears as a straight line with slope $-q$. This is written as $P(S>s) = s^{-q}$ and is quantified by grouping data according to consecutive ranges of severity and examining the frequency that wars fall into these groups. It turns out that the Power Law may be applied to many phenomena [6]. An example of the Power Law applied to cyber-crime data [7] is illustrated in Fig. 1. It is the straight line with an approximate slope of -0.7 (Note that variable b in the figure is negated in the Power Law formula).

Fig. 1 is an example of how the Power Law is often misapplied. For identification (ID) theft in the U.S., Circle A shows that the Power Law misrepresents data from 1 to 10,000 or about half of the entire range of the graph. Circle B shows that the data does not match the Power Law fit for greater than 10^7. Critically, the Power Law fails as a probability when $q<1$ unless the use is properly qualified. A proper qualification will recognize that "data held to be power-law distributed represent samples from some underlying population. As these samples often cover a narrower scale range than that of the population as a whole they are truncated" [8]. A q value less than one indicates that the exceedance probability decreases slower than the increase in severity. In such "long-tail" cases, the severity increases arbitrarily, causing the mean to become mathematically divergent. The slope associated with the Power Law fit to identification theft data in Fig. 1 is less than one, meaning that it is invalid as a probability distribution for the range indicated and, therefore, cannot be used in

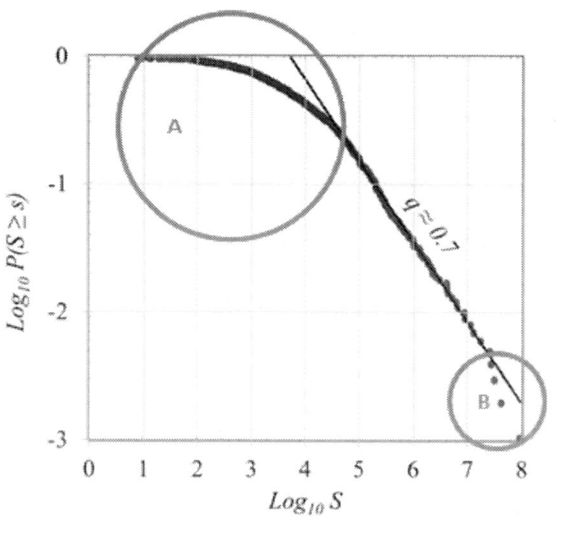

Figure 1. Normalized ID theft data and Power Law fit reported by [7].

mathematical decision criteria (e.g., a likelihood ratio test) that may be used to compute minimum risk.

Curvature in log-log data, such as that observed at both ends of the data in Fig. 1, suggest the applicability of logarithmic distributions other than the Power Law, like the log-normal distribution [9]. A Log-Normal (LN) distribution is a normal distribution applied to the logarithm of the statistic. Curvature in the integral of LN data is evident in many plots meant to demonstrate the applicability of the Power Law. The LN is a symmetric distribution, but often data will appear non-symmetric. A non-symmetric distribution skewed toward higher statistics is the log-gamma (LG). Conspicuously absent from disaster modelling literature is application of the LG to severity, except for one [10] linking LG and LN distributions of combat deaths to economic theory [11]. When plotted in a log-log graph, the middle section of the integral of the LN and LG PDFs will always appear somewhat straight, explaining why the Power Law is so often misapplied. Application of the Power Law in these cases is not only mathematically invalid, but it fails to reveal the true nature of the underlying phenomena.

Finding a valid exceedance probability is not straightforward. The Power Law erroneously serves as a panacea for this difficulty. The deficiencies noted in Fig. 1 illustrate how the Power Law is misapplied to cyber-risk. A better quantitative method is needed to estimate exceedance probabilities. An approach based on the spread of known computer viruses would be the best way to proceed. However, the data needed for such an approach is not available and/or public. Another method is needed.

III. METHOD

A novel alternative to the Power Law is demonstrated here with empirical interstate war and coronavirus pandemic fatality data that relates frequency distribution for severity S (deaths per state) to frequency distributions for vulnerability V (deaths per case or combatant), exposure E (cases or combatants per capita), and population P (population per state) by (1). Because all three of these variables are found to conform to parametric distributions associated with random variables, each may be viewed as a random variable.

$$S = VEP \quad (1)$$

In war, deaths are "transmitted" from one combatant to another by contact following geographic movement, much like how an airborne biological virus is transmitted. Similarities between interstate war and a global pandemic, including the finding that war is a network phenomenon [12], lead us to posit that the statistics of interstate war are representative of these and similarly networked phenomena. War data used in this study are from the Correlates Of War (COW) Project. Combat death statistics were obtained from the COW War Data, 1816 - 2007 (v4.0) [13]. Population and military personnel (i.e., combatant) statistics were obtained from the COW National Material Capabilities (NMC) (v5.0) dataset [14]. The two datasets were combined manually for this study. The data involves 93 wars. However, proper application of game theory [15] requires that these wars be differentiated by participating nations, of which there are 337. Due to missing military personnel data for some of these wars, the number of states is reduced to 250. Other defects further reduce the set to 236 states. Moreover, it is reported that 25 of these warring states lost more combatants than reported in the NMC database. In these cases, we limit the number of combat dead to be 100% of the combatants.

The magnitude and variability of S for interstate war, measured in terms of combat dead, is represented by the red lines in Fig. 2(a). The solid red line with square markers indicates combat deaths taken directly from the COW War Data set. The thick semi-transparent red line with no markers indicates combat dead computed using (1). The solid green line with circle markers is the distribution of state populations taken from the NMC dataset, which represents P in the equation. The solid blue line with solid diamond markers indicates the distribution of combatants per capita, also taken from the NMC dataset, which represents exposure E. The distribution of vulnerability V, or deaths per combatant, taken from the interstate war dataset, is indicated by the solid orange line marked by triangles. In all graphs, solid lines with solid markers indicate empirical data, whereas dotted lines with no markers indicate parametric fits to data.

Curves in Fig. 2 appearing to the right of zero on the logarithmic axis are greater than one, while those to the left of zero are numbers between zero and one. The calculated deaths per nation S, a number greater than one, is the product of a random number P and likewise greater than one, with two random variables E and V that are both fractions. For this reason, the red curves are situated between the green curve and zero on the x-axis. The fact that the thick semi-transparent red curve overlaps the solid line with square markers is a good indication that estimation of deaths using $S=VEP$ accurately reflects what is reported in empirical data. Small mismatches are mainly attributed to inaccurate army sizes reported in the COW NMC dataset.

Parametric fits are important because they help to determine if the data are mathematically well-behaved, discern what processes underly the phenomena, and applicable to risk-minimizing formulae. The distribution of state populations P follows a negatively Skewed LN (SLN) distribution. The E and V curves follow an LG distribution, described by (2). The distribution of combat deaths S follows an LG distribution.

$$f(x;\alpha,\beta)=\frac{1}{\beta^{\alpha}\Gamma(\alpha)}x^{\alpha-1}e^{-x/\beta} \quad (2)$$

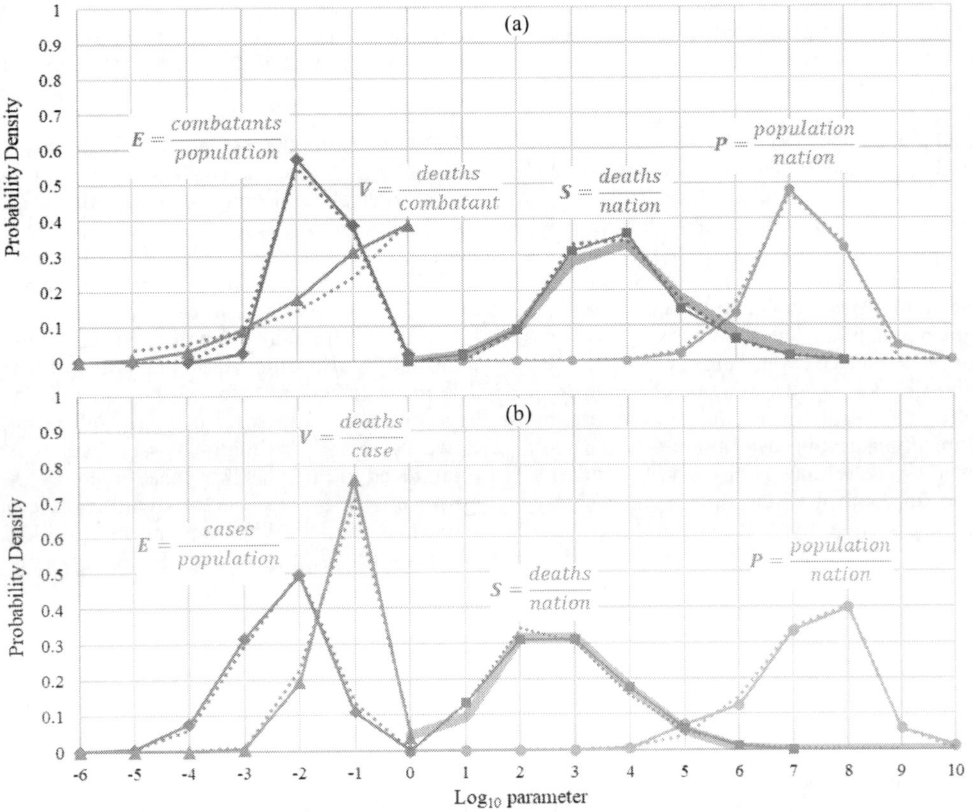

Figure 2. PDFs for (a) interstate war (top) and (b) the COVID-19 pandemic (bottom). Solid lines with solid markers indicate empirical data, dotted lines with no markers indicate parametric fits to data, and the thick semi-transparent line indicates the curve computed using the relation $S = VEP$.

Fig. 2(b) reports the *S*, *V*, *E*, and *P* curves associated with the coronavirus pandemic derived from Our World In Data (OWID) statistics [16]. Of the 217 nations reporting data, only 199 are used because zero values reported by 18 nations cannot be included in a logarithmic graph. The coronavirus graph is presented just below and in alignment with the interstate war graph using the same scales to help the reader compare and contrast the two sets of curves. The meaning of the solid and dashed lines is the same as for Fig. 2(a). It turns out that the same parametric functions fit the coronavirus data, except with different parameters.

Similarities and differences between phenomena are more evident when their data are separated into constituent random variables in this way. The similarities between the cases of interstate war and COVID-19 appear to be mostly a result of similar population data. The only difference between the population distribution for these cases is that the interstate war data spans 191 years from 1816 to 2007, whereas the COVID-19 pandemic population data is taken only from 2020. The most striking difference between the two are their vulnerability curves. For interstate war, there is a 40% chance that a nation loses all its combatants in a war. Compare this to the COVID-19 pandemic, where there is a zero probability that all exposed to the virus will die, but an 80% chance that 10% of those exposed will die. At first glance, these curves appear to be associated with two different parametric distributions because the V distribution for interstate war looks like an exponential. This difference is resolved by the fact that an exponential distribution is a gamma distribution for certain combinations of parameters. In other words, they both can be considered gamma distributions applied to the logarithm of the statistic.

Comparison of *S*, *V*, *E*, and *P* data for interstate war and the COVID-19 pandemic appear to make clear that two very different phenomena have real-life implications for the other, possibly due to common or similar underlying phenomena (e.g., both involve networks), and that the same might be true for cyber phenomena. One may choose different populations to study, or the populations themselves may change. However, for a given threat (e.g., war, coronavirus, etc.), we suspect that distributions for *E* and *V* may be common to or similar for these different populations. Thus, we can use this knowledge to estimate underlying distributions for *E* and/or *V* and use them in (1) to determine *S* for a given population under consideration. In contrast to the threat, vulnerability, and consequence model used by the Federal Emergency Management Agency (FEMA) where *Risk=TVC* [17], ours is based on a population because the threat and severity both derive from the population itself and exposure expresses the population's ability to convey the threat.

IV. RESULTS

We apply the method to the case of a hypothetical computer virus that spreads like COVID-19 and inflicts a combat-like mortality rate on Internet-connected computers. For this case, the population distribution is taken to be the number of people per nation with access to the Internet. For all nations, OWID [16] reports the fraction of people with Internet connections, which is multiplied by the population of the respective state. For *E* and *V* distributions, we intend to use those associated with the coronavirus pandemic and interstate war, respectively. Before doing so, however, we would like some evidence that these distributions are appropriate for modelling a computer virus. Unfortunately, there is no quantitative data available that directly serves this purpose.

The Privacy Rights Clearinghouse (PRC) is one of the few organizations to publish an online database quantifying different types of cyber-crime [18]. However, this database does not provide any statistics about the number of attacks or infiltrations per capita or the number of records per attack or infiltration. That is, the database does not help quantify *E* or *V*. Only the distribution of *S* can be discerned from the PRC data. Our approach in this case is to "reverse-engineer" the vulnerability distribution using (1) by first positing that the exposure distribution is the same as for the coronavirus. We then adjust the vulnerability distribution until the relation *S=VEP* produces an *S* distribution that matches the distribution of the PRC data. State populations in the U.S. were taken from Wikipedia [19]. The result of this process applied to "datalossdb" records in the PRC ID theft database is reported in Fig. 3. As before, *S=VEP* is represented by the thick semi-transparent red line and the empirical data for S is represented by the solid red line with square markers. The resulting *V* distribution is more consistent with the vulnerability associated with interstate war than to vulnerability associated with the coronavirus, a finding that gives us some confidence that the respective *E* and *V* distributions for the Coronavirus and interstate war can be applied to our hypothetical computer virus.

Fig. 4 reports the exceedance probability for *S* computed using *P* and *E* distributions from the coronavirus pandemic and a reverse-engineered *V* distribution. Only a thick semi-transparent red line is reported (i.e., no solid line with square markers) because the severity distribution is based on *S=VEP* and there is no *S* data with which to compare directly. However, we can compare the *S=VEP* curve to the exceedance probability for the PRC ID theft data, which is indicated by the solid black line with solid square markers. The main difference between the curves is that they diverge beginning at a value of 5 (i.e., 100,000) on the x-axis. The Power Law approximation associated with the PRC is reproduced in Fig. 4 as the black dotted line. Our best fit of a power law to the PRC data is with a slope of -0.65, which rounds to -0.7, the value reported by Maillart and Sornette [7]. As with the Power Law fit in Fig. 1, the fit in Fig. 4 diverges from the data for s values less than 4.5 and greater than 7.5.

Parametric fits to each of the four PDFs (i.e., *S*, *V*, *E*, and *P*) for each of the four phenomena (i.e., interstate war, the COVID-19 pandemic, U.S. ID theft, and hypothetical global computer virus) are recorded in Table 1. For the hypothetical virus, a non-skewed LN distribution (α=0) fits the population of internet-connected devices, which is slightly different than the other populations fit by a SLN distribution. The curve for the computed severity of the hypothetical computer virus appears to follow an LG distribution, which is the same as for interstate war and the coronavirus pandemic.

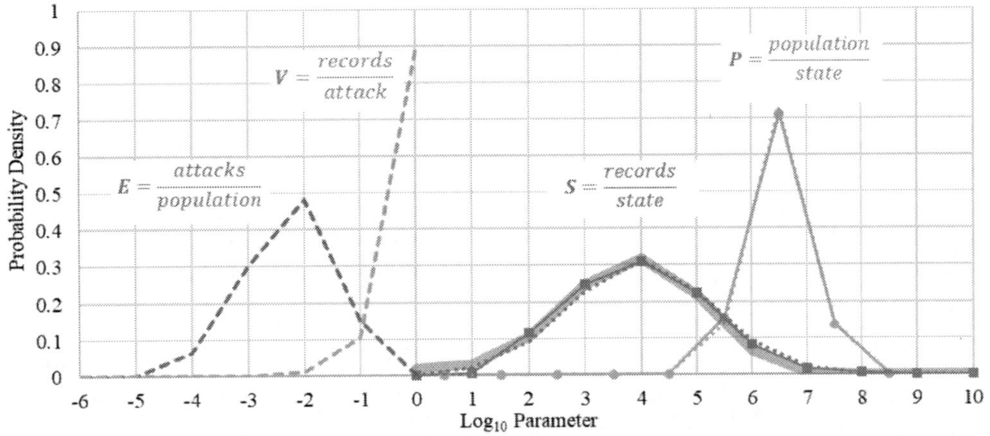

Figure 3. PDFs for ID theft in the U.S. The severity distribution is based on Privacy Rights Clearinghouse data [18]. The population distribution, which is Internet access per nation, is based on OWID [16]. Curve formats have the same meaning as for curves in Fig. 2.

Parametric distributions that mimic empirical data are valuable to decision formulae. What is particularly important in the case of logarithmic severity distributions, like those in this study, is that the parametric fits adequately model the high-severity portion of the data. Consider the data and fits to the data in Fig. 4. The data represented by the solid black line is turning downward, gaining a more negative slope whereas the black dotted line (i.e., the Power Law fit) is a straight line with negative slope 0.7. The Power Law approximation cannot be used in probabilistic decision formulae because it is divergent for slopes equal to or greater than negative one. Conversely, the LG fit represented by the dotted red line, which faithfully mimics the solid red data line, is valid for use in such formulae because it becomes increasingly negative. As can be seen in these exceedance probabilities, there is a portion in the middle that is approximately straight, which creates the temptation to report the distribution as a Power Law. This tendency is particularly prevalent for war statistics [20].

Results should not be overinterpreted. The method is not useful for investigating microscopic causes of cyber-risk, although it can be used to posit or confirm the macroscopic result of microscopic causes vis-à-vis parametric distributions. However, the method is a better bookkeeping and estimation tool for uncertainty in the constituents of risk when the threat is created and propagated by the population. FEMA's model is applicable to threats that are independent of the population (e.g., earthquakes).

V. CONCLUSION

Risk is the product of probability and severity. Exceedance probability is the mathematical object connecting both. The magnitude and variability of the severity S of a computer virus can be computed in terms of frequency distributions representing the subject population, P, that part of the population exposed to the risk, E, and the vulnerability of the exposed, V. Currently there is not enough cyber risk data to calculate S directly, so the advantage of

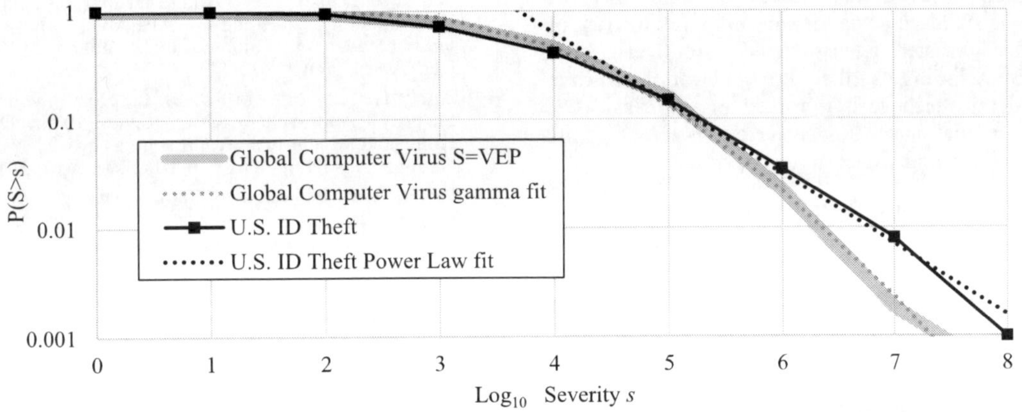

Figure 4. Exceedance probability functions, $P(S>s)$, for U.S. ID theft (solid black with square markers) and a highly "contagious" global computer virus (thick semi-transparent red) developed using the S=VEP relation, with power law fit to U.S. ID theft data (dotted black) and log-gamma fit to $S=VEP$ curve for the global computer virus (dotted red).

TABLE 1. PARAMETRIC FITS TO PROBABILITY DENSITY FUNCTIONS.

	Interstate War	**Coronavirus Pandemic**	**Records Theft**	**Computer Virus**
P	SLN ξ=8, ω=1.2, α=-3	SLN ξ=8.4, ω=1.5, α=-3	SLN ξ=7.8, ω=1.2, α=-2	SLN ξ=7, ω =0.9, α=0
E	LG α=17, β=0.13	LG α=14, β=0.20	LG α=14, β=0.20	LG α=14, β=0.20
V	LG α=1.0, β=2.0	LG α=5.5, β=0.35	LG α=1.0, β=0.50	LG α=1.0, β=0.50
S	LG α=9.8, β=0.34	LG α=4.0, β=0.6	LG μ=3.5, σ=1.3	LG α=4.0, β=0.6

this method is that the PDF of S, from which the exceedance probability function is derived, may be computed indirectly using more readily obtainable or representative probability densities for *V*, *E*, and *P*. The Power Law is divergent when applied to the cyber-risk so it should be avoided for these purposes in favor of methods such as the one proposed here. The method was applied to a hypothetical computer virus given the propensity to spread like COVID-19, predicated on the hypothesis that the frequency distributions associated with interstate war, COVID-19, and computer viruses manifest similar network behavior. Results are consistent with this hypothesis.

The PDF associated with the logarithm of severity for a worldwide computer virus is fit by a gamma distribution. This parametric distribution can be used in operational computer software designed to detect and react to cyber threats in real-time, in stochastic decision formulae enabling authorities to optimally choose among alternative cyber preparedness or resilience measures, or in actuarial equations to determine insurance premiums for cyber risks.

. Using data from Tab. 1, we compute the logarithmic variance of the computer virus to be 1.44 ($=\alpha\times\beta^2$) and the logarithmic standard deviation to be 1.2, which is equal to a factor of 16 ($=10^{1.2}$). For x-axis values greater than 6 in Fig. 4, the exceedance probability varies by an order of magnitude in one standard deviation, meaning that the risk of a global cyber disaster is associated with very high uncertainty. This finding is likely to hold for a real-live computer pandemic because it is rooted in empirical U.S. cyber-crime data that has been corrected in terms of its population, exposure, and vulnerability distributions.

DISCLAIMER

The opinions, conclusions, and recommendations expressed or implied are the authors' and do not necessarily reflect the views of the Department of Defense or any other agency of the U.S. Federal Government, or any other organization.

REFERENCES

[1] M. Eling and W. Schnell, "Ten Key Questions on Cyber Risk and and Cyber Risk Insurance," The Geneva Association, Zurich, Switzerland, 2016.

[2] L. Danon et al., "Networks and the Epidemiology of Infectious Disease," Hindawi Publishing Corporation, Interdisciplinary Perspectives on Infectious Diseases, Volume 2011.

[3] V. H. Standley, F. G. Nuño, and J. W. Sharpe, "Modeling Interstate War Combat Deaths," International Journal of Modeling and Optimization, vol. 10, no. 1, pp. 1-8, 2020.

[4] T. G. Lewis, Critical Infrastructure Protection in Homeland Security - Defending a Networked Nation, Hobeken, New Jersey: John Wiley & Sons, 2015.

[5] L. F. Richardson, The Statistics of Deadly Quarrells, Chicago: Quadrangle Books, 1960.

[6] L. Cederman, "Modeling the Size of Wars: From Billiard Balls to Sandpiles," The American Political Science Review, vol. 97.1 , no. April 2015, pp. 135-50, 2003.

[7] T. Maillart and D. Sornette, "Heavy-Tailed Distribution of Cyber-Risks," Physics of Condensed Matter, vol. 75, no. 3, pp. 1-16, 2008.

[8] G. Pickering, J. M. Bull, and D. J. Sanderson, "Sampling power-law distributions," Tectonophysics, vol. 248, pp. 1-20, 1995.

[9] L. Benguigui and M. Marinov, "A classification of natural and social distributions Part one: the descriptions," 2015. [Online]. Available: https://arxiv.org/abs/1607.00856 [retrieved: August, 2021]

[10] V. H. Standley, J. W. Sharpe, and F. G. Nuño, "Fusing attack detection and severity probabilities: a method for computing minimum-risk war decisions," Computing, 102, pp. 1385–1408 2020.

[11] J. von Neumann and O. Morgenstern, Theory of Games and Economic Behavior, 3rd ed., Princeton N.J.: Princeton University Press, 1953.

[12] M. O. Jackson and S. Nei, "Networks of Military Alliances, Wars, and International Trade," PNAS, vol. 112, no. 50, pp. 15277-15284, 2015.

[13] M. R. Sarkees and F. Wayman, Resort to War: 1816 - 2007, Washington DC: CQ Press, 2010.

[14] D. J. Singer, S. Bremer and J. Stuckey, "Capability Distribution, Uncertainty, and Major Power War, 1820 - 1965," in Peace, War, and Numbers, Beverly Hills, Sage, 1972, pp. 19-48.

[15] T. C. Schelling, The Strategy of Conflict, 1st ed., Cambridge: Harvard College, 1960.

[16] C. Appel et al. "Data on COVID-19 (coronavirus) by Our World in Data," The Oxford Martin Programme on Global Development, [Online]. Available: https://github.com /owid/covid-19-data/blob/master/ public/data/README.md. [retrieved: August, 2021]

[17] Analysis, Committee to Review the Department of Homeland Security's Approach to Risk, "Review of the Department of Homeland Security's Approach to Risk Analysis," The National Academies Press, Washington D.C., 2010.

[18] P. R. Clearinghouse, "Data Breaches," Privacy Rights Organization, 13 January 2020. [Online]. Available: https://privacyrights.org/data-breaches. [retrieved: August 2021].

[19] "List of states and territories of the United States by population," Wikipedia, 5 November 2020. https://en.wikipedia.org/wiki/List_of_states_and_territories_of_the_United_States_by_population.

[20] R. González-Val, "War Size Distribution: Empirical Regularities Behind the Conflicts," Defence and Peace Economics, vol. 27, issue 6, pp. 838-853, 2014.

Evaluations of Information Security Maturity Models

Measuring the NIST Cybersecurity Framework Implementation Status

Alsaleh, Majeed
King Fahd University of Petroleum and Minerals.(KFUPM), Dhahran, Saudi Arabia
e-mail: g198925300@kfupm.edu.sa

Niazi, Mahmood
King Fahd University of Petroleum and Minerals.(KFUPM)., Dhahran, Saudi Arabia
e-mail: mkniazi@kfupm.edu.sa

***Abstract*—Many organizations with critical infrastructure sectors and other businesses have started to adopt the National Institute of Standards and Technology (NIST) cybersecurity framework. As cybersecurity is a long-term investment, organizations adopting the framework need to sustain their cybersecurity capabilities and ensure growth toward the maturity level needed to deliver the desired outcome. Therefore, the maturity capability of the cybersecurity program needs to be assessed regularly. Several capability maturity models can be used to measure the progress of implementing the cybersecurity program. However, attempts are still being made to define a capability maturity model to be used specifically for measuring the cybersecurity programs that adopt the NIST cybersecurity framework. With the aim of identifying and applying evaluation criteria, this paper reviews multiple existing maturity models and compares their scale levels definitions and the used assessment methodology. The researchers determined the criteria based on subject matter experts' feedback. A survey was conducted to define the values of the criteria that organizations are looking for in order to select the best-fit capability maturity models to use in measuring the progress of NIST CSF implementation.**

Keywords-cyber security; information security; maturity model; measurement metrics.

I. Introduction

The National Institute of Standards and Technology (NIST) issued the Cyber Security Framework (CSF) in 2014 [1] as a response to the Executive Order signed by President Obama on February 12, 2013 [2]. This framework was quickly adopted by many organizations around the world. In a study by Gartner [3], the framework was expected to grow in usage from 30% in 2015 to 50% by 2020. However, after the Executive Order signed by President Trump on May 11, 2017 [4], the framework is expected to be adopted by more organizations worldwide. The executive order clearly places the accountability for managing the cybersecurity risk on the heads of executive departments operating critical infrastructure and heads of federal agencies; thus making the compliance to the framework requirements involuntarily. The growth of the framework implementation has been fast outside the United States of America too. For example, many Oil and Natural Gas (ONG) companies around the world have adopted the framework [5].

The NIST issued an update to the framework, with new features added and more clarifications for some of the terms used to measure cybersecurity such as, the term compliance [6]. The update also addressed the supply chain as one new cybersecurity category was added to the previous 22 categories. Moreover, the link between the framework and the Internet of Things (IoT) was established as a possible area of risks associated with operational technology and cyber-physical system environments [7]. Table I below summarizes the structure of the core components of the framework along with the key changes and updates in the new version of the framework.

TABLE I: Framework Versions Comparison

Version	Functions	Categories	Sub-categories	Informative References
V1.0 [1]	5	22	98	5
V1.1 [6]	5	23	108	5

One of the key changes in the new version of the framework emphasizes the role of cybersecurity risk management measurement (cost vs. benefit) in a newly added section called "Self-Assessing Cybersecurity Risk". Moreover, the NIST officially recognized the importance of measuring cybersecurity by including it as an item on the Roadmap for Improving Critical Infrastructure Cybersecurity. Using the framework components will enable organizations to measure their risk along with the cost and benefits of mitigating it while deciding which level of risk (risk tier out of the four risk tiers) is acceptable to the organization. This is determined by considering many factors including legal regulatory requirements, the threat environment, and an organization's current risk management practices. The framework suggests leveraging external guidance such as, existing Capability Maturity Models (CMMs) to allow organizations to measure the status of their NIST CSF implementation progress [8].

However, there are varieties of CMMs that may or may not be associated with specific best practices standards or frameworks. For example, industry best practices standards, such as, Control Objectives for Information and Related Technologies (COBIT) and the Information Security Forum (ISF) Standard of Good Practice (SoGP) for Information Security have their own Maturity Models (MMs) that can be utilized to measure the NIST CSF implementation progress [9] [10]. On the other hand, the Systems Security Engineering Capability Maturity Model (SSE CMM) [11], Capability Maturity Model Integration (CMMI) [12], ONG subsector Cybersecurity Capability Maturity Model (ONG C2M2) [13], Information Security Management Maturity Model (ISM3) [14], and Community Cybersecurity Maturity Model (CCSMM) [15] are examples of MMs that can be used to measure the implementation of any given framework. Worth noting is that the wide range of NIST CSFs adopted not only spans many organizations but also covers more areas such as, building cybersecurity [17] and cyber cloud security [18].

Therefore, due to the varieties of available CMMs, organizations may lose some benefits of using a unified CMM or compatible ones that allow smooth mapping to the NIST CSF framework. For example, an organization may not get an accurate progress update if it does not use the same CMM for identifying the baseline (where it stands currently) and the desired higher levels of cybersecurity maturity over time. This is due to various difficulty levels of mapping each CMM to the NIST CSF framework and vice versa [19]. Benchmarking is another benefit that might not be possible if organizations not using a unified CMM or compatible ones that allow smooth mapping to the NIST CSF framework.

This paper's main objective is to identify and apply evaluation criteria through reviewing multiple existing MMs and comparing their scale levels definitions and their used assessment methodologies. The researchers sought the feedback of Subject Matter Experts (SME) through a survey to define the criteria for selecting the best-fit CMMs that can be used in measuring the NIST CSF implementation progress.

This paper consists of seven sections: The first section is the Introduction, and the second section provides an overview of the NIST CSF framework and its components, Section III reviews seven CMMs, Section IV reviews and compares the levels of the CMMs, Section V discusses the survey, Section VI analyzes the survey results, and Section VII is the Conclusion.

II. The NIST Framework Components

The NIST CSF has three components: 1) the profile, 2) the risk tiers, and 3) the core functions [6]. The three components can be utilized by organizations in a variety of ways, considering the current situation of the organization, that is, whether they are at the very initial stages of implementing a cybersecurity program or are already adopting existing best practices and standard frameworks. The framework is not meant to be a substitute for any existing cybersecurity program of the organization, but to complement and allow for more improvement opportunities to strengthen the cybersecurity program.

A. The Profile Component

This component of the framework is considered the tool for capturing the organization's current cybersecurity status. It is utilized to document the current and the planned risk tiers and determine which of the cybersecurity activities should be selected for implementation in improving the current situation and to track progress to achieve the desired security status.

B. The Risk Tiers Component

The risk approach followed by an organization for managing the cybersecurity risk and the processes in place influence the organization's placement in one of the four risk tiers defined by this component. Yet the risk tiers do not indicate the maturity of the cybersecurity program of the organization [6] [8] [20].

C. The Core Functions Component

The core functions component is the part of the framework where all controls are listed as "subcategories". The latest version of the framework [6] has 108 subcategories as against the 98 subcategories of the previous version [1]. The subcategories account for 23 categories that can be looked at as processes of cybersecurity activities or objectives to be achieved by implementing some or all subcategories.

While the previous version of the framework has 22 categories, the new version has added one more to address the supply chain. The categories then make the core five functions: Identify, Protect, Detect, Respond, and Recover. The five functions shape the high-level and strategic view of the organization's efforts in managing its cybersecurity risk and the implemented cybersecurity program. Table II provides examples of the subcategories of the framework.

TABLE II. Examples of Subcategories of the NIST CSF Framework

Function	Category	Sub-Categories
Protect	(PR.DS) Data Security	PR.DS-1: Data-at-rest is protected
		PR.DS-2: Data-in-transit is protected
		PR.DS-3: Assets are formally managed throughout removal, transfers, and disposition

III. Capability Maturity Models

This section will review the selected CMMs and analyze their levels, domains, and assessment methods.

A. *Community Cyber Security Maturity Model (CCSMM)*

This model was originally designed to measure the capability maturity of cybersecurity practices run by communities [15]. It is not meant to assess individual organizations, though it was also extended later to cover organizations and states. The model is structured to address the improvement of four areas on a scale of five levels [16]. The improvement areas are called dimensions, namely planning, policies, awareness, and information-sharing. The maturity of these dimensions is measured in five levels starting with "Initial" as the lowest level, through "Established", "Self-Assessed", and "Integrated" till "Vanguard", which is the highest maturity level. The model uses assessment criteria that help check the level of the community with respect to the four dimensions, which range from minimal or little at the initial level to mandatory, fully integrated, full-scale, or "vanguard", which is the fifth level. The scale levels and the dimensions are measured as per the satisfaction of the criteria used to verify the status of cybersecurity implementation. Table III illustrates the criteria of the CCSMM.

B. *Information Security Management Maturity Model (ISM3)*

This model was originally designed as an extension of quality management, that is, ISO 9001 for Information Security Management (ISM) systems, to focus on the common cybersecurity processes of organizations and not on controls. As an extension of the quality assurance standard, the ISM3 is used to build a quality assurance process framework [14]. The five ISM system configuration levels are like maturity levels that measure organizations' progress in implementing cybersecurity programs.

The five maturity levels of the model are 1) undefined, 2) defined, 3) managed, 4) controlled, and 5) optimized. The domains of the models are grouped into the following four categories, each of which includes the required processes for achieving every maturity level:

1. General (3 processes)
2. Strategic management (6 processes)
3. Tactical management (11 processes)
4. Operational management (25 processes)

This model provides optional certifications related to ISO 9001 at each maturity level and ISO 27001 at Levels 4 and 5. Table IV illustrates the processes used in the ISM3.

TABLE III. CCSMM Criteria For Verifying Cybersecurity Maturity

5. Vanguard	Awareness is mandatory by the business	Fully integrated	Full-scale combined exercises and assessment of complete fusion capability	Continue to integrate cyber in Continuity of Operations Plans (CO-OP)
4. Integrated	Leaders and organizations promote awareness	Formal information-sharing internal and external to the community	Self-directed cyber exercises with assessment	Integrate cyber in CO-OP
3. Self-Assessed	Leaders promote awareness	Formal local information sharing	Self-directed tabletop cyber exercises with assessment	Include cyber in COOP; formal cyber incident response/recovery
2. Established	Leadership is aware of cyber threats	Informal information-sharing	No assessment but aware of requirements	Aware of the need to integrate
1. Initial	Minimal cyber awareness	Minimal information-sharing capabilities	Minimal cyber assessments and policy evaluations	Little inclusion of cyber in the community's COOP
Levels\ Diminutions	Awareness	Information Sharing	Policies	Plans

TABLE IV. ISM3 CRITERIA FOR VERIFYING THE PROCESS CAPABILITY MATURITY

5. Optimized	for a **high investment** in ISM processes that are managed to result in a **highest** risk reduction with **compulsory use of process metrics**			
4. Controlled	for a **high investment** in ISM processes that are managed to result in a **highest** risk reduction			
3. Managed	for a **significant investment** in ISM processes that are managed to result in a **highest** risk reduction			
2. Defined	for a **moderate investment** in ISM processes that are managed to result in a further risk reduction			
1. Undefined	for a **minimum investment** in **essential** ISM processes that are managed to result in a significant risk reduction			
	GP1	SSP1 . . . SSP6	TSP1 . . . TSP11	OSP1 . . . . OSP2
Levels\ Categories	General	Strategic Management	Tactical Management	Operational Management

C. Process Assessment Model (PAM) for the COBIT Framework

PAM is a process capability base assessment model for assessing information technology enterprises' implementation of COBIT 5 [9] [21]. The model is structured to address the improvement of 37 processes on a scale of six levels [14]. The 37 processes are defined and classified into five categories (domains). Each process is assessed against nine pre-defined attributes distributed among the maturity levels.

A standard rating scale of four status levels is used to further evaluate and score each attribute as defined in the ISO/IEC 15504 standard [14]. The rating scale measures and scores the percentage of achievement; it considers a process in achievement range from 0 to 15% as "not achieved", a process in achievement range between 15% and 50% as "partially achieved", a process in achievement range between 50% and 85% as "largely achieved", and process in achievement range between 85% and 100% as "largely achieved". The levels commence with Level 0 that indicates "Incomplete Process" and then Levels 1 to 5 to indicate the statuses of "Performed Process", "Managed Process", "Established Process", "Predictable Process", and "Optimizing Process", respectively.

The 37 processes have been classified under the five categories as follows:

1. Evaluate, Direct, and Monitor (5 processes)
2. Align, Plan, and Organize (13 processes)
3. Build, Acquire, and Implement (10 processes)
4. Deliver, Service, and Support (6 processes)
5. Monitor, Evaluate, and Assess (3 processes)

Table V illustrates the attributes used in the PAM.

D. Information Security Forum (ISF) Standard of Good Practice (SoGP) for Information Security

The ISF MM assesses, in combination, the activities performed and the supporting processes' capabilities [10]. The maturity level is an indication of how comprehensive the implementation of high-level activities is along with the capabilities of the processes supporting the activities that maintain and sustain the performance consistency and effectiveness. The model is structured to assess the processes' capabilities by evaluating the 21 domains in which each domain covers one information security discipline. The 21 domains are grouped into the following five strategies:

1. People (2 domains)
2. Strategic (6 domains)
3. Technical (6 domains)
4. Connections (2 domains)
5. Crisis (5 domains)

The model uses a scale of six levels that starts with Level 0, which indicates that the process is "Incomplete". Levels 1 to 5 represent the following process statuses: "Performed", "Planned", "Managed", "Measured", and "Tailored". The maturity level is defined by the number of requirements to be met in each activity. A standard rating scale of three status levels is used to further evaluate and score each activity. The rating scale measures and scores the percentage of requirements met; it considers the implementation of 0 to 15% requirements as "Not Met", implementation between 15%

TABLE V. PAM CRITERIA FOR VERIFYING THE PROCESS CAPABILITY MATURITY

5. Optimizing	Process: 1) Innovation 2) Optimization				
4. Predictable	Process: 1) Measurement 2) Control				
3. Established	Process: 1) Definition 2) Deployment				
2. Managed	1) Performance management 2) Work product management				
1. Performed	1) Process performance				
0. Incomplete	No attributes				
Levels\ Categories	Evaluate, Direct and Monitor	Align, Plan and Organize	Build, Acquire, and Implement	Deliver, Service, and Support	Monitor, Evaluate, and Assess

and 85% of requirements as “Partially Met”, and implementation of more than 85% of requirements as “Met”.

Table VI illustrates the assessment criteria of the ISF MM.

E. Systems Security Engineering Capability Maturity Model (SSE CMM)

The SSE MM was developed to address the absence of a comprehensive framework for evaluating security engineering practices in order to measure and improve the performance of security engineering principles [11]. The model's scope is the security engineering secure system lifecycle, from designing to commissioning and decommissioning. Thus, this model can be applied to organizations that provide security engineering services.

The model was designed to be a fixable tool that can measure process improvement, process capability, or the trustworthiness of the process outcome.

The model has been structured to assess process capabilities by evaluating all the practices (called best practices)

TABLE VI. ISF MM CRITERIA FOR VERIFYING PROCESS CAPABILITY MATURITY

5. Tailored	The activity is performed, planned, managed, measured, and subject to **continuous improvement. It is tailored** to specific areas.																	
4. Measured	The activity is performed, planned, managed, and is **monitored.**																	
3. Managed	The activity is performed and planned, and there are sufficient organizational resources to support and **manage** it.																	
2. Planned	The activity is performed and supported by **planning** (which includes the engagement of stakeholders and relevant standards and guidelines)																	
1. Performed	The activity is **performed.**																	
0. Incomplete	The activity is **not** performed.																	
Levels\ Categories	D1	D2	.	.	D6	D7	.	.	D12	D13	D14	D15	.	.	.	D19	D20	D21
	Strategic					**Technical**				**Connections**		**Crisis**					**People**	

under each process. The model uses a scale of six levels that begins with Level 0, which indicates that the process is "Not Performed". Levels 1 to 5 represent the following process statuses: "Performed Informally", "Planned and Tracked", "Well Defined", "Qualitatively Controlled", and "Continuously Improving", respectively. The model assesses about 60 security practices that are classified under 11 process domains that address the major areas of security engineering.

Moreover, the model has been expanded to assess over 60 practices performed under 11 process domains in the project and organizational areas. The model uses general assessment criteria that check the capability of the process based on the applied practices. Table VII illustrates the assessment criteria for SSE CMM.

TABLE VII. SEE CMM CRITERIA FOR VERIFYING PROCESS CAPABILITY MATURITY

5. Continuously Improving	Improving Organizational Capability
4. Qualitatively Controlled	Establishing Measurable Quality Goals Objectively Managing Performance
3. Well Defined	Defining a Standard Process Performing the Defined Process Coordinating the Process
2. Planned and Tracked	Planning Performance Disciplined Performance Verifying Performance Tracking Performance
1. Performed Informally	Base Practices are Performed
0. Not Performed	No process is performed
Levels\ Categories	PA1 . . PA11 PA22 Security Engineering Process Areas (PA1 …) | Project and Organizational Process Areas (PA11 … PA22)

F. Capability Maturity Model Integration (CMMI)

The new version of the CMMI was announced by the CMMI institute in early 2018 [12]. After expanding the model to include services and supplier management later in the same year, the model now consists of 22 process areas grouped into four categories: project management, process management, engineering, and support [12]. The model's objective is to build organizational capability for improving performance for their selected activities, which may include cybersecurity.

The model is structured to assess the process categories by evaluating all 22 practices under each process area. The model uses a scale of five levels, which includes Level 1 "Initial" that indicates that no process area has been performed. Levels 2 to 5 represent the process statuses of "Managed", "Defined", "Quantitatively Managed", and "Optimizing".

The model assesses the 22 process areas that are performed and distributed over the four maturity levels (Levels 2 to 5). The distribution of the process areas is as follows: 7 in maturity level 2, 11 in maturity level 3, 2 in maturity level 4, and 2 in maturity level 5. Each process area consists of best practices, guidance, or activities to be performed. Table VIII illustrates the assessment criteria for CMMI.

G. Oil and Natural Gas Subsector Cybersecurity Capability Maturity Model (ONG C2M2)

This model was originally designed as a derivative of the Electricity Subsector Cybersecurity Capability Maturity Model (ES-C2M2) to serve the ONG subsector [13]. The model has been structured to address the implementation of a set of cybersecurity practices, grouped into 10 domains, on a scale of four levels.

Each domain consists of a number of practices that are categorized into the following groups of objectives:

1. Risk Management (three objectives)
2. Asset, Change, and Configuration Management (four objectives)
3. Identity and Access Management (three objectives)
4. Threat and Vulnerability Management (three objectives)
5. Situational Awareness (three objectives)
6. Information Sharing and Communications (two objectives)
7. Event and Incident Response, Continuity of Operations (five objectives)
8. Supply Chain and External Dependencies Management (three objectives)
9. Workforce Management (five objectives)
10. Cybersecurity Program Management (five objectives)

Each domain is assessed independently and scored cumulatively where all the practices in a given level and its predecessor levels are implemented. Unlike other MMs, ONG C2M2 defines a different set of evaluation criteria for each objective to verify the implementation of practices. Table IX provides examples of the evaluation criteria for one objective.

TABLE VIII. CMMI CRITERIA FOR VERIFYING PROCESS CAPABILITY MATURITY

5. Optimizing	1. Causal Analysis and Resolution 2. Organizational Performance Management	
4. Quantitatively Managed	1. Organizational Process Performance 2. Quantitative Project Management	
3. Defined	1. Decision Analysis and Resolution 2. Integrated Project Management 3. Organizational Process Definition 4. Organizational Process Focus 5. Organizational Training	6. Product Integration 7. Requirements Development 8. Risk Management 9. Technical Solution 10. Validation 11. Verification
2. Managed	1. Configuration Management 2. Measurement and Analysis 3. Process and Product Quality Assurance 4. Project Monitoring and Control 5. Project Planning 6. Requirements Management 7. Supplier Agreement Management	
1. Initial	No process area has been addressed	
Levels	PA1 . . . . PA11 . . . . PA22	
Categories	Process Management | Project Management | Engineering | Support	

TABLE IX. EXAMPLES OF EVALUATION CRITERIA FOR ONG C2M2 OBJECTIVES

	Manage Asset Configuration
MIL1	a. Configuration baselines are established for inventoried assets where it is desirable to ensure that multiple assets are configured similarly.
	b. Configuration baselines are used to configure assets at deployment.
MIL2	c. The design of configuration baselines includes cybersecurity objectives.
MIL3	d. Configuration of assets are monitored for consistency with baselines throughout the assets' life cycles.
	e. Configuration baselines are reviewed and updated at an organizationally defined frequency.

The model maturity scales, called Maturity Indicator Levels (MILs), include MIL 0, which indicates that no practice has been performed, and MILs 1 to 3, which indicate the statuses of "performed but Ad-hoc", "Defined and Resourced", and "Governed and Effectively Resourced", respectively.

IV. SCALE LEVELS OF CAPABILITY MATURITY MODELS

Table X compares the seven CMMs and gives an insight into the similarity of the descriptions and the meanings of the levels.

A. Level 1: Practice Existence

All CMMs define the first level as the mere existence of the assessed practice in the organization. However, each CMM leverages a slightly different language to convey the same meaning. SSE focuses on the "base practices" that are categorized by the statement "you have to do it before you can manage it." Whereas, both ISF and ONG focus on the concept of "performed practices" to emphasize their existence. Finally, PAM requires processes to be "implemented"

TABLE X. A COMPARISON OF THE LEVELS OF CMMS

Levels/ CMM	Level 1	Level 2	Level 3	Level 4	Level 5
SSE CMM [11]	Performed Informally	Planned and Tracked	Well Defined	Quantitatively Controlled	Continuously Improving
PAM [21]	Performed Process	Managed Process	Established Process	Predictable Process	Optimizing Process
ISF [10]	Performed	Planned	Managed	Measured	Tailored
CMMI [12]	Initial	Managed	Defined	Quantitatively	Optimizing Managed
CCSMM [15]	Initial	Established	Self-Assessed	Integrated	Vanguard
ISM3 [14]	Undefined	Defined	Managed	Controlled	Optimized
ONG [13]	Performed but Ad-hoc	Defined and Resourced	Governed and Effectively Resourced	N/A	N/A

due to its process-oriented nature. It is worth noting that such processes are not required to be documented at this level by the PAM. This is also true for the ONG model, as practices are explicitly stated to be "ad-hoc". This formality aspect is less clear in the other models, though it can be implicitly inferred by contrasting this particular level with the next levels. Cybersecurity can be assessed against this level for the presence of its core best practices. Therefore, a cybersecurity CM would consider this level as the first level.

B. *Level 2: Practice Formalization*

Apart from SSE, all CMMs define this level around formalizing practices by involved stakeholders through documenting and endorsing process/procedure requirements such as, inputs/outputs, clear roles and responsibilities, and planning of resources. Cybersecurity can be assessed against this level for the formalization of its core best practices into organization-wide processes/procedures. Therefore, a cybersecurity CM would consider this level as its second level. SEE, on the other hand, defers this level to the third level and requires an intermediate level before practice formalization, which is focused on project-level formalization. Projects are regarded by the SSE as learning opportunities for the organization, from which formal processes/procedures are later established. Common lessons learned are the basis for the later formalized processes/procedures. Projects can be formalized similar to processes/procedures, though only at the project level.

Other CMMs implicitly consider this intermediate level as part of Level 1. Such projects can be seen as more than ad-hoc practices but also less than formalized processes/procedures. Projects tend to have a shorter lifespan and are more focused on the group of practices. Whereas, processes/procedures tend to have a much longer lifespan and apply to the whole organization. Therefore, it is safe to include this SSE level under Level 1 by expanding the definition of existent practices to ad-hoc and formalized projects.

C. *Level 3: Practice Governance*

Again, except SSE, all CMMs define this level as establishing governance over formalized practices by defining and enforcing organizational structures with proper authority/accountability, policies/standards/guidelines, and job specifications in terms of required knowledge/skills. This level is as far as ONG goes; hence, it lacks the subsequent levels. PAM, however, extends the definition of this level by requiring a certain degree of the Planning, Doing, Checking, and Adjusting (PDCA) lifecycle for a more flexible and agile style of governance. Cybersecurity can be assessed against this level for the governance of formalized organization-wide processes/procedures. Therefore, a cybersecurity CM would consider this level as its third level.

D. *Level 4: Practice Monitoring*

All CMMs, excluding the ONG one, define this level around the quantification of outcomes by governed processes/procedures against organizational goals using metrics for measuring performance and enabling informed optimizations based on facts. Stockholders set the operational limits of these metrics and are kept informed on the metrics on an agreed-upon regular basis. Cybersecurity can be assessed against this level for the monitoring of governed processes/procedures. Therefore, a cybersecurity CM would consider this level as its fourth level.

E. Level 5: Practice Optimization

All CMMs, excluding the ONG one, define this level as the requirement of regular/continuous improvement cycles of monitored processes/procedures. This level is associated with operational excellence programs in first-class worldwide companies, which satisfy their specific/unique needs. Improvements are based on data from monitoring desired operational limits. It is important to note that improvement must be sustainable over a considerable number of years to claim this level. Cybersecurity can be assessed against this level for the optimization of monitored processes/procedures. Therefore, a cybersecurity CM would consider this level as its fifth level.

V. EVALUATION CRITERIA

To identify the best fit CMM for measuring the maturity of organizations that are adopting or planning to adopt NIST CSF, we sought the opinions of SMEs. Interviews were conducted with four SMEs in the field of cybersecurity, information security management, information systems audits, and internal control management. The feedback of the interviews was analyzed, and the common areas of focus were combined to draft the survey questions. The drafted survey focused on four aspects related to the CMM: the scale, domains, assessment criteria, and administration.

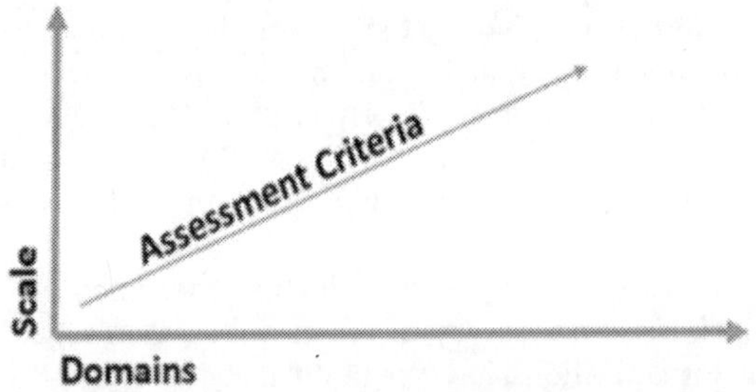

Figure I Common Areas of Focus for SMEs for Evaluating CMMs

Scale: Capability Maturity Models represent the organization's capability through various numbered levels. However, the majority are five-level scales. The descriptions of those levels vary.

Domains: Each CMM assesses the capability maturity of the activities that build, cumulatively or by stages, the maturity level based on requirements defined as domains. The NIST CSF provides informative resources for mapping the number of framework domains to functions/categories/subcategories. Additionally, some frameworks map their domains with the NIST CSF functions/categories/subcategories.

Assessment Criteria: There are two types of assessment criteria: one that assesses each domain activities with the same generic question/s for each level over the different domains and the other uses specific questions about each level or even about each domain for verification.

Administration: Some of the CMMs were originally designed to be used with specific frameworks, while many are generic and not linked to any specific framework. Some are freely available, and others are licensed. Training and assessment guides could be provided in various formats, including in-class and hands-on practices. Some are associated with industry certificates, while others are not.

VI. SURVEY DESIGN AND ANALYSIS

To address the common areas of focus, we designed a survey consisting of 16 questions and shared the draft with the interviewed SMEs. The final sets of survey questions were communicated to many organizations in the oil and gas industry. Given the short survey period, twelve cybersecurity professionals responded to the survey. Of the participants, 58% were Governance, Risk, and Compliance (GRC) specialists (that is, 25% compliance specialists, 17% governance, and 17% as risk specialists). Another 25% of the participants were senior information system auditors. Furthermore, 8% of the participants were compliance officers, and 8% were process performance assessors. The key selection criteria of the participants were their roles, profession, and involvement in cybersecurity capability implementations and maturity assessments.

The feedback received on the survey was analyzed, and top organizational preferences were considered for constructing the evaluation criteria for comparing the reviewed CMMs. Table XI illustrates the selected criteria and compares them with each CMM.

Q1: Does your organization adopt the NIST CSF or is it planning to?

Of the responses, 75% were that their organizations are currently adopting the NIST CSF, and 25% are that their organizations were planning to adopt the framework.

Q2: Is there any governance requirement that mandates the adoption of the NIST CSF?

More than 66% of organizations are adopting or planning to adopt the framework due to governance requirements. The remaining are voluntarily adopting the framework.

Q3: How many times have you assessed your organization's maturity?

While all organizations assessed their cybersecurity maturity at least once, more than 58% did the assessment more than three times.

Q4: Did you use the same CMM in all the assessments?

Out of all the organizations that did the assessments more than once, 75% used the same CMM for the assessment and 25% used different CMMs.

Q5: Did you use or do you plan to use the result for benchmarking?

It was found that 90% of the organizations either have used the result of the assessment or are planning to use it for benchmarking with other organizations in their field of operation.

Q6: Did you use or do you plan to use CMMs to certify your organization?

Including the certification as part of the assessment goals was the intent of 50% of the organizations.

Q7: What is your preference related to training?

More than 90% of the organizations prefer that the selected MM provide training in various formats, including in-class.

Q8: Did you use or do you prefer using a CMM linked to a framework?

It was found that 75% of the organizations prefer that the selected MM be linked to a framework.

Q9: Did you use or do you prefer using a CMM that is mapped to the NIST CSF functions/categories/subcategories?

It was found that 75% out of the organizations preferred to use a CMM linked to a framework or preferred to have the linked CMM mapped to the NIST CSF functions/categories/subcategories in general.

Q10: Would you prefer that the mapping was done by the NIST or the CMM owner?

More than 66% of the organizations want the mapping to be done by the NIST, specifically as part of the informative references.

Q11: What is the preferred level of mapping?

More than 66% of the organizations prefer "one-to-one" mapping, while 25% prefer "close to one-to-one" mapping, and the remaining have no preferences.

Q12: What are the scale levels you have used or prefer using?

More than 83% of the organizations prefer using a five-level scale CMM.

Q13: Do you prefer using the descriptions of the scale levels as they are or do you modify them?

More than 66% of the organizations prefer using the description of the scale levels as they are, while the remaining preferred to modify it.

Q14: Did you use or do you prefer using generic criteria or specific criteria for assessing each domain in each level?

In terms of the assessment methods, more than 83% of the organizations prefer using generic criteria for assessing each domain of each level. The remaining prefer using specific criteria for assessing each domain of each level.

Q15: Did you use or do you prefer using assessment criteria that allow different weights for the assessed process/activity?

More than 66% of the organizations have used or are planning to use assessment criteria that allow different weights for the assessed process/activity. About 16% do not prefer using criteria that allow different weights. Moreover, the same percentage of organizations have no preferences regarding the weights specified.

Q16: What is the scoring preference?

Finally, 50% of the organizations preferred the use of a cumulative scoring method, 25% of the organizations preferred using a non-cumulative, and 25% of the organizations preferred using a combined scoring method (non-cumulative for compliance and cumulative for performance).

As shown in Table XI, none of the reviewed CMMs has a one-to-one mapping to the NIST CSF framework. ISM3 gets first place for satisfying all other evaluation criteria (8 out of 10), followed by PAM, which satisfied 7 out of 10.

VII. CONCLUSION

There exist several CMMs that can be used to measure the progress of implementing a cybersecurity program. However, with the evolving risk of cybersecurity threats, specifically for organizations with critical infrastructure, the adoption of the NIST CSF has been widely popular. Yet no specific CMM has made a clear-cut model to be used specifically for measuring the cybersecurity programs that adopt the NIST cybersecurity framework. Many factors need to be considered by an organization in choosing one CMM versus another; additionally, one CMM should be used over time to accurately measure the progress of implementing the NIST CSF and to maintain and sustain the desired maturity level. Moreover, benchmarking with other organizations has been deemed necessary for sharing the lessons learned and best practices for maintaining and sustaining the high cybersecurity maturity level efficiently and effectively. This is another reason for organizations to use a unified CMM or compatible ones that allow smooth mapping to the NIST CSF framework.

This paper has come up with evaluation criteria based on SMEs' feedback and a survey of the most common requirements that organizations have regarding choosing a CMM for measuring the progress of their implementation of NIST CSF. The criteria considered four aspects for selecting the CMM. These aspects are the scale, domains, assessment criteria, and administration. This article also reviewed seven CMMs: CCSMM, ISM3, PAM for the COBIT framework, ISF SoGP for Information Security, CMMI, SSE CMM, CMMI, and ONG C2M2. The reviews of these CMMs considered the models' scales, domains, and assessment methods. Further, the paper compared the models based on the above aspects as well, as determined the evaluation criteria.

The result showed that all models did not meet the "one-to-one" mapping criterion and did not allow the use of weighted values for each control. ISM3 meets the remaining criteria followed by PAM for COBIT. However, no evidence indicates that these two CMMs are as wildly used as the NIST CSF. Future studies could aim to identify which CMM is in the top quadrant in practical life.

TABLE XI. THE EVALUATION CRITERIA AND THEIR VALUE VERSUS EACH CMM

CMM/Evaluation Criteria	SSE	PAM	ISF	CMMI	CCSMM	ISM3	ONG
Certification	✗	✗	✗	✓	✗	✓	✗
Training in various formats, including in-class	✓	✓	✓	✓	✓	✓	✓
Linked to a framework	✗	✓	✓	✗	✗	✓	✗
Mapped to NIST CSF functions/categories/subcategories	✓	✓	✓	✗	✗	✓	✗
Mapping done by the NIST	✗	✓	✗	✗	✗	✓	✗
"One-to-one" mapping	✗	✗	✗	✗	✗	✗	✗
Five-level scale	✓	✓	✓	✓	✓	✓	✗
Generic criteria for assessing each domain of each level	✓	✓	✓	✗	✗	✓	✗
Weighted value for each control	✗	✗	✗	✗	✗	✗	✗
Cumulative scoring methodology	✓	✓	✗	✓	✓	✓	✓

Additionally, in the future, case studies on organizations that have implemented the NIST CSF should be reviewed. Furthermore, the possibility of one-to-one mapping of NIST CSF to other frameworks or domains of CMMs needs to be assessed.

REFERENCES

[1] National Institute of Standards and Technology. NIST: "Framework for Improving Critical Infrastructure Cyber Security," [Online]. Available from: http://www.nist.gov/cyberframework/upload/cybersecurity-framework-021214.pdf, 2014. [retrieved: 2021.04.25]

[2] B. Obama, "Executive Order 13636, Improving Critical Infrastructure Cybersecurity," [Online]. Available from: http://www.gpo.gov/fdsys/pkg/FR-2013-02-19/pdf/2013-03915.pdf, February 12, 2013. [retrieved: 2021.04.25]

[3] Gartner: "Gartner Webinar, Framework for Improving Critical Infrastructure Cybersecurity," [Online]. Available from: https://www.gartner.com/user/registration/webinar?resId=3163821, 2015. [retrieved: 2021.04.25]

[4] D. Trump, "Executive Order 13800, Strengthening the Cybersecurity of Federal Networks and Critical Infrastructure," [Online]. Available from: https://www.gpo.gov/fdsys/pkg/FR-2017-05-16/pdf/2017-10004.pdf, May 11, 2017. [retrieved: 2021.04.25]

[5] M. Nygaard and S. Mukhopadyay, "Dragonstone Strategy Kickoff Report (No. LLNL-TR-805864)," Lawrence Livermore National Lab (LLNL), Livermore, CA (United States), 2020.

[6] NIST: "Framework for Improving Critical Infrastructure Cyber Security," [Online]. Available from: https://nvlpubs.nist.gov/nistpubs/CSWP/NIST.CSWP.04162018.pdf, 2018. [retrieved: 2021.04.25]

[7] I. Lee, "Internet of Things (IoT) Cybersecurity: Literature Review and IoT Cyber Risk Management," Future Internet, 12(9), p. 157, 2020.

[8] S. Almuhammadi and M. Alsaleh, "Information Security Maturity Model for NIST Cyber Security Framework," [Online]. Available from: https://airccj.org/CSCP/vol7/csit76505.pdf, 2017, 2018. [retrieved: 2021.04.25]

[9] Information Systems Audit and Control Association. ISACA: "COBIT 5: A Business Framework for the Governance and Management of Enterprise IT," 2012.

[10] Information Security Forum. ISF: "Time to Grow Using Maturity Models to Create And Protect Value," in Information Security Forum (ISF), 2014.

[11] Carnegie Mellon University. CMU: "Systems Security Engineering Capability Maturity Model (SSE-CMM) Model Description Document Version 3.0," 1999.

[12]Capability Maturity Model Integration Institute. CMMI: "The CMMI Institute Announces CMMI Development V2.0," 2018.

[13] Department of Energy. DoE: "Oil and Natural Gas Subsector Cybersecurity Capability Maturity Model (ONG-C2M2 v1.1)," Department of Energy, Washington, DC: US, 2014

[14] V. Aceituno, "Information Security Management Maturity Model (ism3) v2. 10, Stansfeld," ISM3 Consortium, 2007
[15] G. White, "The community Cyber Security Maturity Model in Technologies for Homeland Security (HST), 2011 IEEE International Conference on IEEE, pp. 173–178, 2011.
[16] N. Sjelin and G. White, "The Community Cyber Security Maturity Model," Cyber-Physical Security. Springer, Cham, pp. 161–183, 2017.
[17] M. Mylrea, S. Gourisetti, and A. Nicholls, "An Introduction to Buildings Cyber Security Framework," Computational Intelligence (SSCI), 2017 IEEE Symposium Series on IEEE, pp. 1–7, 2017.
[18] N. Le and D. Hoang, "Capability Maturity Model and Metrics Framework for Cyber Cloud Security," Scalable Computing: Practice and Experience, vol. 18, no. 4, pp. 277–290, 2017.
[19] D. Proença and J. Borbinha, "Information Security Management Systems: a Maturity Model Based on ISO/IEC 27001", International Conference on Business Information Systems, Springer, Cham, 2018.
[20] A. Dedeke, "Cybersecurity Framework Adoption: Using Capability Levels for Implementation Tiers and Profiles," IEEE Security & Privacy, no. 5, pp. 47–54, 2017.
[21] ISACA: COBIT Process Assessment Model (PAM): Using COBIT 5, ISACA, 2013.

Internet of Things in Healthcare: Case Study in Care Homes

Tochukwu Emma-Duru
School of Computer and Engineering
University of Huddersfield
Huddersfield, United Kingdom
e-mail: Tochukwu.emma-duru@hud.ac.uk

Violeta Holmes
School of Computer and Engineering
University of Huddersfield
Huddersfield, United Kingdom
e-mail: V.Holmes@hud.ac.uk

Abstract— **The Internet of Things (IoT) involves the interconnection of devices and humans to the Internet. IoT is rapidly being adopted in different sectors of life, including the health sector. Numerous sensing devices are used to gather patients' information, generating a large volume of data. The traditional applications and algorithms are not efficient in processing and managing the patients' data, which presents a challenge. Much research on the Internet of Things in healthcare focuses mainly on hospitals with little focus on care homes. This research uses care homes as a case study as these are regarded as the homes of service users for an extended period of time, much longer than the time they spend in hospitals. This research proposes a system that would enable healthcare staff to monitor the pressure sores in service users with low mobility and provide them with a secured system against attacks from cyber criminals. The system implements the use of sensors to monitor pressure exerted from bedridden service users in real-time using ThingSpeak, provides a secure system by implementing two-factor authentication (2FA) for caregivers for safe login, transmitting data securely over a safe network using raspberry pi 4 as the edge devices, and applying machine learning to help monitor the network for intrusion detection from hackers. With the current gap in research in care homes, this paper emphasises the need for the adoption of real-time monitoring and having a secured system framework for care homes to improve their services provided.**

Keywords – Internet of Things, IoT Security, Edge devices, Esp8266, Embedded Systems, Bedsores, IoT Healthcare.

I. INTRODUCTION

A. *Importance of IoT In Healthcare*

The Internet of Things (IoT) is a concept that is believed to be the future of the Internet. It is the interconnectivity of devices with humans, thereby linking the virtual world with the physical world and is seen as a massive network of things: people-to-people, people-to-devices, devices-to-devices [1]. Communication in IoT thrives from the constant advancements in Wireless Sensor Networks (WSN), Radio Frequency Identification (RFID), Mobile Communication, Cloud technology, among a few others. IoT has hugely helped advance people's standard of living and made life easier as devices and the different sectors of life are adopting smart technology. With the rapid adoption in the utilization of IoT applications, CompTIA predicted that roughly 50.1 billion devices would be connected to the Internet by 2020 [2] of which the number of devices connected to the internet has increased. The Internet of Things has in recent years become the key focus of research as millions of devices are becoming intelligent and being used in different fields such as healthcare, business, security, schools, asset tracking, agriculture, automobiles, smart cities, smart homes, smart metering [3].

The architecture of an IoT system is made up of a variety of layers built with sensors and actuators embedded as part of their structure. While the sensors gather information from its surroundings and process this data to produce useful information, actuators, on the other hand, adjust or modify the condition of their environment based on the information received from the sensors. Some examples include transceivers, thermometers, thermostats, cloud administrations, etc. With the accelerating growth and rapid adoption and use of these smart devices, the security of the sensitive data being shared, the applications and platforms on which they are used becomes top priority to avoid data being compromised. From a functionality and implementation point of view, the IoT systems architecture should be built with a very high and secure level of cryptographic abilities to ensure data authentication, integrity, confidentiality, and validation. Systems having these security features would be protected against all forms of attacks from hackers and cybercriminals that target vulnerable systems with low security.

The constant expansion and growth of the Internet of Things has led to the emergence of Edge Computing. Quite a high number of IoT edge devices that are used very often have high vulnerabilities, and users of these devices are advised to use the inbuilt security features in each device to avoid cyber-attacks [4]. This paper presents an overview of the IoT systems architecture, IoT enabling technology, and its security at the edge. We focus on the application of IoT in healthcare by monitoring pressure sores in patients with low mobility.

The rest of this paper is organized as follows: Section II discusses the literature review of IoT security in healthcare. Section III is the methodology. Section IV addresses the experimental setup. Section V presents the conclusion and future work.

B. Monitoring Pressure Sores

Pressure sores, also called bedsores, are known as injuries to the skin and the underlying tissues due to continuous pressure being applied on the skin for a prolonged period, which results in a shortage of blood flow. This pressure occurs most of the time around parts of the body that are quite bony and prone and faced with continuous friction, immobilization, and malnourishment [5]. Pressure sores have long posed a massive burden in healthcare [6]. People at risk of developing pressure sores are mostly the elderly, disabled patients in wheelchairs, and bedridden patients in hospitals and care homes. In care homes, high profile beds are used especially for patients that are prone to bedsores. Pressure relief cushions are used in chairs and wheelchairs as well to help relieve pressure when sitting.

While in bed, hourly repositioning is done for patients to relieve pressure on the sides laid. It is also done when patients sit in their recliners and wheelchairs; these actions are known as pressure relief mechanisms. Patients are assisted to stand up for a few minutes and if they can, take a short walk to help relieve the pressure that has built up while they were seated for a while. Barrier creams are also regularly applied to the pressure points to protect the skin and act as a barrier. Moody et. al. [7] proposed a platform that shows the pressure distribution map of the body, collects information from sensors embedded in the patient's bed, has the data analysed to create a timestamp, and has the actuators readjust its surface profile to make sure pressure is distributed all over the body.

Different solutions have been proposed to reduce bedsores, like smart beds, sensors, and artificial intelligence to monitor the whole body lying in bed or sitting in a chair. Nair et al. [8] proposed a smart air mattress that can inflate and deflate, thereby relieving the body pressure. Benet et al. [9] also proposed an algorithm that automatically detects parts of the body that have been relieved by pressure points from under a supine subject without assumptions or input by users.

II. RELATED WORK

Much research is being carried out in the use of IoT and its security in the healthcare sector with the main focus on hospitals, and not necessarily in care homes, and this is what this research focuses on. In care homes recently, IoT is being deployed like using sensor mats to detect falls, wearable devices to monitor the patients' vitals, temperature sensors, humidity sensors, and a few others. Many care homes still implement the traditional method of storing patients' data and monitoring sensors via their care plans and daily logbooks. Real-time monitoring of patients' vitals and information in care homes is not common. It is mostly their personal records and information that can be accessed online, and it is mostly managers, nurses and senior carers who have access to these. Most existing research focuses on highlighting the trends and current challenges, and proposing more solutions which IoT can offer the health sector in general as carried out by [10], but there has been little research on implementing a more secured IoT system. Most care homes do not implement two-factor authentication (2FA) to ensure a more secure system, and it is just staff login details that grant them access to the system. This is not very safe and can be very detrimental should a third party hack the system and steal or alter patient's information; that is what this research is focusing on, providing a 2FA system for more security and providing a more secure system while transmitting these patients' data using edge devices. [11] presented the main problems facing narrowband IoT (NBIoT) currently and presented some solutions to help tackle these challenges. [12] addressed the important areas of IoT technologies for smart sensors, big data analytics and advanced health care systems. They used various case studies to identify possible perspectives by highlighting ongoing research issues like interoperability, scalability, security, and device-network-human interfaces. [13] focused on the applications and networks of IoT devices in healthcare, attacks on these devices, the security requirements for the IoT systems, and the organizational approach towards the development and implementation of IoT security. [14] investigated the current IoT security and privacy requirements and provided a new framework that sorts out all aspects of these security and privacy measures, requirements, and recommendations in healthcare. [15] shed light on the importance of IoT-based elderly healthcare systems and their classification by reviewing different research studies focused on developing and utilising these systems. This research also addressed the security and architecture of IoT systems in healthcare and how they are implemented in the home and hospital. [16] designed a system for smart homes to assist care for people with special needs for a prolonged period. The system tracks and analyses how residents behave at different time intervals and provide caregivers with reports and alerts. [17] proposed a novel healthcare IoT system model that provides information on the current health status of patients. Using a Raspberry Pi 3, patients can get an immediate response about hospitals close to them and if the physicians are available to see them. [18] proposed a multi-agent approach to advanced continuous threat detection using machine learning for predictive analysis in identifying security vulnerabilities and patterns to make predictions and recognize outliers.

A. IoT Systems

The IoT systems involve simple, smart devices ranging from wearables to more complex systems such as the recently developed self-driving cars. These devices aim to bring more comfort to the lives of people. IoT systems have improved the quality of life of people greatly. It has made room for everything around us to be automated. Every sector of life uses IoT to improve the services they provide [19]. A combination of all these smart systems gave rise to smart healthcare, smart transportation, smart homes, and smart industries.

B. Security Issues in Internet of Things (IoT)

With the security of the IoT being a top priority, many researchers propose different solutions using different technologies to help reduce cyberattacks [20]. Many research projects have been carried out to address the modelling of the system, its design, setup and the IoT enabling technologies that allow for the proper functioning of the system and, most importantly, its security. The continuous integration of IoT and its applications has drawn attention to several security issues which should be addressed. The more devices become a part of the Internet framework, the more global exposures would give rise to more security vulnerabilities giving room for attackers and cybercriminals to exploit these security flaws. Hewlett Packard, in a survey, stated that a high percentage of IoT devices that are often used are vulnerable and defenceless to attacks [21]. IoT devices can be exposed to these security risks due to inadequacies in their systems design, which may lack security features such as authentication and authorization and have deficient communication media.

Some of the main security issues in IoT include Botnet, Malware attacks, Man-in-the-Middle attacks, and Denial of Service attacks [22]. Hackers can attack IoT devices due to the default software configuration, inconsistent software updates and the extended distance between the patch release and its installation [23]. Security in IoT is crucial and needs to constantly be maintained to protect the billions of devices connected to the Internet.

The design of the IoT system should involve the following security features:

- Confidentiality
- Integrity
- Authenticity
- Authorization
- Availability

C. Edge Devices in Healthcare

IoT in healthcare consists of edge devices used to sense and process data. These edge devices connect a very high number of sensing devices that are smart [24]. They come between the source of information and the cloud [25]. Edge devices provide healthcare with smart systems that allow for speedy health diagnosis and help in providing precise, effective treatments. IoT sensors and its healthcare applications have greatly changed and improved the healthcare approach, with the number of IoT healthcare devices estimated to be more than 162 billion in the year 2020 [26]. The structure of Edge-based IoT healthcare has aided remote monitoring with the help of smart sensors for patients. Data obtained from sensors are sent over to the edge devices for prepossessing before they can be trained using machine learning to also help in monitoring illnesses in real-time and treat these diseases. Solutions for remote monitoring of patients in real-time and the secured transmission of their health reports have for many years been the main area of research for health researchers [27]. [28] suggested the use of computers and microcontroller-based monitoring systems like the electrocardiogram (ECG) and heartbeat sensors to monitor the heartbeat and notify high heart rate. Because of their limited resources, Edge devices are quite vulnerable to different types of threats that could affect their performance. Hence, the cryptographic algorithms should be deployed to increase security.

D. Embedded Devices and Edge devices in IoT

Edge Computing means data being processed at the edge of a network as close to the source of data as possible. It is the expansion of the Internet of Things that led to Edge Computing. Commonly, edge devices are regarded as microcontroller-based systems [29]. As data is being collected from various IoT Edge devices, it is first pre-processed before it is sent to the cloud. Unlike the centralized cloud computing, edge computing is a distributed architecture even though it is based on cloud technologies. With traditional cloud computing being centralized and having all its computation and storage done in a single data centre, it faces some limitations with the continuous emergence of new technology that needs low latency, real-time response and decision making. This is where edge computing comes into play as it is used to improve cloud computing [30]. Data generating devices are considered edge devices. Edge devices in the IoT context are mostly microcontroller-based systems that are resource-constrained and are short of memory and computing power, and they could also be remotely located, meaning they need to optimize their power consumption as they rely on small batteries. Some embedded devices in IoT include Raspberry pi, Jetson Nvidia, etc.

Edge devices directly interact with the physical environment by using RFID tags, sensors, actuators, and embedded devices. The edge layer, which is a critical component of IoT application, is a major target to attackers as they try to gain access to the whole system in the bid to take it down. Figure 1 below shows the architecture of edge devices.

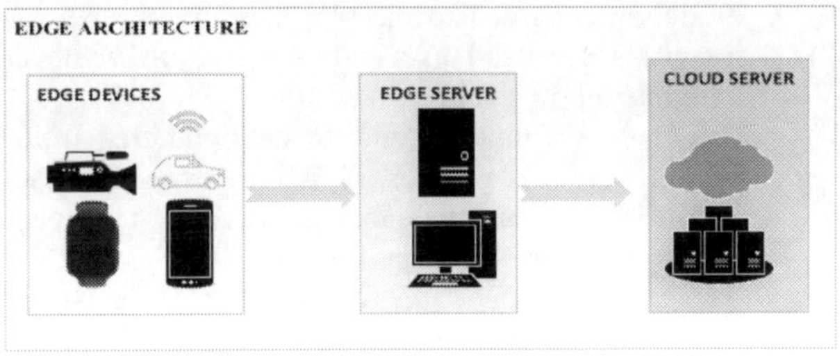

Figure 1. Edge Architecture

E. Security at the Edge in Healthcare

Statistics published a few years back showed that one sector that faced the highest level of threat was the health sector [31]. Security and privacy are major concerns to the security of patient's data. The slightest form of attacks on both patients' personal data, tampering with their medication file, can be catastrophic to the patient and life-threatening [32]. Because of these security concerns, ongoing research on data security concentrates mainly on developing and implementing encryption, authentication, and solutions for wearable and implantable devices [33]-[35]. [36] evaluated a case study for patient biosignal data and designed a structure that uses edge devices to process the data sent to the cloud and enhance the processing and response time while maintaining a very high-level accuracy and data privacy.

F. Artificial Intelligence (AI) Tools For IoT Security in Health Care

Artificial Intelligence is a combination of different technologies. AI in healthcare deploys different software and algorithms to emulate human intelligence to process complex medical data and carry out analysis, tasks, reasoning, detecting patterns and solve problems with no direct human input [37]. AI has brought a massive change in diagnosing diseases, patient care and medical analysis [38]. Since its adoption in healthcare, AI has proven to be the most efficient technology used to process big data and enabling results analysis in real-time [39]. Some of the AI tools for security in healthcare are Machine Learning, Deep Learning, Big Data, Cloud Technology [40] and Blockchain. Based on research conducted, many papers use deep neural networks to tackle privacy and security in healthcare systems [41].

- Machine Learning is an aspect of artificial intelligence that uses intelligent software to enable machines to work effectively. Training models in machine learning are Supervised and Unsupervised. Some of the ML algorithms are Decision Trees, support vector machine (SVM), K-Nearest Neighbour (KNN), Logistic Regression (LR), Naives Bayes, Discriminant Analysis. Popular software used for ML is MATLAB.
- Deep Learning can be defined as learning by example using neural network architecture. It is a specialized ML technology where computer models are trained to classify data given such as images, sounds and texts and, with a result, achieve a high level of accuracy.
- Big Data is a huge amount of data gathered from billions of IoT devices. Analysts expend these gathered data, and valuable information retrieved and conveyed to organizations. This valuable dataset can affect an organisation's decision-making strategies, hence the need to employ advanced technology to help manage the high volume of data.
- Cloud Technology can be used to store data that is easily accessed over the Internet or network. Cloud Computing works with smart devices such as sensors and allows this sensing data to be saved and used for intelligent monitoring and actuation.
- Blockchain technology allows the storage and exchange of data based on peer-to-peer (P2P) network. Blockchain is open-ended and its operation is decentralised.

III. METHODOLOGY

The research adopted in this investigation consists of investigating IoT, edge computing, security in IoT and on edge, and experimentation to evaluate a secured IoT system. A combination of qualitative and quantitative research will inform the design of such IoT systems for healthcare applications.

A. Qualitative Research

A survey was carried out in care homes, and this was aimed at nurses and carers who work with elderly patients who are prone to developing pressure sores. This survey aimed to identify the gap in knowledge in the use and adoption of IoT in healthcare to help reduce the occurrence of bedsores and the need for IoT systems and security. The following information was gathered to help gain a better understanding of the current situation;

- The time intervals that service users are turned to prevent sores from developing
- If pressure sores are monitored in real-time
- How the patients' data are viewed and logged
- Security measures currently in place
- The security measure that they would be applied to prevent attacks and detect intrusion.

Below shows some feedback from the survey conducted:

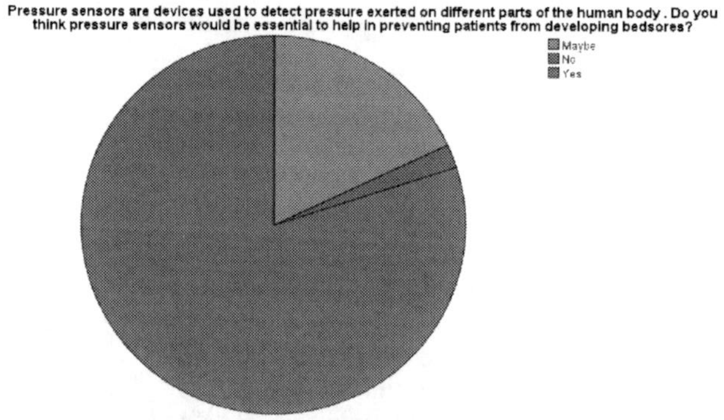

Figure 2a. Adoption of pressure sensors monitoring

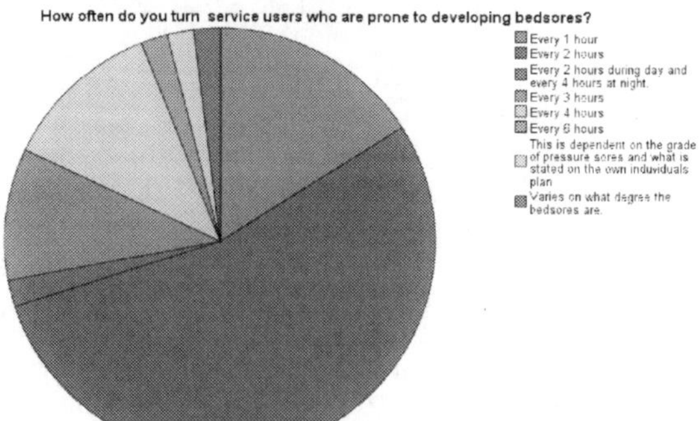

Figure 2b. Time interval of turns

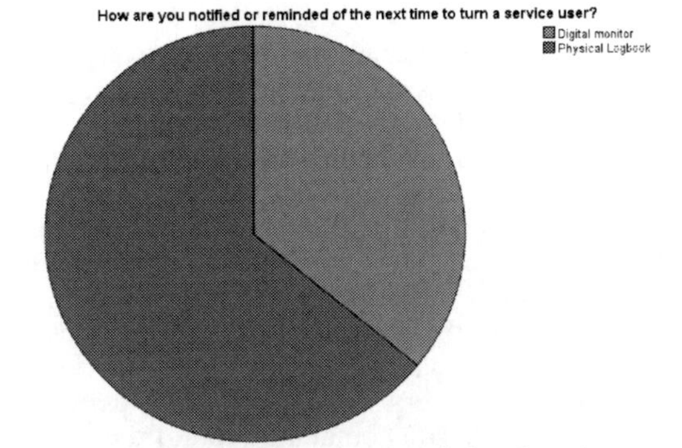

Figure 2c. Paper-based reminder of turn times

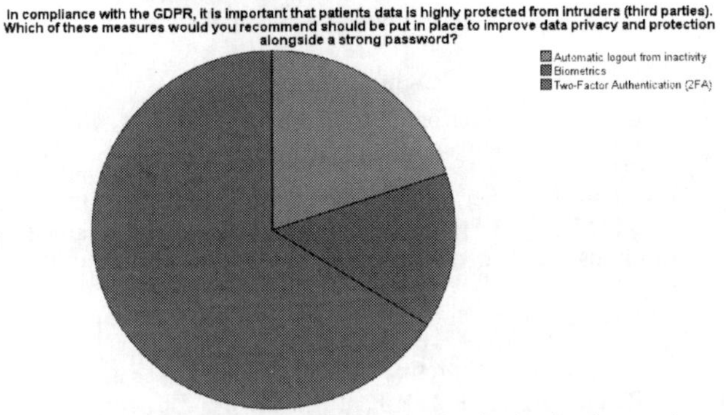

Figure 2d. Preference of the Two-factor authentication implementation

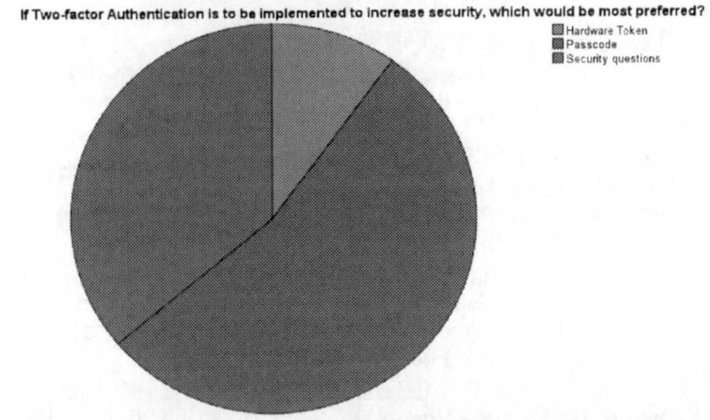

Figure 2e. Preference of the passcode for the two-factor authentication

Many healthcare staff are used to the traditional method of periodically checking on the patients and turning them. Many times, these patients are turned even before the next expected reposition time. Moreover, with this constant turn, not to forget, these carers hurt their backs with the frequent bending positions while repositioning patients. An IoT system in place would save the health staff time of checking patients' position and the level of pressure being exerted by different parts of the body, but they would be able to monitor the pressure being applied on the skin in real-time.

B. *Quantitative Research*

With the information gathered from the survey, experiments would be performed to design the system required to monitor patients prone to developing sores in real-time. A secured system using edge devices to monitor and detect intrusion by deploying machine learning would be developed.

IV. EXPERIMENTAL SETUP

The IoT based system would enable the healthcare staff to monitor patients' vitals in real-time. This system will help prevent sores from developing in these patients. Different service users are turned at different time intervals depending on the skin's vulnerability to developing sores, everyone hour, two hours, or three hours, but the most common is two-hourly turns. Certain parts of the body are more prone to sores than other parts. The pressure sores monitoring system would monitor the pressure exerted in real-time on the ThingSpeak network so the health staff can keep track of the pressure being exerted on that part of the body and reposition the patient as needed. This system is designed to gather, process, store and analyze the data.

The system consists of the pressure sensors, LED, Arduino UNO, Esp8266 and ThingSpeak network cloud platform.

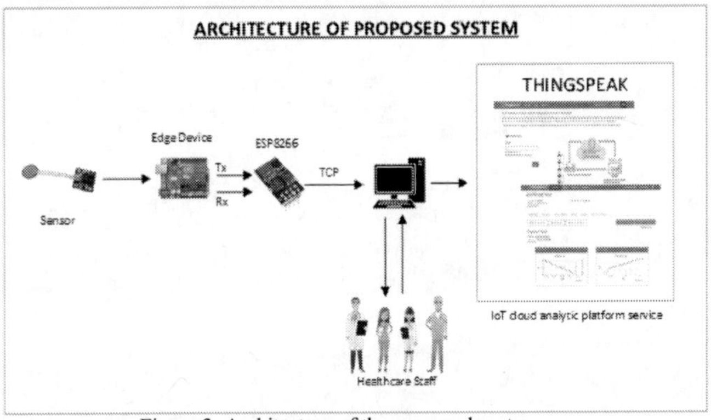

Figure 3. Architecture of the proposed system.

A. *Obtaining sensing data*

The pressure sensor reads when pressure is exerted on different body parts and passed through to the edge device and the cloud network. To provide a more secure system, a two-factor authentication (2FA) system would be deployed. Staff would be required to input a passcode while logging into the platform through a webpage.

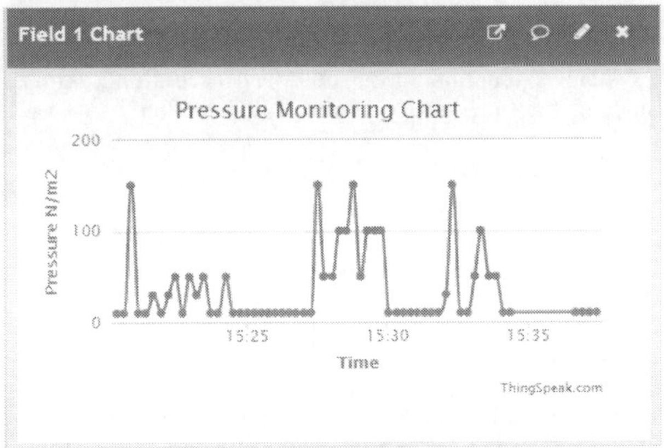

Figure 4. Real time pressure monitoring on ThingSpeak

B. *Creating a Secured Website and Implementing the Two-Factor authentication (2FA).*

A webpage was designed where the 2FA would be required to get into the system. The staff would need an authentication code to log into the system not just the traditional login method involving staff email and password. The authentication code was used based on the feedback that was received from the survey that was conducted.

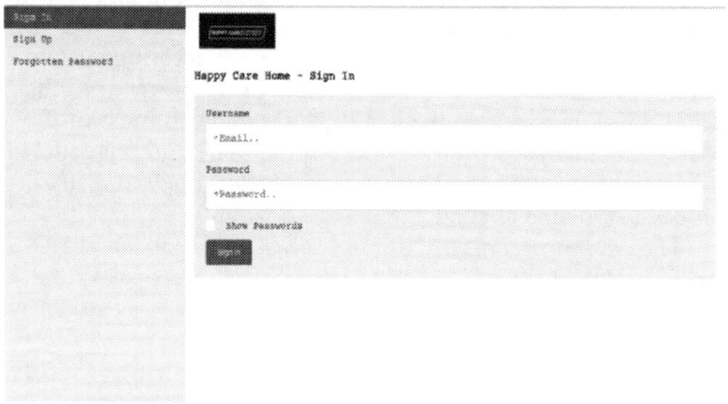

Figure 5. Staff login page

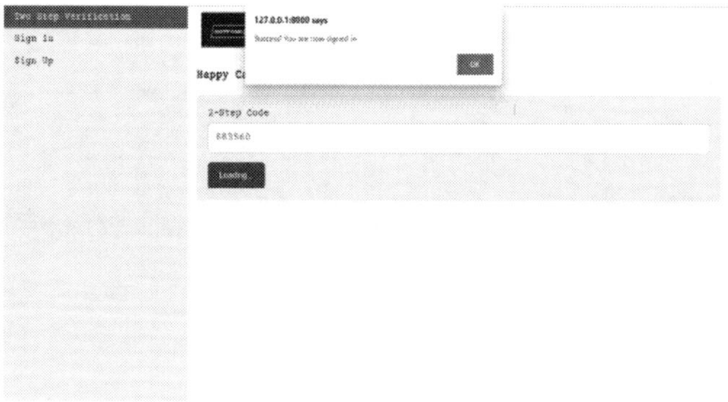

Figure 6. Authentication page

C. *Obtaining the data from ThingSpeak and applying ML*

The sensor will be connected to the edge device, which would transmit the data safely over the network through the transceiver ESP8266, acting as a gateway to ThingSpeak. ThingSpeak provides a secured Transport Layer Security (TLS) protocol. The data obtained would be used in MATLAB to train the model to detect intrusion. To test that the system is functioning, unauthorized access data would be injected into the system for intrusion detection.

V. CONCLUSION AND FUTURE WORK

In this paper we present our research on the IoT application in care homes. The care staff are still using the traditional paper-based methods of logging patients' data as evident from the survey conducted. There is a need for a safe IoT system for storage, transfer, and easy retrieval of patients' data on the cloud. The proposed IoT system is designed to fill this need. The system will enable a transfer of data from the IoT based sensors, such as pressure sensors, to the cloud (TTN and ThingSpeak) and will have strong security features. Two-factor authentication (2FA), which was implemented is proving to be one of the safest security features to ensure data protection and security and prevent unauthorized access. The staff will be able to access the cloud platform, record the data on the system and retrieve real-time information on patients' data. In addition, the proposed system would involve analysis of the data on the ThingSpeak platform and using machine learning algorithms in MATLAB to run simulations and train machine learning models to detect safety breaches. Future work would be focused on evaluating the effectiveness of the proposed system in a case study that will involve a monitoring of pressure to prevent pressure sores. The effectiveness of the system will consider the safe communication of the sensors data, storage, and retrieval of the information on a cloud and safe access to the data by the home care staff.

REFERENCES

[1] A. Iwayemi, "Internet of Things: Implementation Challenges in Nigeria", American Journal Of Engineering Research (AJER), Volume-7(Issue-12), pp-105-115, 2018. Available from http://www.ajer.org.

[2] CompTIA | Sizing Up the Internet of Things. 2015 Available from https://www.comptia.org/content/research/sizing-up-the-Internet-of-things.

[3] K. Mekki, E. Bajic, F. Chaxel, and F. Meyer. "A comparative study of LPWAN technologies for large-scale IoT deployment", ICT Express. 2019;5(1):1-7

[4] M. Abomhara and G.M. Køien, "Security and privacy in the Internet of Things: current status and open issues", IEEE International Conference on Privacy and Security in Mobile Systems (PRISMS), 201433

[5] G. Brandeis, W. Ooi, M. Hossain, J. Morris, and L. Lipsitz, "A longitudinal study of risk factors associated with the formation of pressure ulcers in nursing homes", J Am Geriatr Soc, vol. 42, pp. 388-393, 1994.

[6] F. Boussu, V. Koncar and C. Vasseur, "Novel approach of ulcer prevention based on pressure distribution control algorithm", in Proc IEEE Mechatronics and Automation, pp. 265-270, August 2011.

[7] B. Moody, J. Fanale, M. Thompson, D. Vaillancourt, G. Symonds, and C. Bonasoro, "Impact of staff education on pressure sore development in elderly hospitalized patients", Arch Intern Med, vol. 148, pp. 2241-2243,1988.

[8] P. Nair, S. Mathur, R. Bhandare and G. Narayanan, "Bed sore Prevention using Pneumatic controls", 2020 IEEE International Conference on Electronics, Computing and Communication Technologies (CONECCT), 2020. Available: 10.1109/conecct50063.2020.9198410

[9] S. Bennett, R. Goubran, K. Rockwood and F. Knoefel, "Monitoring the relief of pressure points for pressure ulcer prevention: A subject dependent approach", 2013 IEEE International Symposium on Medical Measurements and Applications (MeMeA), 2013. Available: 10.1109/memea.2013.6549722.

[10] G. Manogaran, N. Chilamkurti and C. Hsu, "Emerging trends, issues, and challenges in Internet of Medical Things and wireless networks", Personal and Ubiquitous Computing, vol. 22, no. 5-6, pp. 879-882, 2018. Available: 10.1007/s00779-018-1178-6 [Accessed 10 September 2021].

[11] S. Anand and S. K. Routray, "Issues and Challenges in Healthcare Narrowband IoT", in International Conference on Inventive Communication and Computational Technologies (ICICCT 2017), 2017, pp. 486 - 489.

[12] F. Firouzi, B. Farahani, M. Ibrahim and K. Chakrabarty, "Keynote Paper: From EDA to IoT eHealth: Promises, Challenges, and Solutions", IEEE Transactions on Computer-Aided Design of Integrated Circuits and Systems, vol. 37, no.

12, pp. 2965-2978, 2018. Available: 10.1109/tcad.2018.2801227.

[13] S. El-Gendy and M. Azer, "Security Framework for Internet of Things (IoT)". 15th International Conference on Computer Engineering and Systems (ICCES), pp. 1-6, 2020. Available: doi: 10.1109/ICCES51560.2020.9334589

[14] E. Fazeldehkordi, O. Owe and J. Noll, "Security and Privacy in IoT Systems: A Case Study of Healthcare Products", 2019 13th International Symposium on Medical Information and Communication Technology (ISMICT), 2019, pp. 1-8, doi: 10.1109/ISMICT.2019.8743971

[15] M. Elkahlout, M. M. Abu-Saqer, A. F. Aldaour, A. Issa and M. Debeljak, "IoT-Based Healthcare and Monitoring Systems for the Elderly: A Literature Survey Study", 2020 International Conference on Assistive and Rehabilitation Technologies (iCareTech), 2020, pp. 92-96, doi: 10.1109/iCareTech49914.2020.00025.

[16] C. Coelho, D. Coelho and M. Wolf, "An IoT smart home architecture for long-term care of people with special needs", 2015 IEEE 2nd World Forum on Internet of Things (WF-IoT), 2015, pp. 626-627, doi: 10.1109/WF-IoT.2015.7389126.

[17] S. Yattinahalli and R. M. Savithramma, "A Personal Healthcare IoT System model using Raspberry Pi 3", 2018 Second International Conference on Inventive Communication and Computational Technologies (ICICCT), 2018, pp. 569-573, doi: 10.1109/ICICCT.2018.8473184.

[18] Á. MacDermott, P. Kendrick, I. Idowu, M. Ashall and Q. Shi, "Securing Things in the Healthcare Internet of Things", 2019 Global IoT Summit (GIoTS), 2019, pp. 1-6, doi: 10.1109/GIOTS.2019.8766383.

[19] K. Jaiswal, S. Sobhanayak, A. Turuk, B. SahooL, B. Mohanta and D. Jena, "An IoT-Cloud based smart healthcare monitoring system using container based virtual environment in Edge device", in Proceedings of 2018 International Conference on Emerging Trends and Innovations in Engineering and Technological Research (ICETIETR), 2021, pp. 1-6.

[20] O. Alfandi, S. Khanji, L. Ahmad and A. Khattak, "A survey on boosting IoT security and privacy through blockchain", Cluster Computing, vol. 24, no. 1, pp. 37-55, 2020. Available: 10.1007/s10586-020-03137-8.

[21] Hewlett-Packard Enterprise Development LP HP P-Class Smart Array Gen9 RAID Controllers. Citeseerx.ist.psu.edu. from http://citeseerx.ist.psu.edu/viewdoc/summary?doi=10.1.1.729.9133.

[22] S. Okul and M. Ali Aydin, "Security Attacks on IoT", 2017 International Conference on Computer Science and Engineering (UBMK), pp. 1-5. Available: 10.1109/UBMK.2017.8093577

[23] R. Gurunath, M. Agarwal, A. Nandi and D. Samanta, "An Overview: Security Issue in IoT Network". IEEE Xplore, (978-1-5386-1442-6), 2018, pp. 104-107.

[24] J. Li et al., "A Secured Framework for SDN-Based Edge Computing in IoT-Enabled Healthcare System", IEEE Access, vol. 8, pp. 135479-135490, 2020. Available: 10.1109/access.2020.3011503

[25] R. Anusuya, D. Karthika Renuka and L. L.Ashok Kumar, "Review on Challenges of Secure Data Analytics in Edge Computing", in 2021 International Conference on Computer Communication and Informatics (ICCCI -2021), Jan. 27 – 29, 2021, Coimbatore, INDIA.

[26] A. O. Akmandor and N. K. Jha, "Smart health care: An edge-side computing perspective", IEEE Consum. Electron. Mag., vol. 7, no. 1, pp. 29–37, Jan. 2018.

[27] S. Amin and M. Hossain, "Edge Intelligence and Internet of Things in Healthcare: A Survey", IEEE Access, vol. 9, pp. 45-59, 2021. Available: 10.1109/access.2020.3045115

[28] Y. Hao, Y. Miao, L. Hu, M. S. Hossain, G. Muhammad, and S. U. Amin, "Smart-edge-CoCaCo: AI-enabled smart edge with joint computation, caching, and communication in heterogeneous IoT", IEEE Netw., vol. 33, no. 2, pp. 58–64, Mar. 2019

[29] S. Shapsough, F. Aloul and I. Zualkernan, "Securing Low-Resource Edge Devices for IoT Systems", 2018 International Symposium in Sensing and Instrumentation in IoT Era (ISSI), 2018. Available: 10.1109/issi.2018.8538135.

[30] I. Sittón-Candanedo, R. Alonso, J. Corchado, S. Rodríguez-González and R. Casado-Vara, "A review of edge computing reference architectures and a new global edge proposal", Future Generation Computer Systems, vol. 99, pp. 278-294, 2019. Available: 10.1016/j.future.2019.04.016.

[31] IBM 2016 Cost of Data Breach Study United States, I. Corp,Washington, DC, USA, Sep. 2016. https://resources.idgenterprise.com/original/AST-0185855_SEL03094USEN.PDF

[32] G. Thamilarasu, A. Odesile and A. Hoang, "An Intrusion Detection System for Internet of Medical Things", IEEE Access, vol. 8, pp. 181560-181576, 2020. Available: 10.1109/access.2020.3026260.

[33] R. V. Sampangi, S. Dey, S. R. Urs, and S. Sampalli, "A security suite for wireless body area networks", 2012, arXiv:1202.2171.[Online].Available:http://arxiv.org/abs/1202.2171

[34] A. S. Sangari and J. M. L. Manickam, "Public key cryptosystem based security in wireless body area network", in Proc. Int. Conf. Circuits, Power Comput. Technol., Mar. 2014, pp. 1609_1612.

[35] W. Li and X. Zhu, "Recommendation-Based Trust Management in Body Area Networks for Mobile Healthcare", 2014 IEEE 11th International Conference on Mobile Ad Hoc and Sensor Systems, 2014, pp. 515-516, doi: 10.1109/MASS.2014.85.

[36] A. Alabdulatif, I. Khalil, X. Yi and M. Guizani, "Secure Edge of Things for Smart Healthcare Surveillance Framework", IEEE Access, vol. 7, pp. 31010-31021, 2019. Available: 10.1109/access.2019.2899323.

[37] N. Al-Milli and W. Almobaideen, "Hybrid Neural Network to Impute Missing Data for IoT Applications", 2019 IEEE Jordan International Joint Conference on Electrical Engineering and Information Technology (JEEIT), 2019. Available: 10.1109/jeeit.2019.8717523.

[38] W. Almobaideen, R. Krayshan, M. Allan and M. Saadeh, "Internet of Things: Geographical Routing based on healthcare centers vicinity for mobile smart tourism destination", Technological Forecasting and Social Change, vol. 123, pp. 342-350, 2017. Available: 10.1016/j.techfore.2017.04.016.

[39] C. Ieracitano et al., "Statistical Analysis Driven Optimized Deep Learning System for Intrusion Detection", Advances in Brain Inspired Cognitive Systems, pp. 759-769, 2018. Available: 10.1007/978-3-030-00563-4_74..

[40] S. Gopalan, A. Raza and W. Almobaideen, "IoT Security in Healthcare using AI: A Survey", 2020 International Conference on Communications, Signal Processing, and their Applications (ICCSPA), pp. 1-6, 2021. Available: 10.1109/iccspa49915.2021.9385711.

[41] P. Ghosal, D. Das and I. Das, "Extensive Survey on Cloud-based IoT-Healthcare and Security using Machine Learning", 2018 Fourth International Conference on Research in Computational Intelligence and Communication Networks (ICRCICN), pp. 1-5, 2018. Available: 10.1109/icrcicn.2018.8718717.

What Influences People's View of Cyber Security Culture in Higher Education Institutions? An Empirical Study

Tai Durojaiye
Information Security Group
Royal Holloway University of London
Egham, Surrey, United Kingdom
Email: Tai.Durojaiye.2019@live.rhul.ac.uk

Konstantinos Mersinas
Information Security Group
Royal Holloway University of London
Egham, Surrey, United Kingdom
Email: Konstantinos.Mersinas@rhul.ac.uk

Dawn Watling
Department of Psychology
Royal Holloway University of London
Egham, Surrey, United Kingdom
Email: Dawn.Watling@rhul.ac.uk

***Abstract*—The education sector is considered to have the poorest security culture score amongst many sectors. Human aspects of cyber security including cyber security culture which have often been overlooked in the study of cyber security have not been fully explored in Higher Education Institutions (HEIs). The lack of understanding of cyber security culture, unclear definition of the concept and guidance on how to measure and foster it, are challenges HEIs face. To address this lack of knowledge and understanding, we explore the factors that influence people's view of cyber security culture in UK HEIs. We interviewed senior HEI leaders, academics, professional services staff, and students (19 participants in total) in three UK universities of similar characteristics. We find that communication necessary to influence security culture in HEIs is lacking. There is lack of policies/frameworks in place to guide user behaviour. We also observe that IT expectations are not well defined, and phishing exercises create problems between the IT team and users. There is no onboarding security training and awareness for students which make up the largest percentage of the HEI populace. We recommend that senior HEI leaders invest in training and awareness programmes for IT staff and other users, focusing on communication, engagement, collaboration, and social engineering. We also recommend that senior HEI leaders prioritise the creation and implementation of a cyber security strategy, on which policies and other security efforts could be based. The adoption of these recommendations could influence the mindsets of users towards engaging in safe cyber security behaviours and by doing so improving the culture of security in HEIs.**

Keywords- Cyber security culture; Higher Education Institutions (HEIs); security behaviour; communication; phishing; training.

I. INTRODUCTION

The increasing use of technology in the twenty-first century continues to yield huge benefits to nations, organisations, and individuals in their day-to-day activities. Modern technological advancements such as Artificial Intelligence (AI), Internet of Things (IoT), big data, 5G, cloud computing and blockchain have affected different areas of society [1][2]. The application of these technologies has brought improvements to different industry sectors, ranging from medical to education. However, the reliance on technology also has its challenges. The application of the technological advancements in different domains translate into more data being generated. With the increase in the attack surface (that is, the total of all exposures of an information system) [3] due to the abundance of data generated, organisations become easy targets for cyber attacks.

Huge volume of data has caused organisations and users to be prime targets for cyber attacks and hackers [4]. Cyber attacks use innovative approaches. Cyber attacks and hackers use different methods, and in some instances, they use advanced technology to prevent staff and students from gaining access to the needed data and networks. This is a major threat in HEIs, where the availability to information could be denied by cyber attacks [5]. According to [5], most UK HEIs are not well prepared to defend their human and information assets from breaches, phishing attacks, and other security vulnerabilities.

Users continue to pose a threat to the information assets of HEIs. As the PwC Information Security Breaches Survey [6] reports, three quarters of large organisations suffered staff-related security breaches while for small businesses it was one third, a respective percentage rise of 17% and 9% from 2014 to 2015. When organisations were questioned about the single worst breach suffered, 50% attributed the cause to inadvertent human error. This was a percentage increase of 19% from 2014 to 2015.

Human error can be attributed to accidents or negligence. The importance of paying attention to human error is further corroborated by the IBM survey which states that nine out of ten information security incidents are caused by some sort of human error [7].

Thus, it is reasonable to hypothesise that human factors constitute a challenge for HEI leaders too. The approach many organisation leaders have taken to reduce the risk posed by cyber threats is focusing on and increasing their investments on technical controls [8]. Traditionally, the focus of risk mitigation in information security has been on technical solutions. Despite following this approach to defend the organisation ecosystem, cyber security breaches have not declined [9]. While technical solutions offer some protection, it is not a panacea for all cyber security breaches. Hence, this calls for additional defence to be employed [10].

Over the years the approach to information security has evolved and gone through many stages. As study [11] shows, the information security evolution moved from the initial stages where information security was characterised solely by technical approach, best left for technical experts [12] to a stage where efforts were made to understand and address the human element as an essential security factor [13].

The industry is now at a stage where researchers and organisations are becoming more aware of the importance of the often-overlooked area, that is, the human aspect of cyber security with emphasis on Cyber Security Culture (CSC). This stage is characterised by researchers defining CSC, identifying, and attempting to address the gaps that exist in the domain [14]. Although there are studies that indicate associations between CSC and characteristics such as attitudes and social norms, there are only indirect associations between CSC and secure behaviour [15].

While some organisations have different training and awareness programmes in place, a study of CSC definitions [16] shows the ineffectiveness of security awareness and education demonstrating that training itself is not enough. Therefore, more research is required to gain a deeper understanding of the human aspect of cyber security.

An understanding of CSC will provide an insight which could be used to address users' unsafe security behaviours. There are gaps that have been identified based on extant literature on CSC, which argue that the field lacks guidance on how to foster it. For instance, the descriptive and theoretical solutions offered by researchers can be impractical to apply in organisational settings, tool validation is needed, and guidelines and practices are needed for developing and implementing security culture in organisations. Also, a gap exists between awareness levels, respective practices, and behaviour [16]. Security culture improvement is needed in organisations to maintain a healthy posture.

Importantly, there are limited empirical studies on CSC in HEIs. Cyber security culture is ill-defined and there are no clear guidelines on how to foster security culture. The education sector lacks understanding about this important domain. The consequence of this is that users exhibit certain security behaviours which make their institution a prime target for cyber attacks. If we know personnel and students' perception of CSC, then we will better understand why they exhibit such security behaviours which put their institutions at risk of cyber breaches.

In this paper, we focus on CSC in the education sector. Our aim is to explore what influences personnel (senior management members, academics, professional services/ administrative staff) and students' views of CSC in HEIs. It is when we understand what is happening in this domain and in this environment, that effective strategies, methods, and appropriate course of action could be proposed and taken to defend information assets in the institutions. Then, plans could be made to instil security behaviours in people which will lead to a healthy security posture in HEIs.

II. BACKGROUND AND IMPORTANCE

The sector is an attractive target for ransomware attacks enabled by phishing operations. Many HEIs around the world and in the UK suffer from cyber attacks on a regular basis. A Joint Information Systems Committee (JISC) report [17] indicates that UK HEIs are not well prepared to defend themselves and recover from cyber attacks if and when they happen. In a survey of CSC in 17 industry sectors, distributed across 24 countries, the Security Culture Report [18] confirms that the education sector has the poorest security culture score among other poor performers such as transportation and energy and utilities.

The education sector continues to be an increasingly attractive target for cyber attacks because of the wealth of information repositories it holds. Information ranges from intellectual property to information about staff, students, and alumni. Cyber attacks in UK HEIs are increasing and are becoming more targeted at users in this sector because of its poor security culture. Indicatively, breaches have been reported at University of Greenwich [19], and University of Edinburgh [20]. This could lead to financial and indirect losses, such as reputational damage, cost of containing the breach, etc. The security solutions that have often been proposed and offered by organisations and security professionals have little or no involvement with users. With a new perspective, we make some recommendations.

We identified three UK universities with similar characteristics to conduct interviews. In the next section, we discuss our research methodology.

III. CURRENT STATE OF CYBER SECURITY CULTURE

CSC studies have been conducted in different sectors, such as banking and finance, healthcare, and government organisations. CSC related work has focussed on the definitions of information security culture (ISC) and CSC, with the two considered to be similar. Although, there are similarities between ISC and CSC, there is no universally agreed definition of CSC [16].

Researchers have also developed models and frameworks to provide guidance in the understanding of CSC. Some of these have built on Schein's iceberg model of organisation culture [21]. The STOPE framework [22] have been used as a basis to develop another framework such as the Information Security Culture Framework (ISCF) in [23].
Other areas that are important for building and maintaining CSC are management support or involvement, security awareness and training, security policy, communication and change management [24]-[30].

Some of the existing solutions that have been offered are theoretical and conceptual in nature, mainly geared towards industry and not HEI-focussed. The solutions are not adequate for fostering CSC in industry nor in HEIs. Hence, there is the need for some of the solutions to be tested through empirical studies. To the best of our knowledge, there is a lack of empirical studies focusing on the cyber security posture of UK HEIs. In view of the inadequate solutions, we investigate the perceptions of personnel and students of CSC in UK HEIs.

Our goal is to highlight the current problems in UK HEIs through a practical approach, allowing pertinent issues of security culture to emerge. Findings could then be used by researchers as a basis for further CSC investigations in UK HEIs and beyond.

IV. METHODOLOGY

We approached staff in three HEIs, all located in the south of England, that were considered similar in terms of student numbers (between 10,000 and 20,000) and staff numbers. The websites of the three UK universities were used to contact participants (N=19) that fit the criteria of our target group, resulting in interviews with three senior management members, six academics (three of whom have information security background), seven professional services/administrative staff, and three PhD students.

Interviews started with general questions on the role and responsibilities of the interviewee [31][32]. Questions included security perceptions, governance, devolution, university structure and culture. Other questions focused on training and development, security of information and records.

To understand what influences personnel and students' views of CSC, we conducted semi-structured interviews, with questions designed and conducted by a multidisciplinary team of three researchers.

One-to-one interviews were conducted between 29 January 2020 and 21 July 2020. Sixteen interviews were conducted face-to-face while three were done online. The interview duration was approximately 30 minutes. Participant's personal identifiable information was anonymised during data cleaning by one of the researchers and were therefore unidentifiable for the other researchers.

Interviews were recorded, transcribed, and then analysed. Content analysis of the interviews, based on the approach described in [32]-[34], was conducted with support of NVivo software. In total 1961 statements were identified.

We focus on the individual level of the security culture model presented in [11]. The individual level of the model focuses on user attributes and characteristics which impact security attitude and behaviour. We make the model more comprehensive by adapting it to cover more factors related to the user's internal-driven individual notions which affect their security attitude and behaviour. Other relevant dimensions are identified from [18] and the comprehensive model is presented in Figure 1. The individual level is further broken down into the seven dimensions of CSC. The definitions of the dimensions are as shown in TABLE 1. DIMENSIONS OF CYBER SECURITY CULTURE. From the detailed analysis of our interviews, themes, that is, recurring topics emerge.

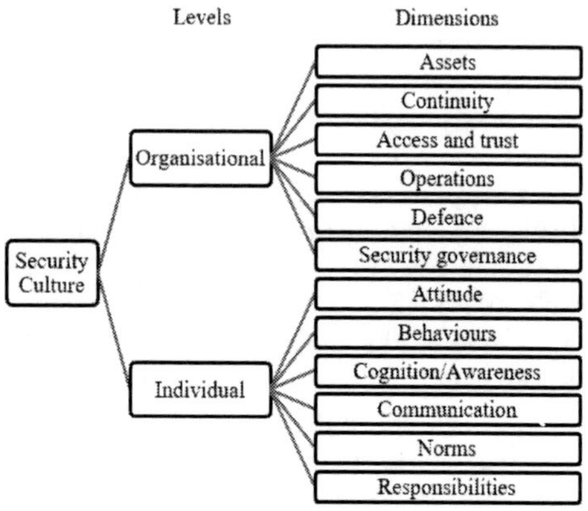

Figure 1. A Comprehensive Security Culture Model [11]

TABLE 1. DIMENSIONS OF CYBER SECURITY CULTURE [18]

Dimension	Definition
Attitude	The feelings and beliefs that employees have toward the security protocol
Behaviours	The actions and activities of employees that have direct and indirect impact on the security of the organisation
Cognition/ Awareness	Employees' understanding, knowledge, and awareness of security issues and activities
Communication	The quality of communication channels to discuss security-related topics, promote a sense of belonging and provide support for security issues and incident reporting
Compliance	The knowledge of written security policies and the extent that employees follow them
Norms	The knowledge of and adherence to unwritten rules of conduct in the organisation
Responsibilities	How employees perceive their role as a critical factor in sustaining or endangering the security of the organisation

V. RESULTS

From the analysis of the 1961 interview statements identified within the 19 interviews, Condensed Meaning Units (CMUs) were generated. A CMU is the shortened version of an interview statement that retains the primary meaning. The relevant CMUs related to CSC dimensions (TABLE 1. DIMENSIONS OF CYBER SECURITY CULTURE) were grouped into codes and were labelled in relation to their content or context; thus, allowing the formation of categories. From the categories, six themes, which reveal underlying meanings, emerge. The themes are: communication; policies and frameworks; IT expectations; moving away from phishing exercises; training, reinforced training and awareness; and CSC measurement.

In this section, we present our findings and the emerging themes from the qualitative analysis; indicative interview excerpts are provided for each finding.

A. Communication

Communication is the main emerging theme in this study that underpins all other themes. Communication is a vital tool which must be mastered and used effectively in collaboration, relationship building, policy conveying, awareness raising and training. The key categories from the study which contribute to the emergence of this theme are communication improvement, beneficial outcomes of collaboration, communication, and information management. The latter captures poor and impersonal communication with users and consists of unclear university cyber security plans, which are poorly communicated with users.

1) Communication Finding 1: Lack of systematic communication from the IT team to users

Communication problems exist in HEIs. As an interviewee explains "there is a lack of systematic communication between the IT services regarding cyber security to staff in general". IT communication is seen as unclear and opaque, and because of this, users have had to form their own judgements based on the little or no information they have about security. The following indicative extracts support this: "I don't even know that. So, I would just like them to be a bit more clear"; "So I feel there's a real [problem], everything is very opaque". While another interviewee understands that the IT team could be busy because of other priorities, they state "They have priorities and that security, because I don't hear about any of this stuff. I don't know. So, I formed judgements because I don't have information".

The following extracts demonstrate the lack of communication from the IT team to users: "I don't think there is enough communication. That's my big thing, just not communicating enough". An interviewee explains the need for the IT team to listen more "I think that generally our IT department do a very good job of communicating, but we don't always do a very good job of listening".

Further, as another user indicates there is a lack of transparency from the IT team: "[IT] haven't told us anything about it. They don't tend to tell us stuff about that. So yeah, maybe they could communicate with us better about what they are doing". Hence, users demand for more communication. An interviewee suggests that communication from the IT team needs to be refined "And clearly they are monitoring phishing emails, and they are sending reminders to people. So 'don't click things' and so on. Let's forget if that is a correct reminder because you can't actually tell people not to click the link [..]. It's part of the job". Thus, there is a query on how people can even do their work if such information is being promulgated without an alternative solution being offered.

Participants highlighted the specific need for pre- and post-phishing communication where phishing exercises have been planned. An interviewee sums this up: "I feel like there should be a message to say like, [..], this was a phishing test" and on post phishing exercises communication "but then definitely there needs to be a clear explanation afterwards as to why they did that and then how students should react and what would be beneficial for them to do in that situation".

2) Communication Finding 2: Collaboration problems exist between the IT team and academics

An observation made is that there are collaboration problems, where academics' offer of their cyber security expertise and this is not embraced by the IT team, as the following extracts indicate: "I try to work with them and to offer help and to try to increase the level of communication and collaboration, that has proved to be difficult". This signifies a challenge in information sharing between academics and IT staff.

3) Communication Finding 3: Communication is impersonal

Another finding from our study indicates that communication is impersonal. There are no names on emails received from IT services. An interviewee says, "I don't like the fact that [..] you don't ever get a signature, you have a conversation with someone over a few emails and you don't know who you're talking to".

B. Policies and Frameworks for Guiding Cyber Security Behaviour

This theme is concerned with the need to have policies and frameworks in place to guide the cyber security expectations and behaviours of HEI information asset users. The policies cover behaviour sets that influence how people practice cyber security. The behaviour sets are compliance with security policy, intergroup coordination and communication, phishing email behaviour, and password behaviour [35]. The policies act as guide for users (including IT staff) in their daily use of information assets and interactions with other users and technology. It also covers regulatory, legal, and compliance information, including General Data Protection Regulation (GDPR).

Our aim is to assess personnel and students' perception of the policies and frameworks that are in place and their impact on influencing user behaviour towards security compliance.

1) Policies and Frameworks Finding 1: Lack of enough policies/frameworks

Our findings show that enough policies and frameworks are not in place for guiding user behaviour in HEIs. With reference to policies and processes that are specific to cyber security an interviewee states "I don't think there are enough, policies and processes in place that people would want to work around it". An interviewee does not feel the HEI security policy defines the boundaries through which they operate, "there is nothing to stop me sending a personal email from my work account, so we don't have anything, I believe, in our terms or policies that prevent you from doing that". Further, another interviewee says, "there is too much writing of policies and not enough doing it", suggesting a lack of policy implementation.

The policies that are in place are not communicated effectively to students and staff. Policy information is shared via employment contract suggesting a passive approach of communication. An interviewee comments "..a lot of it is covered by individual employment contracts with us, or student enrolment with us in those different areas, as to the standards that [we are] required to meet and what they can and can't do with our network and our information assets".

2) Policies and Frameworks Finding 2: Lack of prioritisation

Prioritisation is another problem identified through this research. For instance, an interviewee comments: "I think one of the challenges [the university] has had around cyber security is that it has tried to do everything in terms of policy standard and technology all at once without any real sense of priority and without any real sense of priority based on an intelligent assessment of what the actual threat and risk is". While another interviewee states "Is it in a framework, is it written down? Can I put my hand on it and say, in priority order, these are the most critical data sets and services to the running of this organisation, you know, prioritise these for security and resilience over others? No. I don't think there is"

C. IT Expectations

This theme is about the need for the IT team to engage more with users to understand the challenges that they face in terms of not knowing what is expected of them. The scope of the theme relates to compliance and non-compliance with IT expectations. Its purpose is to explore users' attitude and behaviour towards compliance with IT expectations.

1) IT Expectations Finding 1: IT Expectations are not well defined

IT expectations are not defined clearly. An interviewee says, "that sounds a little bit weak because the expectations are probably not very well defined, as I probably mentioned there is a lack of systematic communication between the IT services regarding cyber security to staff in general". This finding also demonstrates that there is a link between IT expectations and communication.

2) IT Expectations Finding 2: Academics do not see the need for IT compliance

An interviewee comments about the attitude of academics towards compliance, "I think academic ones, they often don't see why they should and don't understand the implication of what they're doing. And you get that in other things like financial regulations and HR regulations as well. They just think that it's getting in their way. They've got things to do and it's the silliness, and they don't understand really the serious implications of what they're doing". And a comparison is made between academics and professional services staff with interviewees commenting that: "Some of us are very into it and others just don't understand and it [is] just blocking their job, which it isn't, but they think it is"; "I think you'll have a higher compliance rate with us than you would with other teams around or other roles around campus". This demonstrates that there is compliance disparity between user groups across the HEI.

3) IT Expectations Finding 3: Users want to comply

Users want to comply with IT expectations because "it's within the framework of the organisation". A senior academic state their willingness to comply "Well, [..] we're in the business of [..] we're information security academics. So, I guess our day job is about- I mean in some sense, one part of our mission is to keep the world secure, to educate people about security practice". An interviewee comments, "so you know, [..] there's no clear guidance on how to behave with stuff like this and what to do if there's a problem."

Although, users are willing to comply with IT expectations, but there are some instances when they may not comply, as the following interviewee extract indicates: "I think we are very likely to comply, because I don't think they are too difficult to comply with. So again, I think there's this trade off, if they expect a lot from us, it will be more difficult to comply with, right? So not asking a lot, but asking something that is reasonable, is, [..] again makes it easier for us to comply". Further, interviewees say they will not comply under certain conditions: "if this is a restriction on my research"; things start to sound unreasonable and they start to become, an obstacle to our work, then the temptation not to comply increases"; "I think we'd only think it's excessive if it was actually hindering us being able to interact".

D. Moving Away from Phishing Exercises

The theme focuses on the observation that was made about how unproductive phishing exercises are and about the need to move away from it. The theme establishes the context for phishing exercises, if at all they are to be done. In which case it needs to be planned, people need to be informed and carried along, this has not been the case in HEIs.

1) Moving Away from Phishing Exercises Finding 1: Phishing exercises create more problems between the IT Team and users

Phishing exercises create problems of distrust and resentment between IT team and users. An interviewee says, "these kind of so-called realistic phishing exercise [..] will probably cause more problems than solving problems because it will cause some confusion, that can potentially even make the functionality fail". Another interviewee comments, "I'd find it a little bit, I guess in a way I'd feel it's a little bit violating that your own university is trying to phish you, even if it's to teach you a lesson, you know, it feels a bit off-putting". Phishing of staff creates anger as these interviewee extracts indicate: "I know some colleagues who were very angry about it, particularly, they thought, they were insulted that they were being phished by the, especially the information security staff"..."but equally I think it annoys people as well".

2) Moving Away from Phishing Exercises Finding 2: Phishing exercises results used to blame others

There is the tendency that phishing exercises results could be used by the university to blame people [36]. This is the undertone of this extract "[..] for those that got caught, it would have been a bit of a wakeup call, I suspect, and it wasn't, and are probably feeling a bit stupid and being a bit cross about it, but actually if they think about it for 30 seconds, they should be quite glad that they clicked on something that was quite innocent and it was helping them raise awareness". Similarly, an interviewee raises a concern about "the risks with these phishing techniques are that they might be just used to blame users and that's, not ideal". In view of aforementioned arguments, some users feel it causes panic and advise that "it is not the way forward".

3) Moving Away from Phishing Exercises Finding 3: Phishing exercises opposed

Phishing exercises are opposed to. For instance, one interview states that there is "a lot of bad feeling from staff who felt that this is not a particular way to go". Due to the negative feelings from users, they have shown resistance to the implementation of phishing exercises.

E. Training, Reinforced Training and Awareness

Training is needed in universities by users and cyber security staff alike. This theme majors on user behavioural change through training and awareness, with a knock-on effect on security culture. The focus of the theme is on all users (including IT staff and students) and how to better equip them to secure information assets. It is through training and awareness that mindsets that influence unsafe user behaviour could be changed.

1) Training, Reinforced Training and Awareness Finding 1: Cyber security training is lacking

Our finding shows that cyber security training is lacking as an interviewee admits, "No. There's no such thing as far as I understand. There's no cyber security training for staff or students as far as I'm aware". Further, another interviewee states that there is "No cyber security training for staff or students". Interviewees recognised that it may be about signposting for the training: "But I've not been on anything [portal] that says, "this is cyber security, and you shall do it"; "there isn't any, what I would describe as dedicated on-boarding training around students for cyber security and institution". The lack of cyber security training could create vulnerabilities and awareness problems that cyber attacks may exploit.

F. Cyber Security Culture Measurement

Cyber security culture is hard to define, grasp and measure [16]. In view of this, it is the observable aspects of CSC that should be measured. These aspects of CSC are training over time, training uptake, incident reporting, cyber security climate, etc. This is an upcoming area of research that is currently being explored. The theme revolves around how to measure the observable aspects of CSC and its implementation across HEIs.

1) Culture Measurement Finding 1: Lack of knowledge about culture measurement

Interviewees feel that security culture is not measured in the HEIs, that it is difficult to measure, and that there is lack of understanding on how to measure it. For instance, interviewees commented that: "I don't think we measure culture, and I don't think most people know how to measure the culture"; "it's quite difficult to measure the culture".

VI. DISCUSSION AND RECOMMENDATIONS

A. Communication

The lack of systematic communication on cyber security between the IT team and users could be due to the absence of the needed training and communication skills among IT staff.

In some HEIs, restructuring of the cyber security and IT teams have led to under-resourced teams with reduced manpower. Hence, IT teams must prioritise and concentrate on technical solutions and approaches, the "traditional means" for defending universities' information assets. Focusing on technical solutions over the human aspect of cyber security could have resulted in the lack of interest in systematic communication with users. The restructuring within universities could also have been influenced by limited financial budget and insufficient cyber security investment, a challenge many Western HEIs face [37]. The same resource issue is a problem Malaysian HEIs experience, which delay the adaptation and implementation of security policies [38].

A reason for unclear communication could be the lack of understanding of what is to be communicated. For example, policies, training content, safe security behaviours or best practices. The communication problem is corroborated by the JISC survey on digital experience insight in UK HEIs [39]. The survey reports that 39% of students state that they were not informed by their institution how their personal data was stored or used. Also, it could be challenging for IT staff to translate technical information into simple layman's language for non-technical users to understand. Conversely, translating information on human aspects of security into technical solutions by IT staff is not an easy task as ENISA reports [40].

The collaboration problem between the IT team and academics could be caused by the lack of engagement in times past, which leaves no room for ideas to be shared and received. The IT team may also see the offer from academics as a way of monitoring their work. The culture of 'us versus them' could also have influenced the IT teams not embracing the offer of help from academics.

Some of the different perspectives provided by academics with information security background is that of their willingness to offer their expertise to assist the IT team and improve the cyber security posture in the HEI. Some feel that it is through the sharing of experiences and best practices that HEIs could be better prepared for security incidents.

Furthermore, issues of distrust caused by the implementation of phishing exercises in HEIs could have strained the relationship between academic and IT staff, thus making collaboration less likely. It is also likely that the IT team and the university have been busy 'firefighting' and have been overwhelmed by the 'catch-up game' with cyber-attacks; as a result, they may not have time for engagement with users.

The impersonal communication from the IT team may be something that IT does not have control over. For instance, not putting an IT staff member's name on a service desk email could have been a senior management decision to increase request response rates. However, interviewees do not comment negatively on IT team's efficiency or excellence.

In view of our findings, a recommendation would be that senior management invest more in training and development for IT teams with specific focus on informing, engaging and persuading.

B. Policies and Frameworks for Guiding Cyber Security Behaviour

The lack of enough policies/framework could have been caused by lack of clear strategy needed to influence these written rules. Also, senior management may not have the expertise required to create polices/frameworks. Furthermore, other priorities could have taken the place of policy creation. The implication of these is that users engage in actions, activities, and habits which they perceive to be right but that may turn out to be detrimental to the security of HEIs assets.

Unclear and insufficient policies will lead to limited knowledge, understanding and awareness among users, as the available policies may not cover some security aspects which need protection. This creates some compliance gaps as some security expectations will not be known and cannot be followed. It then becomes difficult for users to see their role as critical in sustaining the security of their university. Users' attitude could also be affected negatively because they are not aware of frameworks that could guide them. Hence, they may see security as the IT team's problem and may not bother about incident reporting.

At times, policy creation responsibility of senior management is delegated to other staff members, but there is no guarantee that the staff members have the necessary skills to execute the duties. The study [41] shows where duties intended for senior leaders are delegated, outcomes are suboptimal.

It is possible that policies are not in place because they are not prioritised by senior management. Maybe regulatory compliance like GDPR is prioritised over security policies, to avoid reputational damage and fines. Prioritisation issues in policies could be caused by lack of understanding about the risks and threats HEIs face. Also, there is the lack of understanding on how to conduct cyber security measurement. It then becomes difficult for senior management to make decisions about policies, prioritise the allocation of significant but limited resources to address increasing vulnerabilities and cyber attacks.

We observe that HEIs' cyber security strategy is unclear and not fully operational. This means that strategy could not influence policies, resulting in a lack of clarity and prioritisation in policies. Communicating policies will be hindered further because of the problems we identify in the key theme, communication.

To address the aforementioned problems, a recommendation would be that senior management prioritise the creation of a cyber security strategy, around which security policies could be built. This could be a starting point which expands to various cyber security areas. HEI leaders should engage academics' expertise within their institutions, to assist in the creation of policies, something that we did not observe, and which caused additional friction. Policies should specify the expected security behaviours of users. There should also be a way testing users' understanding of policies as communication is not effective until recipients understand the information being conveyed. Additionality, training on using quantitative approach for CSC measurement should be provided to the relevant HEI teams.

C. IT Expectations

IT Expectations Finding 1 indicates that IT expectations are not well defined. The possible cause of this could be that those responsible for defining IT expectations lacks the required understanding. This is similar to the lack of understanding of security culture that results in CSC being ill-defined [16]. Other possible causes of unclear IT expectations could be the lack of cyber security strategy, resource limitations, and time pressures on the IT staff.

The lack of strategic direction and expectations that users see may result in them not having trust in any of the IT expectations that they are advised about. The act of senior cyber security academics approaching IT teams to offer help may indicate that serious problems exit in the IT teams and within its processes.

Also, there could be a knowledge gap between IT staff and academics which might have an influence on the users' attitudes to learning about cyber security. This attitude could have resulted in compliance disparity that we observe among the user groups. For example, we saw reported a higher security compliance rate among administrative staff, who are better informed on security-related processes, in comparison to academics.

Users indicate they will comply with IT expectations if they know what these expectations are. Their willingness to comply is a positive attitude towards security. From our study, we observe that users, ranging from academics to students see the need for compliance and understand its benefits. This compliance readiness is what the HEIs could work with and use for 'nudging' users towards cultivating certain security behaviours in the university [42]. Small changes could be introduced in the design of solutions, where decisions need to be made. For example, nudges could be used where a user needs to decide whether or not to report a security incident. In this way, the user is encouraged to adopt the desired behaviour leading to an incident reporting. While a one-size-fits-all nudge approach may produce a useful outcome, personalised nudges could be more effective, although personalised nudges have been seen as threat to user autonomy [43].

However, compliance even when expectations are known does not always happen. Our study shows that users will resist unrealistic expectations, as common sense implies. It is therefore important for IT staff in HEIs to engage and communicate with users, particularly where expectations could be perceived as borderline/unrealistic. This might enhance user understanding and, thus, compliance.

Extant literature confirms our finding of distrust, and it states that phishing exercises create more problems than solve them [36]. The literature points out the reasons why an organisation should not phish staff as it creates distress, and even distrust between users and security, as some of the interviewees in our research explain.

Given the aforementioned challenges, we recommend that IT expectations are reviewed by a multi-disciplinary team.

D. *Moving Away from Phishing Exercises*

To promote collaboration and engagement between the IT team and users, the implementation of phishing exercises is to be avoided. HEIs represent freedom of expression and openness. Utilising an approach which causes distrust stifles relationship-building and collaboration. Using the outcomes of phishing exercises to blame users could create an environment that is void of transparency and openness. There is a tendency that blaming users could stop them from reporting security incidents or near misses when they occur. Therefore, an opportunity for the IT team to address a vulnerability could be left to a cyber attack to exploit.

It seems that resistance to phishing exercises come from almost all users, except for senior management that might have authorised them in the first place. Even if phishing exercises were to be used, the time needed to think through, and administer non-repetitive innovative exercises by HEIs IT teams may not be available.

Some academics feel phishing exercise could be used to understand the current cyber security state of the university. For example, the level of preparedness of users, which individual needs to be upskilled. Increasing security knowledge in HEIs is seen as important but there is a feeling that there is more to security knowledge that sending out phishing emails and making personnel attend mandatory training.

In line with a senior security staff interviewee, we argue that the implementation of phishing exercises approach should be avoided. We recommend that HEIs senior management investigate the problems caused by implementing phishing exercises in their HEIs from users' perspective. A clear picture could only be seen if senior management examine users' attitude toward security issues, their security behaviours and how critical they now consider their responsibilities to be in securing HEIs information assets, after they have been phished. This is likely to change senior management's opinion towards implementing phishing exercises in their HEIs.

E. *Training, Reinforced Training and Awareness*

The lack of enough cyber security training in HEIs could be because of limited financial resources in HEIs [38]. Also, prioritisation issues identified in policies and ill-defined IT expectations may mean that the most pressing security need is not identified and as a result could not be addressed by training. For example, our study did not observe social engineering training as a matter of priority in HEIs.

The implication of insufficient training is that users engage in unsafe security behaviours that could compromise security. Without adequate training, users are not aware, are uninformed, and are not equipped to deal with current security issues. This could make HEIs and other users susceptible to cyber attacks.

We observe that a link exists between training, communication, and policies. Training can be used to communicate policies to users, thus bringing awareness, understanding, and influencing cyber security culture across the HEIs. Training approach and training content are also important. When training users, storytelling and other approaches that have been found to promote engagement and knowledge transfer should be considered.

As security compliance is influenced by training, it is important for cyber security training to be taken seriously by HEI senior management. Furthermore, there are cloud computing challenges with distant learning following the changes introduced by Covid-19 lockdown which affects education delivery [44].

We recommend that senior management prioritise and invest in trainings, including offering training that focuses on social engineering and other human aspects of security.

F. *CSC Measurement*

An understanding of how to measure CSC and its implementation across institutions is needed. From our analysis, we found that people/universities do not know how to measure CSC. Also, the scales and the matrices that have been promoted by standard bodies such as International Organisation for Standardisation (OSI), National Institute of Standards and Technology (NIST) and Open Web

Application Security Project (OWASP), does not consider the complexity of cyber security, changing technology and human agents [3]. Hubbard and Seiersen [3] argue that compliance with standards and regulations does not improve cyber security risk management and the metrics for assessing the risks are flawed.

If the approach of assessing cyber threats and measuring security risk and culture is flawed or not known, then the true state of security in HEIs may not be determined. This makes informed decisions about resource allocation and other security investments a challenge for HEI senior management. Without the ability for assessing the current state of security through training uptake, incident reporting and behaviour change, we cannot demonstrate that progress has been made in terms of CSC in HEIs.

We recommend that HEIs consider ways of conducting CSC measurement.

VII. CONCLUSION AND FUTURE WORK

Communication is the central theme that must be fully embraced and continuously utilised if CSC is to be developed in HEIs. Communication with its approaches is significant because without it, all the other themes that we identify in this study will not be impactful in HEIs. Thus, we establish that communication is interwoven with the themes – policies and frameworks, IT expectations, moving away from phishing exercise, training, reinforced training and awareness, and CSC measurement. These themes are the factors that influences personnel and students' view of CSC in HEIs.

Currently, the approach of communication in the HEIs we examined needs to change. This includes communication between the IT team and users, as well communication from senior management to HEI staff. While there is information flow from the IT teams to users, we observe that dialogue is lacking. Hence, a new approach is needed that promotes engagement and collaboration.

Training, reinforced training and awareness are necessary to ensure that security information communicated through policies, frameworks and programmes are always at the fingertips and on the minds of users. Hence, training and awareness require an effective communication strategy so that its delivery could make maximum impact and change people's mindsets towards cyber security. In view of this, no-one should be exempted from training, irrespective of their status or hierarchy within the institutions.

There must be a conscious effort and drive from senior management team to create multi-disciplinary team of experts who will champion the promotion of CSC in HEIs and challenge the reactive attitude of "always being in the catch-up game with cyber attacks". The multi-disciplinary team could also be involved in co-creating policies by involving other users and fostering engagement. This approach will be a useful one for replacing phishing exercises which we have proved to be problematic, ineffective and have also been strongly opposed by academics, students, and other users.

The expertise of academics in HEIs have not been fully utilised in the quest to defend the institutions from cyber attacks. We recommend that senior management members kick-start an initiative to engage academics and seek ways of using their expertise, experience, and their innovative approach for defending the information assets of the HEIs. Any solutions that come out of the initiative could be integrated into the university training and awareness programmes and could also be shared with other sectors.

In sum, the implementation of a communication strategy, engagement and collaborative effort will be valuable in developing a cyber security culture and by so doing securing information assets of HEIs and reducing security breaches caused by human error.

There are a few limitations of the study. As in all qualitative analysis, researchers bias could be a concern. To avoid self-reporting bias [45] and maximise the value of our approach, leading questions were avoided. We used open-ended questions, allowing the interviewees to give detailed answers, using their own words. Further, more personnel could have been interviewed in our study. The barrier to this, was the Covid-19 lockdown which affected the response we received from the HEI personnel we contacted.

Our research shows that there is limited or no measurement of CSC in the HEIs that we examined. Hence, future research could investigate how CSC could be measured in different HEIs. Also, research can explore how cyber security training needs of different users in various departments could be identified. Appropriate training can then be geared towards an individual user instead of applying a one-size-fits-all approach. Another aspect that could be researched is HEIs' response to embracing technological change following the disruption introduced by the Covid-19 pandemic.

REFERENCES

[1] C. Kyriazopoulou, "Smart city technologies and architectures: A literature review", in 2015 International Conference on Smart Cities and Green ICT Systems (SMARTGREENS). 2015 International Conference on Smart Cities and Green ICT Systems (SMARTGREENS), 2015, pp. 1–12.

[2] A. A. Rahman, U. Z. A. Hamid, and T. A. Chin, "Emerging Technologies with Disruptive Effects: A Review", PERINTIS eJournal 7(2), p. 19, 2017.

[3] D.W. Hubbard and R. Seiersen, *"How to Measure Anything in Cybersecurity Risk"*. Hoboken, NJ, USA: John Wiley & Sons, Inc 2016. doi: 10.1002/9781119162315.

[4] N. S. Safa, M. Sookhak, R. Von Solms, S. Furnell, N.A. Ghani, and T. Herawan. "Information security conscious care behaviour formation in organizations", *Computers & Security*, 53, pp. 65–78, 2015. Doi: 10.1016/j.cose.2015.05.012G.

[5] J. Chapman. "How safe is your data? Cyber-security in higher education". HEPI Policy Note, vol. 12, Apr. 2019.

[6] PwC [online] Available at: <https://www.pwc.co.uk/assets/pdf/2015-isbs-technical-report-blue-03.pdf> [Accessed: September 2021].

[7] IBM, "IBM 2015 Cyber-Security-Intelligence-Index". Available at: https://essextec.com/wp-content/uploads/2015/09/IBM-2015-Cyber-Security-Intelligence-Index_FULL-REPORT.pdf (Accessed: September 2021).

[8] K. Huang and K. Pearlson, "For What Technology Can't Fix: Building a Model of Organizational Cybersecurity Culture," Proc. of the 52nd Hawaii International Conference on System Sciences, Jan. 2019, pp. 6398-6407.

[9] A. Ahmad, K. C. Desouza, S. B. Maynard, H. Naseer, and R. L. Baskerville, 2020. "How Integration of Cyber Security Management and Incident Response Enables Organizational Learning," Journal of the Association for Information Science and Technology, vol. 71:8, 2020, pp. 939-953.

[10] A. Wiley, A. McCormac, and D. Calic, "More than the Individual: Examining the Relationship Between Culture and Information Security Awareness," Computers & Security, vol. 88, Jan. 2020, doi: 10.1016/j.cose.2019.101640.

[11] A. Georgiadou, S. Mouzakitis, and K. Bounas, D. Askounis, "A Cyber-Security Culture Framework for Assessing Organization Readiness", *Journal of Computer Information Systems*, pp. 1–11, 2020. Doi: 10.1080/08874417.2020.1845583.

[12] B. Von Solms, "Information Security — The Third Wave?", *Computers & Security*, vol. 19(7), pp. 615–620, Nov. 2000. Doi: 10.1016/S0167-4048(00)07021-8.

[13] A. Da Veiga and J. H. P. Eloff, "A framework and assessment instrument for information security culture", *Computers & Security*, vol. 29(2), pp. 196–207, Mar. 2010. Doi: 10.1016/j.cose.2009.09.002.

[14] R. Reid and J. Van Niekerk, "From Information Security to Cyber Security Cultures Organizations to Societies". Information Security South Africa (ISSA), vol. 38, pp. 97-102, 2014.

[15] L.J. Hadlington, "Employees attitudes towards cyber security and risky online behaviours: an empirical assessment in the United Kingdom". International Journal of Cyber Criminology. vol. 12 (1), pp. 269–81, Jan-Jun. 2018.

[16] N. Gcaza and R. Solms, "Cybersecurity Culture: An Ill-Defined Problem", IFIP World Conference on Information Security Education (WISE 2017) pp. 98-109, 2017. Doi: 10.1007/978-3-319-58553-6_9.

[17] Jisc.ac.uk. [online] Available at: <https://www.jisc.ac.uk/sites/default/files/dei-2020-student-survey-question-by-question-analysis.pdf> [Accessed: September 2021].

[18] K. Roer, et al. "Measure to Improve, Security Culture Report 2020". [online] Available at: <https://www.knowbe4.com/hubfs/Security-Culture-Report.pdf> [Accessed: September 2021].

[19] Ico.org.uk. *The University of Greenwich fined £120,000 by Information Commissioner for "serious" security breach.* [online] Available at: <https://ico.org.uk/about-the-ico/news-and-events/news-and-blogs/2018/05/the-university-of-greenwich-fined-120-000-by-information-commissioner-for-serious-security-breach/> [Accessed: September 2021].

[20] D. Sanderson, "*Edinburgh University hit by freshers' week cyberattack"*. [online] Thetimes.co.uk. Available at: <https://www.thetimes.co.uk/article/edinburgh-university-hit-by-freshers-week-cyberattack-0m2xzl0p8> [Accessed: September 2021].

[21] J. F. Van Niekerk and R. Von Solms, "Information Security Culture: A Management Perspective". Computers & Security, Vol. 29 (4), pp. 476-486, 2010.

[22] S. H. Bakry "Development of e-government: A STOPE view", International Journal of Network Management, vol.14 (5) pp. 339-350, 2004.

[23] A. Alhogail and A. Mirza, "Information Security Culture: A Definition and A Literature Review," World Congress on Computer Applications and Information Systems, WCCAIS, pp. 1-7, Jan. 2014. doi: 10.1109/WCCAIS.2014.6916579.

[24] A. Da Veiga and N. Martins, "Information security culture: A comparative analysis of four assessments". Proceedings of the 8th European Conference on IS Management and Evaluation, 2014, pp 49-57.

[25] M. Alnatheer, "Information Security Culture Critical Success Factors". 12th International Conference on Information Technology - New Generations, 2015, pp. 731-735.

[26] M. Bada, A. Sasse, and J.R.C Nurse, "Cyber security awareness campaigns: Why do they fail to change behaviour?" International Conference on Cyber Security for Sustainable Society, 2015.

[27] M. Ioannou, E. Stavrou, and M. Bada, "Cybersecurity Culture in Computer Security Incident Response Teams: Investigating difficulties in communication and coordination," 2019 International Conference on Cyber Security and Protection of Digital Services (Cyber Security), 2019, pp. 1-4, doi: 10.1109/CyberSecPODS.2019.8885240.

[28] R. Knight and J. R. C. Nurse, (2020). A framework for effective corporate communication after cyber security incidents. Computers & Security, vol. 99, Sep. 2020. https://doi.org/10.1016/j.cose.2020.102036

[29] A. Da Veiga, "An approach to information security culture change combining ADKAR and the ISCA questionnaire to aid transition to the desired culture". Information & Computer Security, vol. 26(5), pp. 584-612, Jun. 2018 https://doi.org/10.1108/ICS-08-2017-0056

[30] M. C. Van't Wout, "Develop and Maintain a Cybersecurity Organisational culture". ICCWS 2019 14th International Conference on Cyber Warfare and Security, Academic Conferences and Publishing Limited, pp. 457-466, Feb. 2019.

[31] C.F. Cannell, P.V. Miller, and L. Oksenberg, "Research on Interviewing Techniques". Sociological Methodology, vol. 12, pp. 389–437, 1981.

[32] C. Erlingsson and P. Brysiewicz, "A hands-on guide to doing content analysis", *African Journal of Emergency Medicine*, vol. 7(3), pp. 93–99, 2017. doi: 10.1016/j.afjem.2017.08.001.

[33] H.F. Hsieh and S.E. Shannon, "Three Approaches to Qualitative Content Analysis", Qualitative Health Research, vol. 15(9), pp. 1277–1288, 2005. doi: 10.1177/1049732305276687.

[34] S. Elo and H. Kyngäs, "The qualitative content analysis process", Journal of Advanced Nursing, vol. 62(1), pp. 107–115, 2008. doi: 10.1111/j.1365-2648.2007.04569.x.

[35] A. Ertan, G. Crossland, C. Heath, D. Denny, and R. Jensen, "Cyber security behaviour in organisations" 2020. arXiv preprint arXiv:2004.11768.

[36] Ncsc.gov.uk. "*The Trouble with Phishing"* 2018. [online] Available at: <https://www.ncsc.gov.uk/blog-post/trouble-phishing> [Accessed: September 2021].

[37] J. Ulven and G. Wangen, "A Systematic Review of Cybersecurity Risks in Higher Education". Future Internet, 2021, 13(2), 39, https://doi.org/ 10.3390/fi13020039

[38] W. Ismail and A. Widyarto, "A Formulation and development process of information security policy in higher education". Proc. of the 1st International Conference on Engineering Technology and Applied Sciences, Afyonkarahisar, Turkey, pp. 21–22, April 2016.

[39] Repository.jisc.ac.uk. 2018. [online] Available at: <https://repository.jisc.ac.uk/6967/1/Digital experience_insights_survey_2018.pdf> [Accessed: September 2021].

[40] Enisa. 2018. [online] Available at: <https://www.enisa.europa.eu/publications/cybersecurity-

culture-guidelines-behavioural-aspects-of-cybersecurity> [Accessed: September 2021].

[41] G. Gearhart and M. Miller "Higher Education's Cyber Security: Leadership Issues, Challenges, and the Future", Journal of New Trends in Education, vol. 10 (2), pp. 11–18, 2019.

[42] R.H. Thaler and C.R. Sunstein. Nudge: Improving decisions about health, wealth, and happiness. New Haven: Yale University Press, 2008.

[43] N. E. Diaz Ferreyra, E. Aïmeur, H. Hage, M. Heisel, and C. van Hoogstraten, "Persuasion Meets AI: Ethical Considerations for the Design of Social Engineering Countermeasures", Proc. of the 12th International Joint Conference on Knowledge Discovery, Knowledge Engineering and Knowledge Management, pp. 204-211, Nov. 2020. Doi: 10.5220/0010142402040211

[44] S. Bhagat and D.J. Kim, "Higher education amidst COVID-19: Challenges and silver lining". Information. Systems. Management, 2020, vol. 37(4), pp. 366–371. https://doi.org/10.1080/10580530.2020.1824040

[45] V. Jupp, The SAGE Dictionary of Social Research Methods. SAGE Publications, London Thousand Oaks, California, 2006.

A Potentially Specious Cyber Security Offering for 5G/B5G/6G

Software Supply Chain Vulnerabilities within Certain Fuzzing Modules

Steve Chan
Decision Engineering Analysis Laboratory, VT
San Diego, USA
e-mail: schan@dengineering.org

Abstract—**A plethora of fuzzing Tactics, Techniques, and Procedures (TTPs) have been either proposed or described in the literature for the purpose of discerning software vulnerabilities with efficacy. The benefits of fuzzing have been well documented, such as when researchers found dozens of vulnerabilities in 4G LTE wireless networks, and fuzzing has become prevalent among the disparate actors within the wireless network ecosystem (to include 5G). However, fuzzing implementations are varied, and ironically, in some cases, implementations have utilized software bundles that have contained known "High Severity" Common Vulnerabilities and Exposures (CVE). On the surface, it seems that fuzzing the fuzzing module itself would constitute a simple solution to this issue. However, prototypical fuzzers have coverage issues (i.e., they only fuzz certain lines of code or sections of the software program). In addition, as numerous fuzzers utilize Docker containers, which are essentially inert when not in use, the complexity of the challenge is non-trivial. This paper introduces a fuzzing framework that capitalizes upon a sequence of bespoke grey-box concolic (i.e., hybridized symbolic and concrete execution) fuzzers (one set that fuzzes the next) to better address the coverage issue (as well as more likely to discern CVEs) and leverage their hybridized nature to overcome the disadvantages of black-box (higher computational performance, but lower coverage) and white-box fuzzers (e.g., lower computational performance, but higher coverage). The introduced bespoke grey-box concolic fuzzer architecture has certain advantages over other Coverage-based Grey-box Fuzzers (CGF) via the numerical stability-centric approach by which it selects seeds, undertakes seed scheduling, and operationalizes the seed pool.**

Keywords-cyber security; fuzzing; wireless networks; 5G; autonomous vehicles; grey-box concolic fuzzer.

I. INTRODUCTION

The growth within the 5G arena is well documented in the literature. According to TeleGeography, "nine 5G networks went live globally in Q1 2021, bringing the global total up to 172 networks" [1], and according to the Global Mobile Suppliers Association (GSA), there are now "511 commercially available 5G devices as of June 2021" [1]. To date, the rollout of 5G has occurred by way of three core service categories (a.k.a., "5G triangle"): Enhanced Mobile Broadband (eMBB), Ultra-Reliable Low-Latency Communications (URLLC), and massive Machine-Type Communications (mMTC). These service categories support a wide range of Quality of Service (QoS) needs. The QoS needs differ by application (e.g., fixed wireless access, connected machinery/equipment, video monitoring/ detection, as well as connected/autonomous vehicles) [2]. QoS needs are constantly evolving as existing applications become more sophisticated and emergent applications are designed for the envisioned capabilities of 5G, Beyond 5G (B5G), and the 6G ecosystem.

A key aspect of the 5G/B5G/6G ecosystem is that hardware is principally supplanted with software so that future upgrades will be software-centric. However, this increased utilization of Software-Defined Networking (SDN) within the network core also expands the attack surface opportunities [3][4]. In fact, the literature shows that cyber security researchers have found a plethora of security vulnerabilities (e.g., improper handling of procedures, invalid integrity protection, and security procedure bypasses), via fuzz testing (a.k.a., fuzzing), within wireless networks [5].

It should be of no surprise that governments and industries around the world are concerned about availability (a key aspect of the cyber notion pertaining to the Confidentiality, Integrity, and Availability Triad) being compromised, particularly as pertains to critical/strategic infrastructure and mission-critical applications [6]. Given the recent surge in issued directives, such as the "Improving the Nation's Cybersecurity" (Executive Order 14028, which was issued on 12 May 2021 and proceeded to direct the National Institute of Standards and Technology or NIST to enhance software supply chain security guidelines), it seems ironic that there remains software supply chain vulnerabilities within certain mission-critical software fuzzing paradigms; after all, these are the very mechanisms that are supposed to discern cyber vulnerabilities and enhance the cyber posture. The main contribution of the paper is to introduce a bespoke fuzzing framework that addresses the issues of limited coverage and inadvertent inherent vulnerabilities within certain fuzzing paradigms.

This paper is structured as follows. Section I introduces the problem space. Section II presents background information and discusses the operating environment and the state of the challenge. Section III delineates the referenced software supply chain challenge and presents some experimental findings derived from scrutinizing a particular architectural stack, which supports a mainstay of the 5G network core — the family of Fast Fourier Transform (FFT)-related functions for signal processing. Section IV posits a potential mitigation pathway for the discussed cyber exposure. Section V concludes with some observations, puts forth envisioned future work, and the acknowledgements close the paper.

II. Background Information

Within the 5G/B5G/6G ecosystems, maximizing spectrum efficiency by optimal allocation of frequency/time/power resources is vital, and the orchestration of the involved waveforms is complex. Exemplar waveforms include Generalized Frequency Division Multiplexing (GFDM), Filter Bank Multicarrier (FBMC), Orthogonal Frequency Division Multiplexing (OFDM), Universal Filtered Multi-Carrier Modulation (UFMC), etc. In turn, there are variants of these waveform types. For example, FBMC has two principal variants: Quadrature Amplitude Modulation (QAM) and real-valued Offset QAM (OQAM) (a.k.a. FBMC/OQAM). OFDM, which conjoins the advantages of QAM and Frequency Division Multiplexing (FDM), has an even greater number of variants. UFCM (a generalization of FBMC and OFDM) has greater variants still.

The library of FFT-related functions for signal processing is of critical import, and as just one example, the library is used for spectrum enhancement of the previously referenced Orthogonal Frequency Division Multiplexing (OFDM)-based waveforms within Fifth Generation New Radio (5G NR) development [7]; 5G NR is, in essence, a new Radio Access Technology (RAT) for cellular networks. The involved functions include not only FFT, but also Inverse FFT (IFFT), Real-Valued FFT (RFFT), Inverse RFFT (IRFFT), Short-Time Fourier Transform (STFT), and Inverse STFT (ISTFT), among others. In particular, STFT is a key requisite functionality within the 5G/B5G/6G ecosystem.

Prior research has indicated that the selection and utilization of, by way of example, specific STFT implementations from the available machine learning libraries/toolkits is critical; it is vital for the 5G/BFG/6G researcher/programmer to understand and contend with the implementation intricacies of the numerical algorithms being utilized for the involved functions. For example, signature consistency and dependency intricacies have been shown to result in errors and/or incorrect results, and these issues can cause a non-graceful degradation of the involved system [8]. Clearly, this would be unacceptable, particularly for those applications (e.g., autonomous vehicles), which have mission critical requirements that necessitate a certain QoS (and even Quality of Experience or QoE for some cases). In particular, those applications with mission critical requirements would be extremely sensitive to the issues of data rate (the data packet transfer rate per unit time), latency (the delay before the mandated transfer of data packets begins), and jitter (the variation in the time between data packets arriving).

Network Slicing (NS) is often utilized to satisfy varied NS QoS requirements (e.g., data rate, latency, jitter). Typically, a Service Function Chain (SFC) handles specific traffic within each NS. As each NS has its own cyber characteristics, each SFC will encounter varied cyber requirements. Consequently, the involved fuzzing modules will have varied implementations; each implementation will have its own set of potential cyber vulnerabilities. This challenge is more fully described in subsections A through D below.

A. *Network Slice (NS)*

To support a wide range of applications with varying QoS requirements (and particularly for mission critical QoS requirements), 5G/B5G/6G networks endeavor to provide high data rates with low end-to-end (E2E) latency and minimal jitter. To achieve this, among a myriad of approaches, NS is often utilized. In essence, each NS QoS requirement is met for the particular involved application while the overall involved 5G/B5G/6G network resources are still, ideally, optimally distributed for all involved NS [9].

B. *Service Function Chain (SFC)*

Operationally, NS leverages both Software Defined Networking (SDN) and Network Function Virtualization (NFV). In essence, NFV is the de-coupling of Network Functions (NFs) from a myriad of hardware appliances and the running of NFs as software in Virtual Machines (VMs). The various NFs (e.g., traffic control), which consist of the involved core network and Radio Access Network (RAN) component, are referred to as Virtual Network Functions (VNFs). Each SFC handles specific traffic within the NS, over varied technological and administrative ecosystems, and is an ecosystem in it of itself [10],[11].

C. *Cyber Implications of using SFCs*

The varied ecosystems can equate to physically dispersed, low-cost, short-range, small-cell antennas (e.g., low-power femtocells, picocells, and microcells). Functionally, each of these small-cell antennas leverages the 5G/B5G/6G dynamic spectrum sharing capability, wherein multiple streams of information share the available bandwidth, via a NS. In turn, each NS has its own varying degree of cyber risk [12][13]. To continually evaluate the ongoing risks, oftentimes a fuzzing module (which intentionally injects malformed inputs into the involved software, so as to ascertain failure/vulnerability points) is utilized.

D. *Potential Cyber Vulnerabilities within the Fuzzing Module Itself*

Given that 5G/B5G/6G protocols/specifications are still evolving and actively being defined by standards bodies, (e.g., 3rd Generation Partnership Project or 3GPP, Internet Engineering Task Force or IETF, International Telecommunication Union or ITU), and since each NS has its own associated cyber risks, varying implementations of fuzzing modules exist within 5G/B5G/6G architectural frameworks [14]. On the surface, it seems that the very use of a fuzzing module is in keeping with the spirit of cyber hygiene best practices. However, upon scrutinization of varied implementations, potential cyber vulnerabilities have been uncovered within the fuzzing module itself. In these cases, the fuzzing module represents a potentially specious cyber security offering for 5G/B5G/6G, as it itself is subject to compromise.

Overall, the work presented in this paper differs from prior research in that a particular sequence of bespoke grey-box concolic fuzzers is utilized to mitigate against the known coverage issue and better discern known CVEs. The chosen sequence shows promise in that it overcomes some of the disadvantages of prototypical black-box and white-box fuzzers.

III. EXPERIMENTATION FINDINGS

This paper examined a 5G/B5G/6G architectural framework, which was used in a Technology Readiness Level (TRL) 5 (i.e., laboratory environment) and 6 (i.e., relevant environment). Typically, fuzz testing is conducted in a controlled, isolated laboratory environment (such as in the case of TRL 5), and isolation is often provided, via containerization. The notion of utilizing containers (as a testing target) is predicated upon the notion that it provides enhanced consistency and reproducibility (particularly when using container images) [15].

The previously discussed implementation intricacies (e.g., signature consistency, dependencies) that result in inadvertent errors and/or incorrect results are already problematic enough; however, this paradigm can be exacerbated when it is intentionally exploited. To better delineate this point, first, the containerization aspect is described. Second, some identified vulnerabilities related to the containerization paradigm are presented. Third, further vulnerabilities are identified within underlying legacy supply chains.

A. Containerization Aspect of Fuzzing

Traditionally, containerization has provided the desired isolation paradigm for fuzzing. The often-used workflow for containerization (e.g., specifying configuration, building a Dockerfile — a text file that contains all the commands required to build a Docker images — for each desired image, and using Docker Compose to assemble the images) facilitates reproducible/consistent testing results. Typical fuzzing architectures might utilize, by way of example, either of two container orchestration platforms for containerization: Docker (referring to either Docker Swarm or Classic Swarm, which was initially released in 2014, or Swarmkit, which was initially released in 2016; of note, Swarmkit stemmed from Docker's acquisition of SocketPlane, an SDN technology firm, in March 2015) and Kubernetes. Generally speaking, Docker, by default, prioritizes isolation between containers; this is construed by some to represent higher security. In contradistinction, Kubernetes prioritizes communication between multiple containers within the same pod; this is construed by some to represent higher efficacy, but lower security. Depending upon the specific requirement, the choice of orchestrator (i.e., Docker or Kubernetes) can be made explicitly.

Over the past several years, the leadership for container orchestration, potentially, has shifted from Docker to Kubernetes. In fact, Docker itself adopted Kubernetes and announced native support for Kubernetes at DockerCon Europe in Copenhagen on 17 October 2017. Yet, Docker's architecture enables users to select the desired orchestration engine (Docker, Kubernetes) at runtime. On the Kubernetes side, as of Kubernetes v1.20, Docker (specifically, Dockershim, which communicates with Docker Engine, which was renamed to Docker Community Edition or Docker CE in March 2017) has been deprecated as a container runtime.

Whatever the case may be with regards to the leadership for container orchestration, Docker images remain a mainstay within the development ecosystem. In addition, Docker Compose still remains in wide use for building Dockerfiles. While container images can indeed be built with tools, such as Kaniko (an open-source tool for building container images from a Dockerfile) [16], Podman, Buildah, and Buildkit, etc., Docker images assembled with Docker Compose may be more prevalent for certain facets of 5G/B5G/6G architectural stacks (particularly those utilizing GNU Octave). Indeed, there is a plethora of GNU Octave-related experimentation (e.g., [17]). By way of background information, whereas the utilization of docker run can indeed start up a container, Docker Compose is often utilized to automatically start up multi-container applications. Historically, Docker Compose has been the configuration component of the Docker ecosystem (whereas Docker Swarm was the scheduling component of the Docker ecosystem and determined where to place the containers within the cluster of Docker hosts, which were in the form of physical computer systems or VMs running Linux). Overall, containerization remains an accepted methodology for consistency/reproducibility; yet, this containerization paradigm for fuzzing modules introduces a new set of potential vulnerabilities.

B. Identified Vulnerabilities Related to certain Containerization Paradigms of Fuzzing Modules

The system of Common Vulnerabilities and Exposures (CVE) is a compilation of Information Security (InfoSec) issues. For example, CVE-2020-1971 identified an OpenSSL (wherein the identity of an involved website/web service is validated, and the information flowing between the website/web service and user is encrypted) "High Severity" issue, which had been reported on 8 December 2020 [18]. The Cybersecurity & Infrastructure Security Agency (CISA) noted that, "OpenSSL has released a security update to address a vulnerability affecting all versions of 1.0.2 and 1.1.1 released before version 1.1.1i. An attacker could exploit this vulnerability to cause a denial-of-service condition" [19]. In brief, the vulnerability issue simply affected OpenSSL v1.0.2, which was out of support and no longer receiving public updates; theoretically, OpenSSL v1.1.1i and beyond are no longer vulnerable to the referenced issue, and the matter should be closed. However, the key issue is not simply that there was a vulnerability issue in a deprecated version; more importantly, various

Github commentators/contributors had noted, such as years prior (e.g., [20]) that various bundled OpenSSL versions had been out of date. Yet, various offerings (e.g., various Docker Compose offerings) still continued to incorporate outdated OpenSSL versions, such as can be seen in Table I below.

TABLE I. DOCKER COMPOSE WITH BUNDLED OPENSSL VERSION

Exemplars	Constituent Components of the Bundle			
	Docker Compose Version	***Docker-Py Version***	***CPython Version***	***OpenSSL Version***
Case #1[a]	1.23.2, build 1110ad0	3.7.3	2.7.16	1.1.1c 28 May 2019
Case #2[b]	1.26.0-rc3, build 46118bc5	4.2.0	3.7.6	1.1.1d 10 Sep 2019
Case #3[c]	1.26.2, build eefe0d31	4.2.2	3.7.7	1.1.0l 10 Sep 2019

a. https://dockerlabs.collabnix.com/intermediate/workshop/DockerCompose/version_Command.html
b. https://github.com/docker/compose/issues/7348
c. https://github.com/docker/compose/issues/7686

Cases #1 through #3 represent just a small sample set of the implications of CVE-2020-1971. Additional OpenSSL CVEs are available at the OpenSSL portal (e.g., [21]), and other CVEs are available at the National Vulnerability Database (NVD) (https://nvd.nist.gov) as well as the U.S. Computer Emergency Response Team (CERT)-CISA (https://us-cert.cisa.gov) portals. As discussed, OpenSSL versions affected by CVE-2020-1971, among others, had been bundled with Docker Compose. Yet, despite the published CVEs, it should be noted that certain images of Docker Compose v1.28.0 might still be deploying with OpenSSL v1.1.1h (i.e., vulnerable to CVE-2020-1971); OpenSSL v1.1.1i and above have the security update for CVE-2020-1971. As of the writing of this paper in January 2021, v1.28.2 was the current version of Docker Compose; as of the finalization of this paper in July 2021, v1.29.2 is the current version of Docker Compose. The latest OpenSSL tarball source files can be found here: https://www.openssl.org/source/; this page asserts that the latest stable version is the 1.1.1 series, which is the OpenSSL.org's Long Term Support (LTS) version, which is slated to be supported until 11 September 2023. For convenience, please refer to Table 2 below. The current version (v1.29.2) is bolded for convenience as are the referenced v1.28.0, v1.28.2, and v1.26.2.

TABLE II. DOCKER COMPOSE RELEASE VERSIONS WITH DATES

Release Version	Release Date
1.29.2	2021-05-10
1.29.1	2021-04-13
1.29.0	2021-04-06
1.28.6	2021-03-23
1.28.5	2021-02-26
1.28.4	2021-02-18
1.28.3	2021-02-17
1.28.2	2021-01-26
1.28.0	2021-01-20
1.27.4	2020-09-24
1.27.3	2020-09-16
1.27.2	2020-09-10
1.27.1	2020-09-10
1.27.0	2020-09-07
1.26.2 (Case #3 from Table I)	2020-07-02

Source: https://docs.docker.com/compose/release-notes/

The Docker Compose bundling issue has persisted for quite some time — as far back as 25 June 2015 (e.g., https://github.com/docker/compose/issues/1601) (e.g., [22]). The bundling issue has also been noted in Linux binaries (as well as Mac binaries). Despite the delineated bundling issue, many vendors, who bundle OpenSSL, "will selectively retrofit urgent fixes to an older version of code, in order to maintain [Application Programming Interface] API stability/predictability. This is especially true for 'long-term release' and appliance platforms" [23]. This trend is significant, for in the current environment, 5G App developers are actively leveraging the faster speeds and lower latencies to innovate and release next-generation Augmented Reality (AR) and other immersive experience Applications (a.k.a., apps), which are used by healthcare providers (e.g., collaborative apps for sharing high-resolution medical images for telemedicine triaging), manufacturers (e.g., inspection apps to assist in identifying defects more quickly), and others. As the involved industries require mission-critical QoS, API stability/predictability is paramount. Therein resides the dilemma; many vendors have utilized older software release versions to maintain the requisite stability/predictability. However, this has resulted in the described bundling issues, which contain — in many cases — deprecated versions of various constituent components of the bundle.

For the architectural stack scrutinized, it was found that the containerization implementation, for an extended period of time (until flagged by the author), contained "High Severity" versions of OpenSSL and other components utilized for the involved fuzzing modules. The implication is that the entire fuzzing TTP could have been compromised, and discovered vulnerabilities within the fuzzing target might have been non-logged; the significance of logs has been previously illuminated by various reports, such as the "Verizon Data Breach Report: Detective Controls by Percent of Breach Victims" (which highlighted the fact that 71% of breach victims relied predominantly upon System Device Logs, 20% for Automated Log Analysis, and 11% for Log Review Process), and extensively discussed in the literature [24]; in essence, logs remain a mainstay of a cyber framework.

C. Further Legacy Vulnerabilities within the Fuzzing Module Supply Chain

Given the possibility of discovered vulnerabilities being non-logged, among other paradigms, the notion of a script, which serves to ensure the bundling of an apropos (e.g., patched) OpenSSL version, as just one example of a bundled component, and the notion of a vetted installer (e.g., PyInstaller) that links to an apropos OpenSSL version dynamically, have been discussed extensively [25]. The notion of such a script to check for CVEs on an ongoing basis seems quite simple; however, because Docker containers are essentially inert when not in use, a systematic evaluation of what CVEs are present is non-trivial. In addition, as the constituent components of a bundle are ever-evolving, and as certain sub-components become deprecated, legacy issues are ongoing. For example, as each network operator has its own 5G/B5G/6G network roll-out plan, at least for the interim, each operator's network is actually a patchwork of 2G, 3G, 4G, and 5G networks. Since 5G networks will, for the foreseeable future, continue to interoperate with legacy networks, they will be subject to prototypical legacy vulnerabilities (e.g., spoofing, denial-of-service, etc.). By way of example, network operators will continue to rely upon General Packet Radio Service (GPRS) Tunneling Protocol (GTP) (designed to facilitate data packets moving backing and forth between the wireless networks of different operators, such as when a user is roaming). Furthermore, in addition to fuzzing modules within the 5G/B5G/6G ecosystem containing vulnerable constituent components within their bundles, fuzzing modules within the 4G ecosystem, etc. have also been found to contain the described vulnerabilities. Hence, even if the 5G/B5G/6G fuzzing modules are robustly scrutinized, the fuzzing modules (a.k.a., fuzzers) of the underlying patchwork (i.e., 2G, 3G, 4G) need commensurate scrutinization.

The implications of this underlying legacy patchwork are profound, particularly in the matter of mission-critical QoS and 5G-enabled software defined networks, such as vehicular networks (5G-SDVN), which have been burgeoning (to support the ever-growing autonomous vehicle market). However, the cyber security issues surrounding 5G-SDVN are complex not only because of the underlying legacy patchwork issues, but also because conventional fuzzers are comprised of varied classes — each with certain advantages/disadvantages: black-box (coverage information is not considered and inputs are randomly generated), white-box (coverage is maximized by considering the data structure/logical constraints of the internal implementation, and inputs are crafted, but the time requirement is higher), and grey-box (in contrast to black-box fuzzing, coverage information is considered, but perhaps not to the extent of white-box fuzzing so as to save on time). Among other distinctions, coverage-based evaluation metrics are difficult to ascertain as it is difficult to determine "which parts of a [software] program a fuzzer actually visits and how consistently it does so," and the lack of a standardized methodology for evaluating coverage remains a challenge [26].

IV. A PROSPECTIVE MITIGATION PATHWAY

As discussed, white-box fuzzers produce quality inputs, but the computational overhead is much higher, while black-box fuzzers that focus upon random mutation have computational overhead that is much lower, but have difficulty producing quality inputs [27]. Even state-of-the-art fuzzers are sub-optimal at discerning " 'hard-to-trigger' bugs in applications that expect highly structured inputs" [28]. While grammar-based fuzzers (capable of generating syntactically correct inputs) can indeed be effective, the computational overhead is high and feature engineering is required.

To address these challenges, in this paper, we present a bespoke grey-box concolic fuzzing module, which is comprised of four differing bespoke grey-box concolic fuzzers. A primary grey-box concolic fuzzer is able to achieve higher coverage (on average) and able to more robustly discern which parts of a software program it visits and how consistent it is in doing so; the primary fuzzer is complemented by a secondary fuzzer, which utilizes different classes (from that of the primary fuzzer) for mutating a seed. Together, they comprise an aggregate fuzzer for the test target; this is an improvement upon prototypical fuzzers, which might simply report on the number of lines or basic blocks (a straight-line code sequence that has no branches except to the entry and from the exit), but does not indicate whether it missed visiting certain sectors of the software program. By having a myriad of distinct and disparate classes (e.g., Class 1a Family, Class 2a Family, etc) for mutating a seed and by utilizing differing seed schedules (i.e., varying distributions of the fuzzing time spent among the seeds) for coverage (e.g., Class 1b Seed Schedule, Class 2b Seed Schedule, etc.), the primary and secondary fuzzers constitute a complementary set. In turn, this set is fuzzed by tertiary and quaternary grey-box concolic fuzzers, so as to mitigate against inadvertently not discerning vulnerabilities within the primary and secondary fuzzers themselves. The utilization of distinct and disparate tertiary and quaternary fuzzers (which utilize different classes for mutating a seed as well as seeding schedules) increases the likelihood of increased coverage (on average). The described paradigm is shown in Figures 1 and 2 below, wherein the entirety of Figure 1 is situated within the yellow box of Figure 2, which is roughly based upon [29].

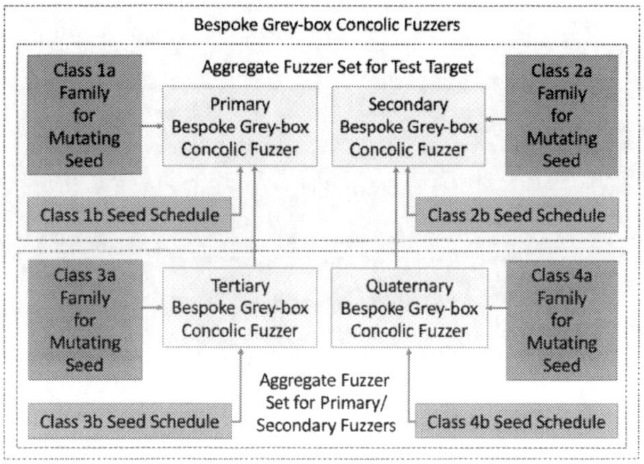

Figure 1. Bespoke Grey-box Concolic Fuzzers

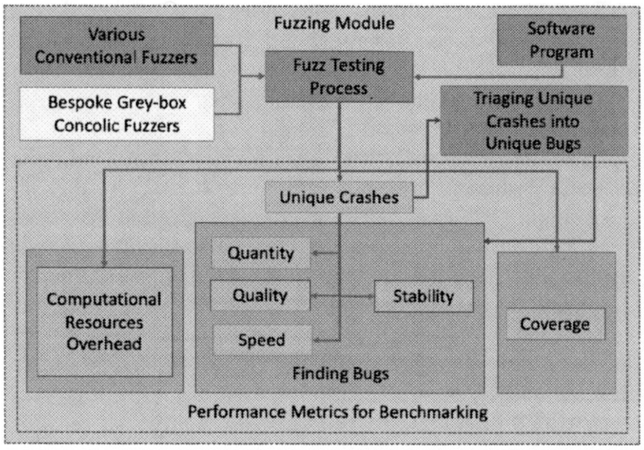

Figure 2. Grey-box Concolic Fuzzing Module

The coverage feedback derived by both primary and secondary fuzzers help to operationalize an underpinning numerical stability-centric Deep [Learning] Convolutional Generative Adversarial [Neural] Network (DCGAN)-facilitated Enhanced Context Module (ECM). The ECM is comprised of a Numerical Stability-Centric Module (NSCM), which in turn contains two Convolutional Adversarial Neural Networks (CANNs), each with a different implementation and version of PyTorch; PyTorch v0.4.1 (more numerically stable) is used in CANN #1, and PyTorch v1.7.0 (less numerically stable) is used CANN #2. The ECM's NSCM, which is shown in light purple in Figure 3 below, directs the aggregate fuzzer set for the test target (a.k.a., directed grey-box concolic fuzzing) to progress more rapidly into deeper code sectors.

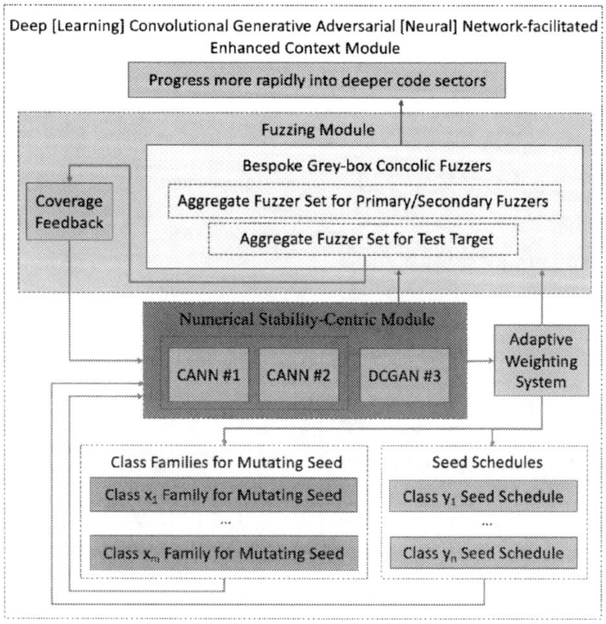

Figure 3. Numerical Stability-Centric Module (NSCM) which Leverages Coverage Feedback and an Adaptive Weighting System for Assigning Relative Weights to Fuzzer Seed Mutations/Schedules

The NSCM architecture is loosely based upon work that had been previously articulated in [8], but this version leverages coverage feedback and utilizes an adaptive weighting system to assign a relative weight to the fuzzer seeds *rw(fs)* that have the potential to achieve greater coverage, as shown in (1) below,

$$rw(fs) = 1/fr(pw(fs))^{e}, \quad (1)$$

where *pw(fs)* is the pathway identifier selected by *fs*, *fr(pw)* is the frequency at which the pathway *pw* is actually selected by the generated inputs, and *e* is a given exponent. The schedule is dynamically updated depending upon the frequency for which each pathway *fr(pw)* is utilized.

Overall, the feedback orientation (e.g., coverage, schedule) provided by the ECM well lends to a runtime coverage feedback paradigm, which in turn lends to, interestingly, enhanced thread-context. In this way, feedback can be operationalized, via the dynamic seed selection, mutation, weighting, and ensuing execution so as to better discern vulnerabilities within even a multi-threaded context [30]. With regards to the inner workings of the ECM of Figure 3, the entirety of Figure 1 is situated within the yellow box of Figure 2, the entirety of Figure 2 is situated within the light blue box of Figure 3, and the various components are described as follows.

A. Grey-box Concolic Fuzzing Module

Standard performance metrics for assessing the Grey-box Fuzzing Module (GFM) include, but are not limited to: (1) Unique Crashes, (2) Computational Resources Overhead, and (3) Coverage. First, Unique Crashes are further translated into unique bugs; it can also further be subdivided into quantity of unique bugs found, quality of bugs found (e.g., common or rare, CVE severity level, etc), speed at which bugs are found (i.e., Time-to-Exposure or TTE), and performance stability for finding bugs (i.e., Relative Standard Deviation or RSD for the number of unique bugs found for the fuzzing iterations; a lower RSD implies higher performance stability) [29]. Second, Computational Resources Overhead reflects the computing resources required by the involved fuzzing paradigm; if a particular paradigm is effective at finding more bugs, but the resources consumed are disproportionate, then that must be taken into consideration. Third, Coverage signifies the intrinsic ability of the fuzzer for exploring new pathways; this is of import for pursuing the desired pathway, which leads to the vulnerable code (i.e., quality versus quantity).

B. Bespoke Grey-box Concolic Fuzzers

The GFM is, in essence, powered by an amalgam of four bespoke grey-box concolic fuzzers: primary, secondary, tertiary and quaternary. Each utilizes distinct class families for mutating the seed as well as a multi-objective optimization seed schedule (whose aim is to decrease the TTE). Furthermore, the seed schedule is further subdivided into seed pool states (e.g., wide area search, targeted search, and assessment). First, for the wide area search, the aim is to seek high-promise pathways. Second, for the targeted search, the aim is to allocate increased weighting (via the Adaptive Weighting System) towards those identified high-promise pathways. Third, for the assessment, the aim is to ascertain and assess promising seeds. The primary and secondary fuzzers form an aggregate fuzzer set for the test target. The tertiary and quaternary fuzzers are tasked with fuzzing the primary and secondary fuzzers. This amalgam of fuzzers comprise the Fuzzing Module.

C. *Deep Learning Convolutional Generative Adversarial Neural Network-facilitated Enhanced Context Module*

The Enhanced Context Module (ECM) encompasses the Fuzzing Module; its purpose is to serve as a macro feedback loop. In essence the ECM selects a seed, mutates it, and serves it as input to the test target. If the input causes a crash, it will be added to the ECM's crash set. Alternatively, if the input segues to new coverage, it will be added to the search seed pool. In turn, the Fuzzing Module derives Coverage Feedback from the Aggregate Fuzzer Set for the Test Target. This then serves an input to the NSCM, which processes the information and informs the Adaptive Weighting System, which dynamically weights the Class Families for Mutating Seed and Seed Schedules. This should segue to a more optimal Seed Schedule for decreasing TTE as well as RSD; the resulting lower RSD/higher performance stability can be attributed to the NSCM and Adaptive Weighting System.

Given the page limitations of this paper, future work will include more quantitative comparison with various CGFs, such as AFLGo (generates input to reach specified target test sectors) [31], FairFuzz (discerns rare branches within the target test and adapts mutation strategies to enhance coverage) [32], MOPT (utilizes Particle Swarm Optimization or PSO to optimize the mutation schedule and reduce TTE) [33], etc.

ACKNOWLEDGMENT

This research is supported by the Decision Engineering Analysis Laboratory (DEAL), an Underwatch initiative. This is part of a VT white paper series on 5G-enabled defense applications, via proxy use cases, to help inform Project Enabler.

V. CONCLUSION

In a not insignificant portion of the 5G/B5G/6G ecosystem cyber cases, the more serious security problems are implementation imperfections (e.g., network protocols); these constitute attack surface areas, which are often exploited. In the case for which 5G/B5G/6G protocols are still evolving and being defined, these implementation imperfections can be amplified. Conventional software cyber security frameworks, which involve code review, risk analysis, penetration testing, and prototypical fuzzing, do not currently suffice for robustly addressing a domain space, such as the 5G/B5G/6G ecosystem, wherein the protocols are evolving at a rapid pace. Indeed, prototypical fuzzers are challenged by the coverage issue, and conventional CGFs are as well. In an endeavor to provide a mitigation pathway, this paper presented an architectural stack comprised of a sequence of bespoke grey-box concolic fuzzers; as the primary grey-box concolic fuzzer (used against the testing target) is designed to work in conjunction with a secondary grey-box concolic fuzzer, so as to better mitigate against coverage issues (e.g., increasing the probability of visiting certain blocks/lines of code of the software program), and both are fuzzed by tertiary and quaternary grey-box concolic fuzzers (which utilize different classes for mutating a seed as well as seeding schedules), so as to mitigate against inadvertently not discerning vulnerabilities within the primary and secondary fuzzers themselves, the likelihood of increased coverage (on average) is enhanced. The feedback for coverage and adaptive weighting, as well as seed scheduling schemas, contribute to the efficacy. Future work will involve more quantitative experimentation.

REFERENCES

[1] "5G Uptake Progresses Across the Globe: Global 5G Connections Reach 298M in Q1 2021, 5G Connections Added in 2021 Nearly Triple that of 2020, 172 5G Commercial Networks Deployed Worldwide," 5G Americas, June 2021.

[2] H. Remmert, "5G Applications and Use Cases," Digi, November 2019.

[3] K. Fysarakis et al., "A Reactive Security Framework for operational wind parks using Service Function Chaining,"2017 IEEE Symposium on Computers and Communications (ISCC), 2017, pp. 663-668, doi: 10.1109/ISCC.2017.8024604

[4] H. Xu, M. Dong, K. Ota, J. Wu, and J. Li, "Toward Software Defined Dynamic Defense as a Service for 5G-Enabled Vehicular Networks," 2019 International Conference on Internet of Things (iThings) and IEEE Green Computing and Communications (GreenCom) and IEEE Cyber, Physical and Social Computing (CPSCom) and IEEE Smart Data (SmartData), 2019, pp. 880-887, doi: 10.1109/iThings/GreenCom/CPSCom/SmartData.2019.00158

[5] C. Cimpanu, "South Korean researchers apply fuzzing techniques to LTE protocol and find 51 vulnerabilities, of which 36 were new," Zdnet, March 2019.

[6] "Department of Defense (DoD) 5G Strategy (U)," Accessed on: Aug 27, 2021. [Online]. Available: https://www.cto.mil/wp-content/uploads/2020/05/DoD_5G_Strategy_May_2020.pdf.

[7] J. Yli-Kaakinen, T. Levanen, M. Renfors, M. Valkama, and K. Pajukoski, "FFT-Domain Signal Processing for Spectrally-Enhanced CP-OFDM Waveforms in 5G New Radio," 2018 52nd Asilomar Conference on Signals, Systems, and Computers, 2018, pp. 1049-1056, doi: 10.1109/ACSSC.2018.8645100

[8] S. Chan, M. Krunz, and B. Griffin, "AI-based Robust Convex Relaxations for Supporting Diverse QoS in Next-Generation Wireless Systems," Proc. of the IEEE ICDCS Workshop - Next-Generation Mobile Networking and Computing (NGMobile 2021), July 2021, pp. 1-8.

[9] B. Han, J. Lianghai, and H. D. Schotten, "Slice as an Evolutionary Service: Genetic Optimization for Inter-Slice Resource Management in 5G Networks," in IEEE Access, vol. 6, pp. 33137-33147, 2018, doi: 10.1109/ACCESS.2018.2846543.

[10] L. U. Khan, I. Yaqoob, N. H. Tran, Z. Han and C. S. Hong, "Network Slicing: Recent Advances, Taxonomy, Requirements, and Open Research Challenges," in IEEE Access, vol. 8, pp. 36009-36028, 2020, doi: 10.1109/ACCESS.2020.2975072

[11] A. Farrel, “Recent Developments in Service Function Chaining (SFC) and Network Slicing in Backhaul and Metro Networks in Support of 5G,” 2018 20th International Conference on Transparent Optical Networks (ICTON), 2018, pp. 1-4, doi: 10.1109/ICTON.2018.8473624.

[12] A. J. Gonzalez et al., “The Isolation Concept in the 5G Network Slicing,” 2020 European Conference on Networks and Communications (EuCNC), 2020, pp. 12-16, doi: 10.1109/EuCNC48522.2020.9200939

[13] B. L. Parne, S. Gupta, K. Gandhi and S. Meena, “PPSE: Privacy Preservation and Security Efficient AKA Protocol for 5G Communication Networks,” 2020 IEEE International Conference on Advanced Networks and Telecommunications Systems (ANTS), 2020, pp. 1-6, doi: 10.1109/ANTS50601.2020.9342780.

[14] J. Knudsen, “How to cyber security: containerizing fuzzing targets,” Synopsys, February 2021.

[15] R. Nagler, D. Bruhwiler, P. Moeller, and S. Webb, “Sustainability and Reproducibility via Containerized Computing,” 2015, pp. 1-2, arXiv:1509.08789 [cs.SE].

[16] "Use Kaniko to build Docker images," Accessed on: Aug 27, 2021. [Online]. Available: https://docs.gitlab.com/ee/ci/docker/using_kaniko.html.

[17] "Octave-x11-novnc-docker," Accessed on: Aug 27, 2021. [Online]. Available: https://github.com/epfl-sti/octave-x11-novnc-docker

[18] “OpenSSL Release Security Update [08 December 2020],” Accessed on: Aug 27, 2021. [Online]. Available: https://www.openssl.org/news/secadv/20201208.txt.

[19] “OpenSSL Release Security Update [25 August 2021],” Accessed on: Jul 19, 2021. [Online]. Available: https://us-cert.cisa.gov/ncas/current-activity/2021/08/25/openssl-releases-security-update

[20] "Update the bundled OpenSSL version #1834," Accessed on: Aug 27, 2021. [Online]. Available: https://github.com/docker/compose/issues/1834.

[21] "[OpenSSL] Vulnerabilities," Accessed on: Aug 27, 2021. [Online]. Available: https://www.openssl.org/news/vulnerabilities.html

[22] "Openssl version used is insecure #1601," Accessed on: Aug 27, 2021. [Online]. Available: https://github.com/docker/compose/issues/1601

[23] “Heartbleed: how to reliably and portably check the OpenSSL version,” Accessed on: Jul 19, 2021. [Online]. Available: https://serverfault.com/questions/587324/heartbleed-how-to-reliably-and-portably-check-the-openssl-version text 10

[24] S. Chan, “Prototype Orchestration Framework as a High Exposure Dimension Cyber Defense Accelerant Amidst Ever-Increasing Cycles of Adaptation by Attackers,” The Third International Conference on Cyber-Technologies and Cyber-Systems, November 2018, pp. 28-38.

[25] “Dynamically linking OpenSSL #1304,” Accessed on: Jul 19, 2021. [Online]. Available: https://github.com/bitshares/bitshares-core/issues/1304

[26] L. Simon and A. Verma, “Improving Fuzzing through Controlled Compilation,” 2020 IEEE European Symposium on Security and Privacy (EuroS&P), 2020, pp. 34-52, doi: 10.1109/EuroSP48549.2020.00011.

[27] P. Chen and H. Chen, “Angora: Efficient Fuzzing by Principled Search,” 2018 IEEE Symposium on Security and Privacy (SP), 2018, pp. 711-725, doi: 10.1109/SP.2018.00046.

[28] X. Wang, C. Hu, R. Ma, B. Li and X. Wang, "LAFuzz: Neural Network for Efficient Fuzzing," *2020 IEEE 32nd International Conference on Tools with Artificial Intelligence (ICTAI)*, 2020, pp. 603-611, doi: 10.1109/ICTAI50040.2020.00098.

[29] Y. Li et al., “UNIFUZZ: A Holistic and Pragmatic Metrics-Driven Platform for Evaluating Fuzzers,” 2020, pp. 1-18, arXiv:2010.01785 [cs.CR]

[30] H. Chen et al., “MUZZ: Thread-aware Grey-box Fuzzing for Effective Bug Hunting in Multithreaded Programs,” 2020, arXiv:2007.15943v1 [cs.SE].

[31] M. Bohem, V. Pham, M. Nguyen, and A. Roychoudhury, “Directed Greybox Fuzzing,” ACM SIGSAC Conference on Computer and Communications Security, 2017, pp. 2329-2344.

[32] C. Lemieux and K. Sen, “Fairfuzz: A Targeted Mutation Strategy for Increasing Greybox Fuzz Testing Coverage,” 33rd ACM/IEEE International Conference on Automated Software Engineering, 2018, pp. 475-485.

[33] C. Lyu, S. Ji, C. Zhang, Y. Li, W. Lee, Y. Song, and R. Beyah, “MOPT: Optimized Mutation Scheduling for Fuzzers,” 28th USENIX Security Symposium, 2019, pp. 1949-1966.

The Life of Data in Compliance Management

Nick Scope
College of Computing and Digital Media
DePaul University
Chicago, United States
Email: nscope52884@gmail.com

Alexander Rasin
College of Computing and Digital Media
DePaul University
Chicago, United States
Email: arasin@cdm.depaul.edu

Karen Heart
College of Computing and Digital Media
DePaul University
Chicago, United States
Email: kheart@cdm.depaul.edu

Ben Lenard
College of Computing and Digital Media
DePaul University
Chicago, United States
Email: blenard@anl.gov

James Wagner
Department of Computer Science
University of New Orleans
New Orleans, United States
Email: jwagner4@uno.edu

Abstract—**Data privacy polices mandate requirements to protect the privacy of individuals, prevent fraud, and support audits. Organizations also implement their own internal data policies to minimize liabilities and protect user privacy. In practice, it is difficult (or impossible with most systems active today) to achieve the desired purpose of these policies due to technological limitations of storage systems. These limitations are ultimately caused by the lack of native database support for data privacy compliance. This paper surveys the principles of data compliance and analyzes the requirements imposed on organizations. We begin by defining data compliance terminology that must be shared between legal and technology domain experts; legislation and litigation examples provide real-world context and motivation for our analysis. Since the data life cycle model is universally accepted in data management, we next discuss how data compliance can be integrated into this model to fully support data management policies. Finally, we consider the open problems with current data storage systems and discuss the requirements for automated privacy regulation compliance.**

Keywords: Compliance Management; Privacy Regulations

I. Introduction

Data management by an organization is bound to data governance policies (e.g., internal requirements or government agency mandates) that define how the data must be stored and used. These policies include data retention (how long the data must be kept), data purging requirements (when the data must be destroyed), and data consent (whether the data can be used for a particular purpose). Failure to comply with these policies could result in large fines, a loss of customers, and an irrecoverable breach of customer data privacy.

Data policies set forth by legislation have been in place for decades. Some examples include the Health Insurance Portability and Accountability Act (HIPAA) of 1996 [8] (patient healthcare data) and the Gramm–Leach–Bliley Act of 1999 [32] (business records of financial institutions); additionally, new policies are continuously introduced, such as California's Proposition 24 of 2020 [7] (which expanded on the previous law "The California Consumer Privacy Act"). Furthermore, there are also instances where organizations must follow additional internal policies or policies of business contacts [10]. We further discuss these motivating examples and more in Section III.

A. Motivation

The data life cycle model is the state-of-the-art structure for organizations to understand and manage their data assets [25]. By examining the data life cycle phases, we can clearly see how compliance must be considered throughout an organization's processes. Since published literature presents several variations of the life cycle phases, we have abstracted the relevant phases from [4], [13], and [23] in Figure 1. Our phase definitions bridge the different goals of domain experts, legal departments, and other stakeholders associated with the data and legal requirements. These were developed to promote discussion on where policy compliance must be considered. For example, some data life cycles model "Usage" as multiple phases (e.g., analysis, reporting). However, for the purposes of privacy compliance, we believe that a single phase captures all necessary aspects of "Usage". To evaluate data lifecycle outside the scope of policy compliance, alternative models may be more applicable. For example, to analyze security considerations, the transition of data between phases would be modeled in further detail. Overall, we use our phases to guide a discussion on future research necessary to remedy the database software shortcomings and facilitate automated compliance management.

Figure 1 illustrates the connections between data life cycle management phases (we detail phase requirements in Section IV). For example, archival phase follows data usage phase; usage phase may also affect the decisions associated with the storage phase. Adding to the complexity, not all data goes through each phase. For example, data may be under an indefinite retention policy, staying in the archival phase and never proceeding to the destruction phase.

B. Contributions

Current systems are missing key functionality, which prohibits complete automated compliance; until these gaps are filled, consumer privacy will suffer. Due to the limitations

Figure 1. Data life cycle phases

in both research and technological implementations focusing on policy compliance, we believe our discussion provides the following contributions:

1) Surveys the current domain challenges and background information on data privacy compliance.
2) Analyzes how compliance must be considered at each phase of the data life cycle to satisfy legal requirements.
3) Discusses the current technological shortcomings that must be explored to automate policy compliance.

II. Domain Challenges

A. Concepts

Business Record: Organizational rules and requirements for data management are defined in units of business records. United States federal law refers to a business record broadly as any "memorandum, writing, entry, print, representation or combination thereof, of any act, transaction, occurrence, or event [that is] kept or recorded [by any] business institution, member of a profession or calling, or any department or agency of government [...] in the regular course of business or activity" [31]. In other words, business records describe any interaction or transaction resulting in new data.

Business records can be represented using different logical layouts. A business record may consist of a single document for an organization (e.g., an email message). In a database, a business record may span many combinations of rows across multiple tables (e.g., a purchase order consisting of a buyer, a product, and the purchase transaction from three different tables). The process of mapping business records to underlying data can vary depending on an organization and the data storage medium.

Policy: A data policy is any formally established rule for organizations dictating the requirements (i.e., how long data must be saved, when data access requires consent, and when data must be purged). Policies can originate from a variety of sources such as legislation or as a by-product of a court ruling (examples in Section III). Companies may also establish their own internal data retention policies to protect confidential data. In practice, database administrators work with domain experts and sometimes with legal counsel to define business records and retention requirements based on the written policy.

Policies can use a combination of time and external events as the criteria for data retention and destruction. For example, retaining employee data until employee termination plus 5 years illustrates a policy criteria that is based on a combination of an external event (employee termination) and time (5 years). The United States Department of Defense (DoD) "DoD 5015-02-STD" [2] outlines the minimum requirements and guidance for any record system related to the DoD, which includes how organizations must preserve and destroy data. Moreover, multiple US government agencies, such as the National Archives, use the same standards.

Policy compliance can be complex due to multiple overlapping policies or criteria for the same business record, or due to different data points belonging to different business records. For example, different rows or columns of a table belonging to an order purchase could be governed by different policies: purchase information (e.g., price) may fall under different retention policies versus customer information (e.g., address). Policy mapping must also consider the potential conflict between multiple policies with data retention and destruction requirements.

Verification: Data curators must be able to query the policies and the status of all business records in storage. Data storage systems must support a standard mechanism for defining the policies, listing or modifying current policies, and checking for potential conflicts (e.g., policies requiring retention and destruction of the same data) or overlap between different policies. For example, if an organization is unable to destroy data when requested by a customer, their refusal must be justified.

Enforcement: Enforcing policies includes archiving and deleting data as required as well as verifying consent when processing data. Enforcing a policy maintains an organization's compliance. Current database management systems do not incorporate automated robust data policy features; as a result, organizations are forced to develop manual solutions for policy compliance. Automated enforcement of policy requirements will both increase compliance and customer privacy.

B. Data Governance Topics

Retention: Retention defines the conditions when a business record must be preserved. Some organizations may choose to delete data once it is no longer needed to minimize liability (e.g, data theft or requested through legal discovery). Others may store the data longer than minimally required (in the gray area between "must be retained" and "must be destroyed"). DoD guidelines state that any storage system must support retention thresholds such as time or event (Section C2.2.2.7 of [2]). Some retention requirements, such as HIPAA with healthcare data, may require a complete historical log of any and all business record updates (e.g., current address and full history of address changes for a patient) [8]. Organizations subject to this level of retention must archive the complete business record before every update to ensure a complete audit trail history was preserved.

Consent: Per GDPR Recital 40, "In order for processing to be lawful, personal data should be processed on the basis of the consent of the data subject concerned or some other legitimate basis" [27]. Additionally, per Article 4(11), "Consent of the data subject means any freely given, specific, informed and unambiguous indication of the data subject's wishes by which he or she, by a statement or by a clear affirmative action, signifies agreement to the processing of personal data relating to him or her." The processing of these business records must be verified according to customer's consent (e.g., marketing versus order processing). Not all processing requires consent; data necessary to complete the business transaction for which data was collected does not require explicit consent.

Purging: In data retention, purging is the permanent and irreversible destruction of data in a business record [20]. Purging requirements establish when a business record must be destroyed. A business record purge can be accomplished by physically destroying the device which stored the data, encrypting and erasing the decryption key (although the ciphertext still exists, destroying the decryption key makes it inaccessible and irrecoverable), or by fully erasing data from all storage. If any part of a business record's data remains recoverable or accessible in some form, then the data purge is not considered to have been successfully completed. For example, if a file is deleted through a file system, but can still be recovered from the hard drive using a forensic tool, this does not qualify as a purge [20].

Some policies require an organization to completely purge business records either after the passage of time, at the expiration of a contract, or purely when the data is no longer needed. Additionally, there are an increasing number of regulations, such as the European Union's General Data Protection Regulation (GDPR) [27], which require organizations to purge business records at the request of a customer. Therefore, organizations must be prepared to comply with purging policies as well as ad-hoc requests.

III. Legal Precedent

Although it is beyond the scope of this paper to provide an overview of all data privacy legislation across different domains, we discuss some of the most impactful government regulations. Private organizations (such as in the financial industry) may set additional policies for any companies that do business with them [10]. Overall, we believe the following examples offer the most significant motivation to increase database support of data privacy compliance.

General Data Protection Regulation: In the European Union, the General Data Protection Regulation greatly expanded consumer power over personal data. This regulation was put into effect May 25, 2018, and is arguably "the toughest privacy and security law in the world" [27]. Any organization which is registered in the European Union, offers goods or services, or monitors behavior of EU residents must comply with GDPR requirements (regardless of whether the organization is based in the EU).

One significant addition to data privacy rights due to GDPR is the "Right to be Forgotten" [12], which allows individuals to request that companies delete all of their personal data. In Recital 65, Recital 66, and in Article 17 GDPR states: "The data subject shall have the right to obtain from the controller the erasure of personal data concerning him or her without undue delay and the controller shall have the obligation to erase personal data without undue delay" [33].

Requesting data deletion does not guarantee that customer's data will be purged. When customers request their data to be deleted, organizations must check if they are legally permitted to do so. If an organization has a retention requirement on this data, they will not be able to purge it despite the request. Without automated verification, organizations must manually check for any applicable retention obligation when deleting data. The "Right to be Forgotten" requests require a response within a month. Thus, without an automated process, organizations must manually process requests within a deadline.

GDPR non-compliance carries significant penalties. On January 15, 2020, TIM was fined €27.8 million by the Italian data protection authority, the Garante, for violations of GDPR [16]. A large number of complaints were filed between January 1, 2017 until early 2019 due to TIM's unwanted promotional calls. Some customers (who did not consent) were contacted over 150 times in a single month. Because TIM did not enforce data consent, this eventually led to being fined due to failing to comply with GDPR.

California Consumer Privacy Act of 2018 & Proposition 24: California passed the California Consumer Privacy Act of 2018 (CCPA) [6], which was greatly inspired by GDPR and offers many similar privacy rights. CCPA went into effect on January 1, 2020 and California Attorney General began enforcing CCPA on July 1, 2020 [5]. Regardless, some privacy advocates believe CCPA did not go far enough to protect data privacy and are still pushing for additional regulations [11]. The California Secretary of State summarizes the position of the advocates for Proposition 24, who believe that this proposition will further increase consumer data privacy [7]. Data retention and management legislation is continuously evolving as Proposition 24 [19] just passed in November 2020.

Proposition 24 exemplifies the continuous battle of privacy advocates against those who are concerned about too much government regulation. Data retention is an evolving field where requirements are continuously changing; organizations must be able to quickly adapt to new and changing requirements. Because systems currently cannot easily add retention protections, any organization which manually added protections with CCPA now must manually update all of those protections due to Proposition 24.

Zubulake v. UBS Warburg: Between 2003 and 2004 in New York, the case of Zubulake v. UBS Warburg resulted in many additional electronic record keeping requirements [34]. According to Li at ABAJournal.com, "Companies were put on notice that they had a duty to preserve data once they reasonably anticipated they might be sued. [...] Otherwise, the consequences could be severe and a party could be hit with sanctions [which] could cripple its ability to mount a defense" [22]. In summary, this ruling clarified that organizations are required to retain all pertinent electronic data if they are aware of a forthcoming lawsuit, even before being explicitly requested to do so.

The plaintiff's attorneys argued that they were not given all of the relevant evidence to her case; the judge concluded that UBS Warburg did not hand over all relevant data. It was determined that the only copies of some relevant data was archived on tapes (which, in turn, made it expensive and difficult to acquire and review). This led to the judge's opinion that "anyone who anticipates being a party or is a party to a lawsuit must not destroy unique, relevant evidence that might be useful to an adversary" [34].

Health Insurance Portability and Accountability Act: In 1996, the United States passed a law that had a significant influence on the way privacy and retention of health care data was managed. HIPAA imposes requirements for both data retention as well as for purging. Per the United States Department of Health and Human Services, HIPAA increases healthcare recipients power over their own data in respect to both privacy as well as transparency [30]. According to research by Annas, HIPAA requires that "[...] a patient's entire medical record can seldom be lawfully disclosed without the patient's written authorization" [1]. HIPAA raised the minimum standards of privacy and medical data, empowering individuals to control their data.

For example, HIPAA Subpart D §164.504 "Uses and Disclosures: Organizational Requirements" [8], requires an individual's data to be destroyed at the expiration of a contract. "At termination of the contract, if feasible, return or destroy all protected health information received from, or created or received by the business associate on behalf of, the covered entity that the business associate still maintains in any form and retain no copies of such information[....]" Therefore, organizations must have a robust data purging process.

HIPAA also requires healthcare recipients in the United States to be clearly informed of their privacy rights. Per the United States Health and Human Services, "The HIPAA Privacy Rule requires health plans and covered health care providers to develop and distribute a notice that provides a clear, user friendly explanation of individuals rights with respect to their personal health information and the privacy practices of health plans and health care providers" [18]. Currently, there is no automatic process in deployed database systems to report all active retention policies and their relevant business records. Any request on which retention policies apply requires a manual lookup process.

IV. Privacy Requirements in the Data Life Cycle

A. Creation

In most organizations, every transaction creates data that could be stored and processed. Whether this data will move on to the storage phase of the life cycle depends on the requirements defined by the owner. In certain industries, such as the financial industry, all transactional data must be stored.

The first step of compliance is mapping the new data to policy requirements. This process typically involves domain experts working with the database administrators and legal professionals. Choosing protections placed on the data must be done immediately, lest retention compliance be violated before protections have been implemented.

Currently, many organizations have standardized processes which include data classification, but this classification is orthogonal to data policy compliance. For example, organizations may automatically label data generated from specific sources as "Internal Only" or "Highly Confidential". These labels indicate that the data must only be accessed by a specific audience but may not align to policy requirements. For example, "Highly Confidential" does not align to any specific requirement dictating when data must be purged.

B. Storage

After data is created, it enters a data storage management system. A number of considerations are factored into the data storage software choice. Organizations with large volume of transactions and a consistent (structured) data will typically deploy a relational database. For data which is less structured and more dynamically evolving, organizations may choose a NoSQL database [17]. Alternatively, keeping data in file documents in a simpler database may satisfy an organization's data storage requirements.

The type of storage used can greatly impact the difficulty in complying with data retention policies. When business records are stored in documents, this task will be simpler. When using advanced databases, the mapping of business records to the stored data is much more complex. When retention and purging requirements correspond to individual files, solutions such as Amazon S3 (which offers a file-level object life-cycle management) facilitate retention and purging compliance. The DoD's "Electronic Records Management Software Applications Design Criteria Standard" (DoD 5015-02-STD) requires systems support both time or event criteria.

Furthermore, most storage solutions require finer granularity than storing a file per business record. As discussed in Section II-A, businesses records may span multiple tuples across tables in relational databases. Prior research addressed retention [28, 3] and purging [29] in relational databases.

C. Usage

The use of data depends on the data owner's policies as well as the organizational need for the data. Common data uses include storing customer information, running statistical analysis to discover underlying trends, and documenting business transactions. Data may be continuously used for an extended duration and for multiple purposes. For example, customer records which are used for shipping orders may also be used for analyzing trends in customer purchase patterns.

Data consent support must be an inherent part of data privacy management. Databases neither offer functionality to define business records (with respect to consent) nor filter on consent for various processing uses (e.g., marketing). Because data privacy regulations require organizations to acquire customer consent when processing data for certain purposes, storage systems must guarantee verification of customer consent. Business records which have not been allowed to be processed must be excluded from the query output. Access control based on the identity of data analyst would not facilitate compliance.

On May 25, 2018 (the day GDPR took effect), Google was found in violation of GDPR [15], leading to a fine of

€50 million. Google was convicted for lack of transparency and failing to acquire user consent for data processing in an instance where consent was required.

D. Archival

HIPAA [9] requires medical data to be retained for at least 6 years. Therefore, organizations have an increased obligation to maintain archived data, even after the data is no longer needed for their operation. Business records that are no longer needed but must be preserved under a retention policy must be moved to an archive until the retention criteria has expired.

In order to reach the archival phase of the data life cycle, data from business records which are no longer needed in usage phase must be under a retention policy. Archived data is the data that has lost its primary relevance but is still required to be available in storage (e.g., historical or reporting purposes). Therefore, archived data does not require regular updates nor is expected to be actively used. Instead, it is stored in a separate repository until it is eligible for destruction (i.e., no longer requiring retention). As long as the data is subject to at least one retention policy, it must remain archived.

Archived business records do not require any updates nor should they be deleted while under retention. In rare situations, data in archive may be returned to active storage for usage (e.g., the result of a lawsuit). Any retention compliant system must purge business records from the archive once they no longer require retention and have a purge policy requirement.

E. Destruction

Once data is no longer needed and is not subject to retention requirements it may enter the destruction phase of its life cycle. Some organizations have data with a retention period "for the life of the company" meaning that it will never enter the destruction phase. On the other hand, some policies, including those from government regulation, explicitly require business records to be destroyed when no longer used nor requiring retention. HIPAA Subpart D §164.504 requires organizations to delete data at the end of a contract if there are no other applicable retention requirements [8]. The Children's Online Privacy Protection Act states that personal information for children can be retained "for only as long as is reasonably necessary to fulfill the purpose for which the information was collected" (Section 312.10 of [14]).

Google has been repeatedly fined for violating GDPR's "Right to be Forgotten" [24]. Google refused to delete customer data at their request despite having no legal basis for retaining the data. France, Sweden, and Belgium have all imposed fines for violations of failing to delete requested data.

To fully comply with purging requirements, systems must implement functionality that allows organizations to define business records and policies, which will automatically be enforced across active databases and backups [29]. This functionality must implement some form of secure deletion to render the required data permanently and irrecoverably destroyed. If any data belonging to a business record requiring purging is recoverable (whether the data exists in the active database, underlying database pages recoverable using forensic tools, or in a backup), the purge policy has not been properly enforced, and the system would not be considered compliant.

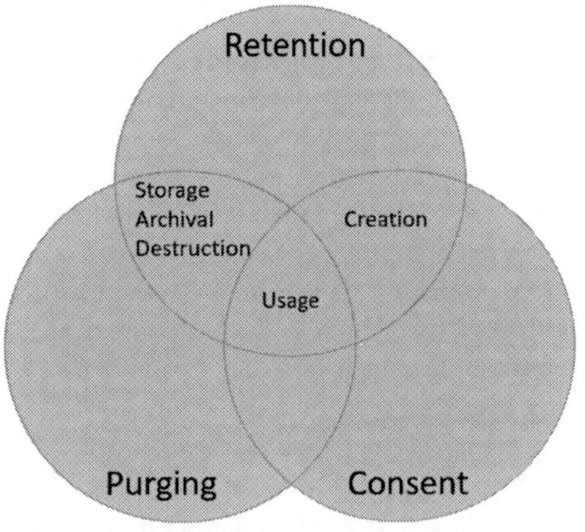

Figure 2. The relationship between life cycle phases and requirements.

V. OPEN PROBLEMS

The complexity caused by data policy requirements coming from a variety of sources (each with their own changes in requirements) means manually achieving compliance is an extremely difficult task. Throughout this paper, we outlined where in a data life cycle each type of compliance must be implemented. Manually achieving compliance requires each individual user to know which policies apply to which business records for each purpose. Therefore, facilitating comprehensive policy enforcement requires automated data policy compliance tools. Regardless of policy type, legacy systems will continue to be a difficult challenge. In this section, we discuss the requirements for the three main areas of data compliance and how they overlap with data life cycle phases.

Retention must be considered during each phase of the data life cycle. On the other hand, purging and consent must only be considered during some of the phases. For example, destruction does not require user consent (although users can request their records to be deleted, they cannot prevent required record purging). Figure 2 provides an overview on where each phase aligns to each governance requirement.

In practice, DBAs work with domain experts and legal counsel to define business records and retention requirements based on policies. Automated systems typically assume that data curators can express business records as a query or as a collection of files. The initial process of mapping the business records and retention policies to database tuples will always be a manual process; any automated system then will reference these definitions to enforce policy compliance.

A. Retention

Retention compliance is achieved by maintaining all relevant business records until some criteria (time or event) has been met. This can be achieved by either 1) blocking transactions which would delete or update protected data or 2) automatically archiving business records in a separate database before deleting or updating data. Either solution requires guaranteeing that update and delete operations automatically cross-reference defined policies and retention criterion.

Databases do not currently offer functionality to enforce retention and archival compliance. Currently, organizations build ad-hoc solutions manually. If any data targeted by a delete or update is protected by a policy, the automated system must either archive the entire business record as-is before executing the transaction [28] or block the transaction [3]. Systems must automatically cross-reference defined business records and retention requirements to archive data when deletes or updates would violate retention requirements. Systems proposed by Scope et al. [28] and Ataullah et al. [3] use triggers in relational databases to enforce retention policies.

Lawsuits may impose sudden and critical retention requirements on various business records. Zubulake v. UBS Warburg expanded on the precedent of organizations being required to retain any applicable business records for the duration of the case [34]. Organizations must be able to easily retain and archive all applicable records.

As shown in Figure 2, retention must be considered at each phase of the data life cycle. Retention must be immediately mapped at creation, and must protect data across storage, usage, archival, and destruction phases. If data prematurely enters the destruction phase from any of the other phases when retention is still required, compliance has been violated.

B. Consent

Regulations such as GDPR require user consent for certain types of data processing. Because the same analyst may process data for a variety of purposes, user-based permissions do not satisfy consent requirements. Therefore, research must implement automated filtering where business records require consent for an input purpose.

Consent must defined at data creation (although customers can revoke or give consent at any time). Additionally, this consent must be applied during data usage depending on whether consent is required. On the other hand, consent policies do not have to be considered during storage, archival, and destruction phases.

One common paradox are customers who demand that all of their data is deleted and to not be contacted in the future. Although the customer is revoking their consent to use their data, the organization cannot delete all of the data without risking contacting them in the future. Thus, organizations must maintain some data on a do-not-contact list, as long as the data maintained on this list is only referenced as a filter.

Although detailed usage requirements are beyond the scope of this paper, we also must note that consent is defined differently by different governing bodies. While some simply require customers to be remain anonymous (but still allowing their data to be used in aggregations), others do not allow any customer data to be included without their permission. Therefore, multiple independent solutions may be required to satisfy the different definitions and requirements.

C. Purging

Purging requires that organizations irreversibly and irrecoverably destroy their data after some criteria has been met. Database administrators must work with domain experts to guarantee that these are mapped as to not conflict with retention policies. If data is prematurely destroyed as the result of a user input or automated policies, this does not violate compliance (unless this violates retention).

Purging must remove data from both all backups (both accessible and inaccessible) and from active storage. If data is recoverable by forensic tools or by backup, compliance has not been achieved. Because data requiring purging is simultaneously stored in systems with data requiring retention, simply destroying the physical storage would satisfy purging compliance at the cost of retention compliance.

Multiple enhancements must be developed to achieve full compliance. First, automated systems must automatically delete all files or tuples in a database as necessary. Once the files or tuples are deleted, they may still be recoverable via forensic means. Therefore, the data must be deleted so that it is no longer accessible to forensic tools. Finally, data must be purged from all backups.

Reardon et al. [26] offered a comprehensive overview of secure deletion, which both provides various approaches and requirements for completely purging data from a storage systems. In their paper, the authors defined three user-level approaches to secure deletion: 1) execute a secure delete feature on the physical medium 2) overwrite the data before unlinking or 3) unlink the data to the OS and fill the empty capacity of the physical device's storage. For all three methods, one requirement is the ability to directly interact with the physical storage device. Therefore, these approaches are only applicable for physically accessible databases (which may not be possible for backups in storage).

Lenard et al. [21] provided an analysis on how long deleted or updated data remains in underlying database pages, which eventually leads to them being included in backups. Therefore, to fully purge data from all storage, it is necessary to both implement steps to remove the data from active storage as well as backups. Scope et al. [29] proposed using a form of cryptographic erasure to purge pertinent business records from backups of relational databases.

D. Performance Considerations

Throughout this paper we outlined the requirements and benefits of automated compliance. This automation does have an associated performance cost. Research by Scope et al. [28] and Ataullah et al. [3] performed experiments detailing the runtime overhead of their additional retention protections.

Balancing performance with automated enforcement is a difficult problem for future research. For example, financial organizations are heavily motivated by system performance. Automated trading system measure execution time in milliseconds. These systems use speed for a competitive trading advantage, but they are also subject to extreme regulations by both the exchanges as well as major government bodies. For these industries, implementing automated compliance will require optimization to minimize impact on system performance. For the necessary functionality enhancements to be widely adopted, these enhancements must both guarantee compliance and minimize system performance overhead.

VI. Conclusion

In this paper, we outlined the data life cycle model and the steps that must be Incorporated into the process to facilitate privacy compliance. Recognizing the data retention needs at each phase of the data life cycle provides a framework for where additional research must be prioritized to satisfy compliance management requirements. Current storage solutions do not have the necessary functionality to automatically enforce data governance policies. Until the necessary functionality is implemented, ad-hoc manual solutions will continue to risk violating privacy regulation requirements. Privacy compliance is only continuing to grow in importance; these issues must be addressed to increase user privacy protections.

Acknowledgment

This work was partially funded by US National Science Foundation Grant IIP-2016548 and CME Group. The authors thank Thamer Al-Johani for comments on the paper draft.

References

[1] G. J. Annas. *HIPAA regulations—a new era of medical-record privacy?* 2003. URL: https://pubmed.ncbi.nlm.nih.gov/12686707/.

[2] Assistant Secretary of Defense for Networks and Information Integration. *Electronic Records Management Software Applications Design Criteria Standard.* https://www.esd.whs.mil/Portals/54/Documents/DD/issuances/dodm/501502std.pdf. Accessed: Aug. 2020. 2007.

[3] A. A. Ataullah, A. Aboulnaga, and F. W. Tompa. "Records retention in relational database systems". In: *Proceedings of the 17th ACM conference on Information and knowledge management.* 2008, pp. 873–882.

[4] A. Ball. *Review of data management lifecycle models.* University of Bath, IDMRC, 2012.

[5] G. A. Brown. *CCPA Enforcement Begins Today.* https://www.natlawreview.com/article/ccpa-enforcement-begins-today. 2020.

[6] *California Consumer Privacy Act (CCPA).* Accessed: Aug. 2020. 2020. URL: https://oag.ca.gov/privacy/ccpa.

[7] California Secretary of State. *Proposition 24: Official Voter Information Guide: California Secretary of State.* URL: https://voterguide.sos.ca.gov/propositions/24/.

[8] Centers for Medicare & Medicaid Services. *The Health Insurance Portability and Accountability Act of 1996 (HIPAA).* Accessed: Aug. 2021. 1996.

[9] Centers for Medicare & Medicaid Services and others. *The Health Insurance Portability and Accountability Act of 1996 (HIPAA).* Accessed: Sept. 2021. 1996. URL: http://www.cms.hhs.gov/hipaa.

[10] *CME Group Rule 536.B.1.* Accessed: Sept. 2021. 2020. URL: https://www.cmegroup.com/rulebook/files/cme-group-Rule-536-B.pdf.

[11] G. Edelman. *The fight over the fight Over CALIFORNIA'S Privacy Future.* 2020. URL: https://www.wired.com/story/california-prop-24-fight-over-privacy-future/.

[12] European Parliament and of the Council. *Regulation (EU) 2016/679 of the European Parliament and of the Council.* https://www.legislation.gov.uk/eur/2016/679. 2020.

[13] J. L. Faundeen et al. *The United States geological survey science data lifecycle model.* US Department of the Interior, US Geological Survey, 2013.

[14] Federal Trade Commission and others. *Children's online privacy protection act of 1998 (COPPA).* Accessed: Sept. 2021. 1998.

[15] C. Fox. *Google hit with £44m GDPR fine over ads.* 2019. URL: https://www.bbc.com/news/technology-46944696.

[16] T. Garante. *Provvedimento correttivo e sanzionatorio nei confronti di TIM S.p.A. - 15 gennaio 2020 [9256486].* 2020. URL: https://www.garanteprivacy.it/web/guest/home/docweb/-/docweb-display/docweb/9256486.

[17] J. Han, E. Haihong, G. Le, and J. Du. "Survey on NoSQL database". In: *2011 6th international conference on pervasive computing and applications.* IEEE. 2011, pp. 363–366.

[18] HHS Office of the Secretary and Office for Civil Rights. *Model Notices of Privacy Practices.* Accessed: Aug. 2021. 2013. URL: https://www.hhs.gov/hipaa/for-professionals/privacy/guidance/model-notices-privacy-practices/index.html.

[19] A. Holmes. *California just passed a major privacy law that will make it harder for Facebook and Google to track people and gather data.* 2020. URL: https://www.businessinsider.com/prop-24-privacy-california-data-tracking-facebook-google-2020-11.

[20] International Data Sanitization Consortium. *Data Sanitization Terminology and Definitions.* Accessed: Feb. 2021. 2017. URL: https://www.datasanitization.org/data-sanitization-terminology/.

[21] B. Lenard, A. Rasin, N. Scope, and J. Wagner. "What is lurking in your backups?" In: Springer International Publishing, 2021, 401–415.

[22] V. Li. *Looking back on Zubulake, 10 years later.* 2015. URL: https://www.abajournal.com/magazine/article/looking_back_on_zubulake_10_years_later.

[23] N. L. of Medicine. *Date Lifecycle.* URL: https://nnlm.gov/data/thesaurus/data-lifecycle.

[24] A. Nicodemus. *Google fined $670K for violating GDPR's 'right to be forgotten'.* 2020. URL: https://www.complianceweek.com/gdpr/google-fined-670k-for-violating-gdprs-right-to-be-forgotten/29186.article.

[25] L. Pouchard. *Revisiting the data lifecycle with big data curation.* 2015. URL: https://www.researchgate.net/publication/305095078_Revisiting_the_Data_Lifecycle_with_Big_Data_Curation.

[26] J. Reardon, D. Basin, and S. Capkun. "Sok: Secure data deletion". In: *2013 IEEE symposium on security and privacy.* IEEE. 2013, pp. 301–315.

[27] *Regulation (EU) 2016/679 of the European Parliament and of the Council.* Accessed: Jun. 2021. 2020. URL: https://gdpr.eu/tag/gdpr/.

[28] N. Scope, A. Rasin, J. Wagner, B. Lenard, and K. Heart. "Database Framework for Supporting Retention Policies". In: *International Conference on Database and Expert Systems Applications.* (to appear). Springer. 2021.

[29] N. Scope, A. Rasin, J. Wagner, B. Lenard, and K. Heart. "Purging Data from Backups by Encryption". In: *International Conference on Database and Expert Systems Applications.* (to appear). Springer. 2021.

[30] Secretary, HHS Office of the and (OCR), Office for Civil Rights. *Your Rights Under HIPAA.* 2020. URL: https://www.hhs.gov/hipaa/for-individuals/guidance-materials-for-consumers/index.html.

[31] United States Congress. 28 U.S. Code §1732. Accessed: Aug. 2021. 1948. URL: https://www.law.cornell.edu/uscode/text/28/1732.

[32] United States Congress. *Gramm–Leach–Bliley Act, Financial Services Modernization Act of 1999.* Accessed: Aug. 2021. 1999.

[33] B. Wolford. *Everything you need to know about the "Right to be forgotten".* 2020. URL: https://gdpr.eu/right-to-be-forgotten/.

[34] *Zubulake v. UBS WARBURG LLC.* 2005. URL: https://sosmt.gov/wp-content/uploads/attachments/E-ZubulakeV.pdf?dt=1519325634100.

Sharing FANCI Features: A Privacy Analysis of Feature Extraction for DGA Detection

Benedikt Holmes
RWTH Aachen University
Aachen, Germany
holmes@itsec.rwth-aachen.de

Arthur Drichel
RWTH Aachen University
Aachen, Germany
drichel@itsec.rwth-aachen.de

Ulrike Meyer
RWTH Aachen University
Aachen, Germany
meyer@itsec.rwth-aachen.de

***Abstract*—The goal of Domain Generation Algorithm (DGA) detection is to recognize infections with bot malware and is often done with help of Machine Learning approaches that classify non-resolving Domain Name System (DNS) traffic and are trained on possibly sensitive data. In parallel, the rise of privacy research in the Machine Learning world leads to privacy-preserving measures that are tightly coupled with a deep learning model's architecture or training routine, while non deep learning approaches are commonly better suited for the application of privacy-enhancing methods outside the actual classification module. In this work, we aim to measure the privacy capability of the feature extractor of feature-based DGA detector FANCI (Feature-based Automated Nxdomain Classification and Intelligence). Our goal is to assess whether a data-rich adversary can learn an inverse mapping of FANCI's feature extractor and thereby reconstruct domain names from feature vectors. Attack success would pose a privacy threat to sharing FANCI's feature representation, while the opposite would enable this representation to be shared without privacy concerns. Using three real-world data sets, we train a recurrent Machine Learning model on the reconstruction task. Our approaches result in poor reconstruction performance and we attempt to back our findings with a mathematical review of the feature extraction process. We thus reckon that sharing FANCI's feature representation does not constitute a considerable privacy leakage.**

***Keywords*—Data privacy; Intrusion detection; Machine learning.**

I. Introduction

Machine Learning (ML) has had great success in solving advanced data-driven problems and its application also yields great performance for solving the Domain Generation Algorithm (DGA) classification problem. Instead of using static IP-addresses or domain names, bots use DGAs to generate pseudo-random domain names and then query the Domain Name System (DNS) to obtain the IP address of their command and control server. The botnet herder knows the DGA generation scheme and is therefore able to register a subset of the generated domains, while the connection is now more difficult for the defender to block. Most of the bot's queries result in non-existing domain (NXD) responses as only the domain names that are registered in advance are resolved to valid IP addresses. ML classifiers can be trained to separate benign NXDs, e.g., caused by typos or misconfigured software, from DGA generated domains. Thereby, DGA activities can be detected even before bots receive instructions from the herder.

For reasons such as the availability, diversity, or size of data, it is uncommon that ML models are trained solely on a large data set obtained from a single source. On the other hand, collecting or sharing sensitive data is a privacy-concern. For ML-based DGA detection on NX traffic, the malicious training samples are publicly sourced, e.g., obtained from DGArchive [1], while samples of benign NXDs are often locally collected and can contain privacy-sensitive information as their disclosure may allow drawing conclusions about sensitive activity on the network, e.g., usage of a particular software or end-user browsing. Deep Learning (DL) is designed to allow models to directly receive raw data as input and therefore privacy-preserving measures are often coupled with the training routine. Non-DL approaches are commonly preceded by a feature extraction stage that performs a data transformation with the goal of reducing size of the data while increasing expressiveness by compressing data samples to finite and fixed length vectors. Whether such transformation can also yield a sufficiently abstract data representation able to hide sensitive information is our main research focus.

In this work, we thus take a step back from the advances in DL-based DGA detection and reconsider a simpler, feature-based DGA detection approach and evaluate its practicability towards privacy-preserving intelligence sharing: FANCI (Feature-based Automated Nxdomain Classification and Intelligence) [2] is the first feature-based classifier that achieves significant performance in DGA detection while only considering few hand-crafted features. Complementing the research on its classification performance [2], we investigate whether FANCI's public feature extractor is prone to malicious inversion. More concretely, we ask whether knowledge of FANCI features threatens the disclosure of the original domain names as the latter could be reconstructable from features. If the feature extraction process can be deemed inversion-resilient, then this allows the risk-free publication of sensitive NX data in the form of FANCI's feature representation and would thus enable to provide data-privacy in otherwise privacy-concerning sharing tasks, e.g., (1) collaborative learning approaches in which many parties join their data or (2) classification outsourcing in which DGA detection is offered as a service.

Our approaches exhibit poor reconstruction performance even when provided with real-world data samples. Consequently, we believe that FANCI's feature extractor is hard to invert, which motivates low-risk publication of feature vector sets for aforementioned sharing scenarios.

The work is structured as follows: Sections II & III elaborate on relevant related work and preliminaries such as FANCI and its feature extractor. Section IV gives a mathematical review of the feature extraction process to assess the limitations of any reconstruction approach. Then, these insights are used to motivate the subsequent data-driven approach, detailed in Section V & VI, in which a DL model is trained to learn a reconstruction mapping based on three large real-world NX data sets. These allow us to asses whether a reconstructor trained on one data set may perform well on another data set at test time. Results, quantified by a normalized edit distance, are presented in Section VII followed by a discussion in Section VIII. Finally, Section IX concludes the paper with an outlook on future work.

II. Related Work

We briefly give an overview of DGA detection methodologies and position ourselves in the research area of ML privacy.

A. DGA Detection

A variety of different DGA detection techniques have been proposed in the past, which can broadly be divided into context-less [2]–[6] and context-aware approaches [7]–[12]. Context-less approaches only use information that can be extracted from a single domain name to determine whether a domain name is benign or malicious while context-aware approaches use additional contextual information to improve classification performance. Previous studies suggest that context-less approaches achieve state-of-the-art detection performance while being less resource intensive and less privacy invasive than context-aware approaches [2]–[4][6].

The context-less approaches can further be divided into feature-based classifiers such as random forests or support vector machines (e.g., [2]), and feature-less classifiers such as recurrent, convolutional, or residual neural networks [3][4][6]. The former group uses domain knowledge to extract hand-crafted features from a single domain name prior to classification. The latter group of approaches consists of DL classifiers that learn to extract valuable features on their own, yet require many training samples.

The main object under study is the context-less and feature-based DGA detector FANCI [2] that comprises a feature extractor and implements a random forest classification module.

B. Privacy in Machine Learning

ML has become the main suspect of privacy research investigating threats and defenses regarding models' and training procedures' natural information leakage of the consumed sensitive training data (e.g., [13]–[18]). The attack class that relates closest to our work is Model Inversion [14][19] which, for a given model output, iteratively searches for the best fit input candidate based on some likelihood maximization scheme, e.g., by misusing loss and gradient of a neural network model. In our work however, the object under study is not a probability-outputting classifier, but rather just a data transformation module. While the general goal of our studied threat and that of Model Inversion are aligned (finding a suitable input for a given output), our work more closely matches the terminology of [17]: There, the term *reconstruction* specifies malicious inversions of the feature extraction stage with the goal to map features back to raw training data samples.

III. Preliminaries

This section briefly introduces FANCI's feature extractor and presents the concept of Sequence-to-Sequence learning, which we leverage as reconstruction tool later in the study.

A. FANCI'S Feature extractor

We utilize the most recent open-source implementation of FANCI's feature extractor [20], which extracts 15 structural, 8 linguistic, and 22 statistical features from domain names as listed in Table I. For some features, an according footnote highlights that the implementation deviates from the definition in the original paper [2], e.g., `contains_ipv4_addr` should also regard IPv6 addresses. The feature extraction recognizes 39 unique characters (letters a-z, digits 0-9 and special characters dot, hyphen and underscore). For our study, we flatten the representation of the feature vector: Feature `number_of_subdomains` is represented as a one-hot encoded vector and clips the number of sub-domains at value 4. Although it is in fact just one feature, we keep the representation via four values. Similarly, we also view each entry of the one-, two-, and three-gram distribution vectors as single feature. Thereby, our feature count differs slightly from the one presented in the original work [2] and we end up with 45-component feature vectors.

As marked in Table I, many of FANCI's features are computed on the Dot-free public-Suffix-Free (DSF) part of the domain which excludes both dot characters and the public valid suffix, which is usually the Top-Level-Domain (TLD). The validity of a suffix is determined by checking against a predefined list that is included in the feature extractor.

For the rest of this work, we formally refer to the feature extractor as a function $E\colon S \to F$ mapping domains from S to the feature space F, where S is the set of strings over the 39-character alphabet with lengths up to 253.

B. Sequence-to-Sequence Learning

Sequence-to-Sequence learning (Seq2Seq) encompasses encoder-decoder models that solve ML tasks related to mapping variable-length input sequences to variable-length output sequences [21][22]. Usually, both the encoder and decoder of a Seq2Seq architecture utilize recurrent units to process the variable-length sequences and work together as follows: The encoder consumes and compresses the input sequence to a fixed-length state while the decoder is trained to create the target sequence from this state. A common use case is machine language translation on token sequences (i.e., words or characters). To train the model, bounds of the output sequences must be encoded in some fashion such that the token-wise decoding

TABLE I
FEATURES EXTRACTED FOR FANCI

Feature	Name	Type	Choices	Normalized by
1	length	integer	250	253
2-5	number_of_subdomains[a]	integer	1	1
6	subdomain_lengths_mean[a]	rational	250	length
7	contains_wwwdot	binary	2	1
8	has_valid_tld	binary	2	1
9	one_char_subdomains[a]	binary	2	1
10	prefix_repetition	binary	2	1
11	contains_tld_as_infix[a]	binary	2	1
12	only_digits_subdomains[a]	binary	2	1
13	only_hex_subdomains_ratio[a]	rational	250+1	1
14	underscore_ratio[a]	rational	250+1	1
15	contains_ipv4_addr[a,c]	binary	2	1
16	contains_digits[a]	binary	2	1
17	vowel_ratio[a,b]	rational	250+1	1
18	digit_ratio[a,b]	rational	250+1	1
19	char_diversity[a,b,c]	rational	250	1
20	alphabet_size[a,b]	integer	38	38
21	ratio_of_repeated_chars[a,b]	rational	38+1	1
22	consecutive_consonant_ratio[a,b]	rational	250+1	1
23	consecutive_digits_ratio[a,b]	rational	250+1	1
	for $n \in \{1, 2, 3\}$:			
24,31,38	n-grams_std[a,b]	rational	1	(features of n-grams are normalized by their respective max value)
25,32,39	n-grams_median[a,b]	rational	250	
26,33,40	n-grams_mean[a,b]	rational	1	
27,34,41	n-grams_min[a,b]	integer	250+1	
28,35,42	n-grams_max[a,b]	integer	250	
29,36,43	n-grams_perc_25[a,b]	rational	250	
30,37,44	n-grams_perc_75[a,b]	rational	250	
45	shannon_entropy[a,b]	rational	≈ 194	log_2(alphabet_size)

[a]Feature ignores public suffix. [b]Feature ignores dots.
[c]Definition of feature in implementation deviates from original paper.

process begins with a start marker and can be stopped once the end marker is encountered or predicted. At test time a sequence can be sampled from the decoder of a trained Seq2Seq model, i.e., beginning with the start marker, the model iteratively predicts the next character with the currently sampled prefix as prior. This sampling technique is commonly referred to as closed-loop, since the predicted characters are fed back into the model at each step.

IV. A MATHEMATICAL REVIEW

Here we view the plain mathematical definition of the feature extraction process as such and assess the invertability of the process. The goal of inversion is to find a valid function $E^{-1}: F \to S$. Due to the feature extractor $E: S \to F$ not being bijective, function E^{-1} can obviously only fulfill $E^{-1}(E(s)) = s$ for samples $s \in R$ of a certain subset $R \subset S$ for which we are concerned that it includes real-world NXDs. Estimating E^{-1} by sampling a complete look-up table would require iterating over all domains in S. In theory, the domain space is of size $|S| = \sum_{i=4}^{253} 39^i \approx 3.55 \cdot 10^{402}$. Size of the feature space F can be estimated based on the multiplication of possible choices for each value in a feature vector (see Table I). For this, we respect the specification's maximum domain length of 253 [23] and choose the minimum length to be four. For the rational-valued features the number of choices is determined by the size of the divisor or if the divisor is another feature, then we view the number of choices as the maximum possibilities for the dividend. Occasionally, the dividend is allowed to be zero, which is denoted by a "+1" in Table I. For the `entropy` feature we estimate the average amount of distinct values it can accommodate. For features that are dependent on others we view the amount of choices as fixed, or "1" in Table I. Finally, we approximate that $|F| \approx 2.71 \cdot 10^{65}$. Consequently, the feature extraction process performs a reduction of order of magnitude $1.311 \cdot 10^{337}$, i.e., there may on average exist 10^{337} pre-images for each feature vector. In the best case, where all pre-images are distributed equally among all images, inversion would thus be impossible.

A. Inference of new Information

It is possible to infer new information about the original domain sample $s \in S$ via the combination of existing features in $f = E(s)$ and thereby more accurately capture the number of possible pre-images. The information is new in the sense that it is not previously held directly as a value in f. Examples of inferable information are listed in Table II. Further, Shannon entropy is computed as weighted sum of character frequencies $H = \sum_{i=1}^{n} freq(x_i) \cdot log(freq(x_i))$ with restrictions $\sum_{i=1}^{n} x_i = p_1$ and $x_i \in \mathbb{N}^{\geq 1} \forall i \in \{1, ..., n\}$. The underlying character frequency distribution $freq(\cdot)$ over n=`alphabet_size` unknown characters is uniquely determined based on p_1 and `entropy`.

B. Limitations

Finding the unique solution for the discrete frequency distribution that matches the entropy feature may require enumerating all solution candidates. Due to the way the entropy is calculated, the number of solution candidates is given by the binomial coefficient $\binom{n-1}{k-1}$. It is further possible to estimate the amount of unique digits (u_d), vowels (u_v) and other characters (u_o) by iterating over all valid allocations of bins in the frequency distribution to one of the three groups such that the sum of frequencies for each group's bins matches with the previously inferred total count (i.e., p_4, p_5 and p_6). There is not necessarily a unique solution to this.

With help of combinatorics we can specify a tighter bound on the number of possible pre-images per feature vector f. First, dsf-struct(f) captures the possibilities to structure the DSF in (1): Given the inferred total occurrences of digits (p_4), vowels (p_5) and others (p_6), one can virtually choose p_4 character slots in the DSF of length p_1 and similarly p_5 slots of the remaining $p_1 - p_4$. The final slots are for the third group. Then, there are $\binom{p_1-1}{p_2-1}$ possibilities to split the DSF into p_2 sub-domains by inserting the $p_2 - 1$ separating dots.

TABLE II
NEW INFORMATION INFERABLE FROM OTHER FANCI FEATURES

ID	New Information	Inference Rule
p_1	Length of the DSF	$p_1 = \frac{\texttt{alphabet\_size}}{\texttt{char\_diversity}}$
p_2	Amount of sub-domains	$p_2 = \frac{p_1}{\texttt{subdomain\_lengths\_mean}}$
p_3	Length of the public suffix	$p_3 = \texttt{length} - (p_1 + p_2)$
p_4	Total digit occurrences	$p_4 = \texttt{digit\_ratio} \cdot p_1$
p_5	Total vowel occurrences	$p_5 = \texttt{vowel\_ratio} \cdot (p_1 - p_4)$
p_6	Occurrences other chars	$p_6 = p_1 - (p_4 + p_5)$

$$\text{dsf-struct}(f) = \binom{p_1}{p_4} \cdot \binom{p_1 - p_4}{p_5} \cdot \binom{p_1 - 1}{p_2 - 1} \quad (1)$$

Secondly, for a fixed valid setting of unique character counts $u = (u_d, u_v, u_o)$ we can estimate the following: Possibilities for digit occurrences in the DSF is determined by the choices of an u_d-large subset of all digits and all permutations of each subset of length of the total occurrences of digits in the DSF, i.e., p_4. Same holds for unique count of vowels (u_v & p_5) and others (u_o & p_6). Since there does not have to be a unique solution for u, one needs to sum over the possible choices for u. Similarly, we can thus capture the total amount of possibilities for the DSF's content by dsf-cont(f) in (2):

$$\text{dsf-cont}(f) = \sum_u \binom{10}{u_d} \cdot \binom{5}{u_v} \cdot \binom{24}{u_o} \cdot u_d{}^{p_4} \cdot u_v{}^{p_5} \cdot u_o{}^{p_6} \quad (2)$$

Finally, the public suffix list used by the feature extractor fixes the amount of choices for the public suffix or TLD with known length to t_f and in total this results in (3), which more reasonably models the number of possible pre-images.

$$\text{pre-images}(f) = t_f \cdot \text{dsf-struct}(f) \cdot \text{dsf-cont}(f) \quad (3)$$

However, the number of pre-images still remains significantly large and improving this manual reconstruction approach ultimately fails due to the lack of more linguistic information: Even if a frequency distribution can be determined, then the allocation of characters to those frequencies remains undetermined as that information is not held in the feature vector itself. Clearly, the function is not bijective and it is impossible to distinguish between equally likely pre-images. Arguing, to which extent more useful information can be extracted or whether a different manual approach would be more beneficial is a complex matter, which is why we attempt to let a DL model learn a reconstruction mapping based on real-world data.

V. METHODOLOGY

In reality, neither the amount of valid pre-images is equally distributed among all possible feature vectors nor are all pre-images for one feature vector equally likely. In fact, real-world examples for benign NXDs and their corresponding feature vectors will only make up a small fraction of the respective domain space S and feature space F: Besides that some subspace of S (and thereby also a subspace of F) is occupied by the malicious samples, benign NXDs that result from typographical errors may still exhibit linguistic characteristics that are of low-entropy. For feature vectors, we argue that there are semantically invalid combinations of features, e.g., `alphabet_size` = 1 while both `vowel_ratio` > 0 and `digit_ratio` > 0. Subsequently, the feature extractor will only act on a restriction of the mapping $S \to F$ in reality.

True pre-image distributions and domain-feature relations are best captured by real-world NXD samples, and hence, we leverage such data sets two-fold: (1) To train a DL model that may learn the distribution of the sample data and (2) as ground truth to assess the reconstruction capability of the trained models. The rest of this section defines the methodology for the experiment, and the evaluation of a DL reconstructor.

A. Attack Model

The context in which the following experiment is conducted is defined by the following aspects: (1) We assume an adversary that is interested in learning the real inputs to the FANCI feature extractor $E : S \to F$ for a foreign feature set $S' \subset S$ of a target, i.e., for any $E(s) = f \in F$, the adversary aims to find a corresponding $s' \in S$ such that $E(s') = f$ holds and some closeness $s' \approx s$ is satisfied (Note, that finding just any $s' \in S$ with $E(s') = f$ is trivial). (2) The adversary is semi-honest, i.e., he reliably participates in any sharing scenario through which he acquires the foreign feature set. (3) The feature extractor is public knowledge. (4) We only consider the disclosure of benign NXDs as privacy critical. (5) We assume feature sets are shared in the clear, hence no interaction with the target is required. (6) We allow the adversary to be in possession of an arbitrary large data set $S'' \subset S$ of benign NXDs that does not intersect with the target's data, i.e., $S'' \cap S' = \emptyset$. (7) We do not restrict the adversary's computational power that he may apply to his own data. Hence, we allow the adversary to train an ML model.

B. Reconstruction Quantification

We leverage existing members from the family of edit distances on the string space to compare pairs of original and reconstructed samples. Due to the possible encounter of unequal lengths, the only suitable candidates are the *Levenshtein* [24] distance metric and its variant *Damerau-Levenshtein*, which both compute a minimum-change distance via the number of character edit operations (substitutions, insertions or deletions) required to transform the one input string into the other. We use the latter of both metrics which additionally considers the transposition of adjacent characters as a single operation. Further, we compute a normalized version for the metric by dividing the resulting minimum-change-distance by the length of the longest of both input strings. This division operation invalidates none of the metric's axioms. Note, however, that the normalized metric is a ratio of edit-operations to string length and which can be interpreted as a lower bound on the percentage of misplaced characters in the longer input string.

Consequently, a metric value of zero indicates equality, while dissimilarity grows in parallel to larger metric values. Thereby, quantifying the closeness, as previously mentioned in the attack model, becomes possible. Note that the choice of any threshold $\varepsilon > |s - s'|$ indicating attack success is subjective, as the metric does not regard a semantic comparison.

C. Benign Data Sets

In the following, we briefly comment on the nature and origin of the real-life benign NXD data we use, that are sourced locally by distinct institutions in different countries.

1) University$_A$: RWTH Aachen University in Germany provided us with a record comprising approximately 26 million unique NXDs recorded in the month of September 2019 by their central DNS resolver. This resolver handles academic and administrative networks, the university hospital as well as networks of student residences.

2) University$_B$: We obtained another data set comprising 8 million unique samples recorded between mid-May 2020 and mid-June 2020 at Masaryk University that is located in the Czech Republic.

3) Association: CESNET is a 27-member association of Czech universities which develops and operates a national e-infrastructure for science, research, and education, including several university networks. We obtained a partial quantity of a one-day recording on June 16th 2020 containing approximately 362k unique samples.

We use the complete record of the Association and draw a random sub-sample in the size of the Association's record from each of the other two institutions' records. Intersections with one another and with malicious samples drawn from the open source intelligence feed of DGArchive [1] (up until September 1st 2020) are removed from all records prior to sub-sampling.

D. Evaluation Setup

In the following experiment, we assess the reconstruction performance of trained DL reconstruction models via the above mentioned distance metrics. More concretely, we train a DL model for each one of the benign data sources and evaluate each of these models against all the data sources including the one on which the individual model was trained on. For each pair of training and evaluation sets we average each metric's scores over all samples. Thereby, we assess the models' capability to reconstruct domains from foreign feature sets.

VI. Data-Driven Reconstruction

The following describes the training setup for the Seq2Seq decoder which is trained on the task of domain sample reconstruction (i.e., learning an inverse mapping $E^{-1}|_R\colon F \to S$ on subset R) using an attack set of benign NXDs and their corresponding feature vectors $\{(f_i, s_i)\}_{i=0}^{n} \subset F \times S$. This is a realistic scenario in any sharing use case where a party receiving a feature set may also be in possession of an own data set of benign NXDs. Basically, we assume that the feature extractor is unknown to the model, and we let it learn the inverse mapping without any domain-specific assistance.

A. Model Architecture

To reconstruct a variable-length domain sample from a fixed-length feature vector, the decoder of a Seq2Seq model is utilized. All models share the same architecture whose design follows a related approach [22]. Beginning with two parallel sequences of two dense layers with 200 units each, this leaves opportunity for the model to manipulate the representation of the input feature vector before the two outputs are used as the initial states for the recurrent unit in the decoder. For the recurrent unit, a single Long Short-Term Memory (LSTM) layer with 200 units is used. Finally, the model ends with a dense layer of size 42 and a softmax activation to output a prediction vector over all relevant characters, which includes the 39 recognized domain characters plus start, end and empty markers used internally for the sequence encoding of domains. In total, the architecture comprises 301,642 trainable weights.

B. Training Setup

For a good balance between training time and model performance, we fix a batch size of 64 for our experiment. Models are trained using the cross-entropy loss to penalize wrong character predictions. Being unaware of any unbalance-bias, a focal loss is used to dynamically down-weigh well-classified samples in the cross-entropy loss during training [25].

Training data is prepared as follows: The test set is a random 20% split of the total data. Another random 5% split of the remaining training data is used as validation set. All entries in a FANCI feature vector are in some finite bounded range of the non-negative rationals and are normalized to the range of $[0, 1]$ by dividing each entry by the upper bound of its value range (see last column of Table I). Domain names are encoded to character sequences with start and end markers.

Each model is allowed to train for at most 1000 epochs, while the training data is shuffled after each epoch and training is stopped early whenever 10 epochs without improvement of the validation loss are exceeded. We follow the common methodology to train a Seq2Seq model and thus employ Teacher Forcing to train the decoder [26]. This essentially sets the input of the decoder to the target sequence shifted by one time step (open loop) instead of feeding the decoder's outputs of previous time steps back into the model (closed loop).

VII. Results

For each domain in an evaluation set, we sample a reconstructed domain from the trained reconstructor models using the normalized feature vector of the original domain as initial state input to the model. Averaged closed-loop reconstruction performance for all combinations of trained models and evaluation sets are given on the left side of Table III.

A. Baseline Reconstruction Performance

Rows in Table III with a highlighted evaluation set show the average Damerau-Levenshtein metric score for the case that the evaluation data is equal to all the data used to train, validate and test the model, and is to be interpreted as baseline reconstruction performance of a trained model.

Although the models achieve a small training and test loss, reconstruction performance is mediocre: For University$_A$, University$_B$ and the Association we measure that on average respectively 47.85, 15.00 and 13.66 character edit operation separate each original domain and its reconstruction. The normalized version of the metric measures an average score for University$_A$ and University$_B$ that is just larger than 0.5, i.e., on average at least 50% of characters in each reconstruction are misplaced. For the Association, we measure a slightly smaller

TABLE III
CLOSED LOOP RECONSTRUCTION PERFORMANCE OF SEQ2SEQ RECONSTRUCTOR & FEATURE SPACE OVERLAP

Network Data Source		**Averaged Reconstruction Performance**		**Feature Space Overlap**				
Training	**Evaluation**	**Dam-Leven.**	**norm.**	**#Unique FV[a] (Training Data)**	**Training ∩ Evaluation**	**% of Eval Data**	**#Unique FV[a] (All Data)**	**% of Total Data**
University$_A$	**University$_A$**	47.85	0.51	288118	-	-	3462	10.3
	University$_B$	23.22	0.72		5789	32.9		
	Association	20.61	0.66		4809	12.1		
University$_B$	University$_A$	72.94	0.75	182786	5789	11.5		30.7
	University$_B$	15.00	0.53		-	-		
	Association	18.61	0.61		12985	41.8		
Association	University$_A$	62.07	0.67	169921	4809	24.6		22.9
	University$_B$	20.01	0.65		12985	30.9		
	Association	13.66	0.46		-	-		

[a]FV = Feature Vectors.

average score of 0.45. It seems that the models' baseline reconstruction performance is similarly bad on all data sets.

B. Transferability

The remaining lines in Table III demonstrate the trained models' reconstruction performance on data from foreign networks, i.e., exactly the scenario which we describe in our attack model. In all cases the reconstruction error is higher than in the baseline cases (score higher than 0.65) with the worst performance (0.75) in the case where the model trained on data from University$_B$ is evaluated on that of University$_A$.

VIII. DISCUSSION

After re-consideration of the mathematical review of the feature extractor, it is plausible that the overall reconstruction performance is poor. After all, FANCI's feature extractor considers only very few features and thereby performs a compression of such extent which is tolerable for good classification performance but hinders good reconstruction quality. In the rest of this section we continue to argue about a quantifiable proof that E is not injective when restricted to the subspace of real-world benign NXDs and review the adversary's theoretical information gain for well-reconstructed domains.

A. Feature Space Overlap

We place our experiment in the scenario in which adversary and target NXD data are disjunct. This does, however, not imply that the sets of feature vectors of each respective data set are also disjunct. Therefore, we also quantify the overlap in feature space for the three data sets used in this study on the right side of Table III. First, it is important to note that although every data set contains approximately 362k unique samples, the amount of unique feature vectors is significantly lower which clearly indicates collisions in the feature space. Secondly, for every combination of two distinct NXD data sets we have an intersection of non-trivial size in the feature space, e.g., 11.5% of University$_B$'s data intersects with University$_A$'s and 41.8% of its data with that of the Association.

A large overlap in the feature space most certainly leads to a degraded reconstruction performance, as for the same feature vector the model may learn to reconstruct a domain different from the one the adversary wants to sample at test time. The worst-performing baseline and transferability reconstructions (training data of University$_B$) coincides with the largest feature space overlap w.r.t. all data sets (see Table III).

B. Top 10% Reconstructions

The adversary has no clear way of estimating the confidence of a single reconstruction without ground truth unless he conducts an own analysis of which type of domains are reconstructed well using a second data set. Hence, we also discuss what he could potentially learn from good reconstructions by taking a closer look at the best 10% of all reconstructions for the transferability cases: The average reconstruction performance for the top 10% lies at 0.276. Further, approximately 45-55% of the top 10% performers are occupied by IPv4 and IPv6 reverse DNS lookups and 20-35% by spam-related or other DNS-related services, e.g., DNS blacklists.

We argue that the models perform so well in reconstructing these types of domains with (1) these domains' contents being well-structured, (2) sharing a large suffix, and (3) standing out by containing a lot of numerical characters. Hence, they occupy the sparse areas of the feature space around features such as a high `digit_ratio`, low `subdomains_lengths_mean` or a True value for features such as `only_digits_subdomains` `contains_ipv4_addr`. Further, these NXDs do not necessarily originate from user typos but rather from misconfigured software. This would also better explain the high occurrence of these types of domains in the data.

The question remains whether knowledge of reverse lookups and spam-services is privacy-sensitive information and we claim the opposite. After all, these domains do not reveal any information about end-user browsing or sensitive tooling usage in the network from which the data was sourced.

IX. CONCLUSION AND FUTURE WORK

In this study we analyzed the data privacy capabilities of the feature-based DGA detector FANCI. The main goal was to answer whether feature vectors of FANCI disclose any sensitive information about the original domain names. We provide mathematical reasoning for the success likelihood for any best-case reconstruction attempt and demonstrate that a manual approach of inferring sensitive information from combination of features has its difficulties and most certainly has its limitations: Reconstruction cannot be easily performed on the basis of a single feature vector.

Therefore, we chose to emulate the logical approach a data-rich adversary would take, namely training an ML model to learn a reconstruction mapping. To provide significance to our results, we make use of three large real-world NXD sets fortunately made available to us. Finally, we find reconstruction performance of the trained models to be worse than desired: On average at least half of all character from a reconstructed domain are misplaced in the baseline cases. The models only perform best on foreign network's data for reverse lookups and other not-sensitive NXDs likely originating from misconfigured software. We find this to be the result of these domains sharing a large portion of the higher-level domains and occupying a special niche in the feature space.

Consequently, our experiment suggest that an ML model aiding in the attack cannot reliably reconstruct NXDs from foreign networks' FANCI feature vectors which would be, however, the main use case in an attack.

Due to its universality, our data-driven analysis approach can be used in the future to perform a similar privacy analysis on other feature extractors used for DGA detection. The general concept of the data-driven analysis approach can also be used for a privacy analysis of feature-based classifiers in other ML use cases.

Acknowledgments

The authors would like to thank Masaryk University, CESNET and Jens Hektor from the IT Center of RWTH Aachen University for providing NXD data. This project has received funding from the European Union's Horizon 2020 research and innovation programme under grant agreement No 833418. Simulations were performed with computing resources granted by RWTH Aachen University under project rwth0438.

References

[1] D. Plohmann, K. Yakdan, M. Klatt, J. Bader, and E. Gerhards-Padilla, "A comprehensive measurement study of domain generating malware," in *USENIX Security Symposium*. USENIX Association, 2016, pp. 263–278.

[2] S. Schüppen, D. Teubert, P. Herrmann, and U. Meyer, "FANCI: Feature-based automated nxdomain classification and intelligence," in *USENIX Security Symposium*. USENIX Association, 2018, pp. 1165–1181.

[3] J. Woodbridge, H. S. Anderson, A. Ahuja, and D. Grant, "Predicting domain generation algorithms with long short-term memory networks." arXiv preprint arXiv:1611.00791, 2016.

[4] B. Yu, J. Pan, J. Hu, A. Nascimento, and M. De Cock, "Character level based detection of DGA domain names," in *International Joint Conference on Neural Networks*. IEEE, 2018, pp. 1–8.

[5] J. Saxe and K. Berlin, "eXpose: A character-level convolutional neural network with embeddings for detecting malicious URLs, file paths and registry keys." arXiv preprint arXiv:1702.08568, 2017.

[6] A. Drichel, U. Meyer, S. Schüppen, and D. Teubert, "Analyzing the real-world applicability of DGA classifiers," in *Conference on Availability, Reliability and Security*. ACM, 2020, pp. 1–11.

[7] M. Antonakakis *et al.*, "From throw-away traffic to bots: Detecting the rise of DGA-based malware," in *USENIX Security Symposium*. USENIX Association, 2012, pp. 491–506.

[8] L. Bilge, S. Sen, D. Balzarotti, E. Kirda, and C. Kruegel, "Exposure: A passive DNS analysis service to detect and report malicious domains," in *Transactions on Information and System Security*. ACM, 2014, pp. 1–28.

[9] M. Grill, I. Nikolaev, V. Valeros, and M. Rehak, "Detecting DGA malware using netflow," in *IFIP/IEEE International Symposium on Integrated Network Management*. IEEE, 2015, pp. 1304–1309.

[10] S. Yadav and A. L. N. Reddy, "Winning with dns failures: Strategies for faster botnet detection," in *Security and Privacy in Communication Systems*. Springer, 2011, pp. 446–459.

[11] S. Schiavoni, F. Maggi, L. Cavallaro, and S. Zanero, "Phoenix: DGA-based botnet tracking and intelligence," in *Detection of Intrusions and Malware, and Vulnerability Assessment*. Springer, 2014, pp. 192–211.

[12] Y. Shi, G. Chen, and J. Li, "Malicious domain name detection based on extreme machine learning," *Neural Processing Letters*, pp. 1347–1357, 2018.

[13] G. Ateniese *et al.*, "Hacking smart machines with smarter ones: How to extract meaningful data from machine learning classifiers," in *International Journal of Security and Networks*. Inderscience Publishers, 2015, pp. 137–150.

[14] M. Fredrikson, S. Jha, and T. Ristenpart, "Model inversion attacks that exploit confidence information and basic countermeasures," in *Computer and Communications Security*. ACM, 2015, p. 1322–1333.

[15] R. Shokri, M. Stronati, C. Song, and V. Shmatikov, "Membership inference attacks against machine learning models," in *Symposium on Security and Privacy*. IEEE, 2017, pp. 3–18.

[16] N. Papernot, P. McDaniel, A. Sinha, and M. P. Wellman, "Sok: Security and privacy in machine learning," in *European Symposium on Security and Privacy*. IEEE, 2018, pp. 399–414.

[17] M. Al-Rubaie and J. M. Chang, "Privacy-preserving machine learning: Threats and solutions," in *Symposium on Security and Privacy*. IEEE, 2019, pp. 49–58.

[18] M. Nasr, R. Shokri, and A. Houmansadr, "Comprehensive privacy analysis of deep learning: Passive and active white-box inference attacks against centralized and federated learning," in *Symposium on Security and Privacy*. IEEE, 2019, pp. 739–753.

[19] M. Fredrikson *et al.*, "Privacy in pharmacogenetics: An end-to-end case study of personalized warfarin dosing," in *USENIX Security Symposium*. USENIX Association, 2014, pp. 17–32.

[20] Fanci: Feature-based automated nxdomain classification intelligence. [Online, retrieved: September, 2021]. https://github.com/fanci-dga-detection/fanci/tree/d6c7d08

[21] K. Cho *et al.*, "Learning phrase representations using rnn encoder-decoder for statistical machine translation," in *Proceedings of the 2014 Conference on Empirical Methods in Natural Language Processing (EMNLP)*. ACL, 2014, pp. 1724–1734.

[22] I. Sutskever, O. Vinyals, and Q. V. Le, "Sequence to sequence learning with neural networks," in *Proceedings of the 27th International Conference on Neural Information Processing Systems - Volume 2*. MIT Press, 2014, pp. 3104–3112.

[23] Rfc 1034: Domain names - concepts and facilities. [Online, retrieved: September, 2021]. https://datatracker.ietf.org/doc/html/rfc1034

[24] V. I. Levenshtein, "Binary codes capable of correcting deletions, insertions, and reversals," in *Soviet Physics Doklady*, 1966, pp. 707–710.

[25] T.-Y. Lin, P. Goyal, R. B. Girshick, K. He, and P. Dollár, "Focal loss for dense object detection," *Transactions on Pattern Analysis and Machine Intelligence*, pp. 318–327, 2020.

[26] R. J. Williams and D. Zipser, "A learning algorithm for continually running fully recurrent neural networks," *Neural Computation*, pp. 270–280, 1989.

The Same, but Different: The Pentesting Study

Jan Roring, Dominik Sauer, Michael Massoth
Department of Computer Science
Hochschule Darmstadt — University of Applied Sciences Darmstadt
Darmstadt, Germany
E-mail: jan.roring@stud.h-da.de, {dominik.sauer,michael.massoth}@h-da.de

***Abstract*—When ordering a penetration test, customers assume that they will receive the same results regardless of who performs the testing. Although well-known standards are commonly used to ensure that results of penetration tests are consistent and reproducible, these results vary widely depending on the chosen service provider. To evaluate this, we had two penetration tests carried out on the same IT environment by independent service providers. While there was some overlap, the results show that the human component has a profound impact on the outcome of a penetration test.**

Keywords*—*penetration test; comparison; standards; human; soft skills.

I. Introduction

As public reports of the German Federal Criminal Police Office show, cybersecurity incidents are on the rise [1]. To protect themselves, more and more companies have the security of their IT systems and applications checked by security experts. In order to identify security vulnerabilities in these technologies, it is common practice to carry out penetration tests [2]. In addition to the identification of threats, a penetration test also includes a risk analysis of each vulnerability, as well as remediation advice, which helps clients to address the most critical issues first [3][4]. In order to provide the best possible added value, as many security vulnerabilities as possible should be identified, so they can be fixed by the client to strengthen the company's security posture.

This paper aims to show how much the quality of penetration tests varies depending on the tester. To show the variability of outcome, two penetration tests are performed on the same IT environment by two independent service providers. To achieve the fairest comparison, the same general conditions apply to both penetration testers. Thereafter, we evaluate how much the results of the two penetration tests differ and what influence the penetration testers have on them.

This paper is structured as follows: Section II provides some background information on penetration testing. Section III describes the experimental setup. The results will be presented and discussed in Section IV. Section V contains our conclusion as well as an outlook on further research opportunities.

II. Background

The following section will be dedicated to the terminology relevant to the paper. In addition to a definition of the term 'Penetration testing', it also includes commonly used standards, as well as the skill set required of a penetration tester.

A. *Penetration testing*

Penetration tests are used to check the security of applications, individual systems or entire networks by simulating an attack by a hacker. The penetration tester uses the techniques and tools of a hacker to uncover security vulnerabilities in the IT environment under review. If possible, identified vulnerabilities are exploited by the penetration tester to prove their existence and investigate possible impacts to better assess the threat potential of a vulnerability. Upon completion of the penetration test, the customer receives a report listing all vulnerabilities found, including a risk assessment and recommendations for remediation. The aim is to find and fix security vulnerabilities before a potential attacker can exploit them [5]–[7].

B. *Commonly used standards*

While a hacker may only need a single vulnerability to gain access, the penetration tester always tries to uncover every possible vulnerability [8]. To ensure that no obvious vulnerabilities are overlooked and results are reproducible, a structured approach is required. Thus, most penetration testers rely on well-known standard approaches when performing penetration tests [9].

Several attempts have been made by governments and the IT security community to standardize the penetration testing process. Therefore, there is a wide choice of standards, each with its own advantages and disadvantages. There is no universal standard that is suitable for all types of penetration tests. Government contracts often require compliance with standards published by the respective national authorities, such as the National Institute of Standards and Technology (NIST) [5] in the US or the Federal Office for Information Security (BSI) [6] in Germany. In addition, there are established standards, such as the Open Source Security Testing Methodology Manual (OSSTMM) [10] or the Penetration Testing Execution Standard (PTES) [11] that are maintained by the IT security community.

Apart from the differing terminology, the process described in each of the previously mentioned standards always has a similar basic structure [7]. It can be divided into several phases, which can be seen in Figure 1.

Some approaches such as BSI [6], PTES [11] or OSSTMM [10] give actionable instructions on what checks to perform in each phase. A more detailed look at these checks reveals that these standards are primarily designed to investigate IT

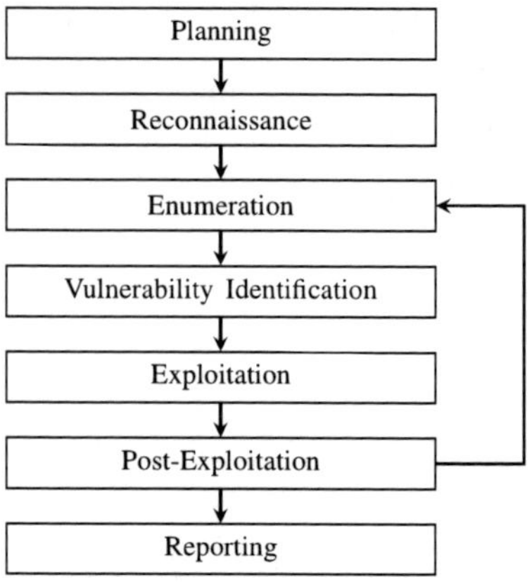

Figure 1. Penetration Testing Process

infrastructures [12]. When it comes to performing penetration testing for web applications, penetration testers typically refer to the OWASP Web Security Testing Guide, which is specifically tailored for this use case [2]. However, this is almost exclusively limited to the technical aspects of web application penetration tests, which is why some penetration testers tend to combine it with one of the aforementioned standards. In addition to such combinations, penetration testers also frequently use their own individual approaches based on the established standards [13][14].

The selection of an appropriate methodology is crucial for the success of a penetration test, as it determines what should be tested and how the penetration tester should proceed. Since the commissioned penetration testers relied on the BSI penetration testing model and the OWASP Web Security Testing Guide, these will be described in a bit more detail below:

a) BSI Penetration Testing Model: In 2003, the German Federal Office for Information Security presented a penetration testing model, which divides penetration tests into the following five phases [6]:

1) Preparation
2) Reconnaissance
3) Analyzing information and risks
4) Active intrusion attempts
5) Final analysis

Throughout the preparation phase, the objectives, scope and further general conditions of the penetration test, like time frame and target systems, are defined together with the customer. In addition, a suitable penetration test is classified and written approval is obtained from the client.

The reconnaissance phase is used to gather information on the target. This includes performing ping and port scans, as well as identifying operating systems and running services to determine possible entry points for an attacker. The tests to be performed are grouped into so-called I-modules. Suitable modules are selected based on the classification made previously.

In the subsequent phase ('Analyzing information and risk'), the previously gathered information is evaluated and potential risks are identified by looking for software versions with known vulnerabilities. In addition, the penetration tester manually searches for common types of vulnerabilities to identify new or more complex vulnerabilities within systems and applications.

To verify the actual existence of vulnerabilities, attempts are made to exploit them in the fourth phase. Through exploitation, the penetration tester aims to gain access to the affected system or read out sensitive data, which may help to escalate privileges or compromise additional systems. So-called E-modules comprise the tests that are carried out during this phase. E-modules, as well as I-modules, are based on the test points of the OSSTMM.

In the last phase ("Final Analysis"), the findings of the penetration test are reviewed and the resulting risks are assessed, depending on which sensitive data could be viewed and which systems could be accessed. Additionally, an action plan is developed with recommendations that can assist in addressing the identified vulnerabilities.

Each phase of the penetration testing process is documented to ensure the reproducibility of the test results and findings. Based on this progress log, a final report is then prepared for the customer, which contains a list of all identified vulnerabilities together with risk assessment and recommendations.

b) OWASP Web Security Testing Guide: The Open Web Application Security Project (OWASP) is a non-profit organization that aims to improve the security of web applications. To achieve this goal, OWASP works closely with the IT security community and provides valuable tools and information through open-source projects [15][16].

One of these projects is the OWASP Web Security Testing Guide, which was released in version 4.2 towards the end of 2020. In addition to the OWASP Testing Framework for developing secure web applications, this guide also includes the Web Application Security Testing Methodology, which can be used to perform web application penetration tests.

The Web Application Security Testing Methodology is divided into a passive and an active phase. During the passive phase, the penetration tester explores the web applications from a user's point of view and tries to gain an understanding of the application's functionality and features. Throughout the active phase, the penetration tester performs the actual tests. For this purpose, the OWASP Web Security Testing Guide offers a comprehensive collection of test points, which are distributed across a total of twelve categories covering different areas of a web application [2]:

1) Information Gathering
2) Configuration and Deployment Management Testing
3) Identity Management Testing
4) Authentication Testing
5) Authorization Testing
6) Session Management Testing

7) Input Validation Testing
8) Testing for Error Handling
9) Testing for Weak Cryptography
10) Business Logic Testing
11) Client-side Testing
12) API Testing

C. Penetration Testing Skill Sets

The selection of a suitable approach by itself is no guarantee for a successful penetration test [17]. In order to maintain adaptability to the customer's needs and new types of technologies, standards should not be too restrictive [18][6]. While a standardized approach can give guidance to the penetration tester and point him in the right direction, at some point the tester may need to deviate from this predefined path. Thereafter, the testing is reliant on the abilities of the tester, which can not be covered by a standard.

Several of the previously mentioned standards describe the required skill sets to successfully perform penetration tests. In order to find vulnerabilities in a system, the penetration tester must understand how it works and how it can be abused. This can require extensive technical knowledge. Furthermore, performing penetration tests can have a negative impact on the customer's systems and networks. To prevent any damage, they should only be carried out by people with experience in IT security. According to BSI [6], penetration testers typically need the following hard skills:

- Knowledge of system administration/operating systems
- Knowledge of TCP/IP and, if applicable, other network protocols
- Knowledge of programming languages
- Knowledge of IT security products such as firewalls, intrusion detection systems
- Knowledge of how to handle hacker tools and vulnerability scanners
- Knowledge of applications/application systems

NIST [5] specifies similar technical know-how as a prerequisite, however, BSI also names 'creativity' as an essential soft skill. According to BSI [6], the creativity of the penetration tester is decisive for the success of the penetration test. Often, breaking into a system is only possible through creative combination of received information, discovered vulnerabilities, along with known tools and methodologies. OWASP [2] also claims that creativity allows for better results in finding vulnerabilities than fully automated tools. Creative penetration testers would therefore be expected to achieve better results than penetration testers who rely solely on the results of their tools [2][6].

According to OSSTMM [18], it is also important that a standardized approach does not interfere with the creativity of the penetration tester and thus negatively affects the quality of the outcome. However, OSSTMM [10] and BSI [6] also agree that creativity should not lead to unsystematic and untraceable penetration testing. Although intuition allows creativity to be applied to penetration testing, it can also lead to mistakes when a penetration tester relies solely on intuition by skipping checks that seem unnecessary [10].

Certificates usually serve as proof of a penetration tester's skills. There is a wide range of certification authorities that offer IT security and, in particular, penetration testing certificates. To obtain such a certificate, participants must pass an examination. Some of them are purely theoretical exams that solely test knowledge and thus only assess hard skills. However, others are more practical and require the successful completion of a penetration test as an exam and thereby also take into account soft skills [6][19].

III. Approach

A research project at Darmstadt University of Applied Sciences called fast electronic identification (SEIN) aims to provide an identification solution that enables fully automated identity verification via the account holder's online banking credentials [20]. To perform this type of identification, several web applications were implemented, which needed to be analyzed for their security through a penetration test.

We took this opportunity to commission two independent service providers to each conduct a penetration test of the SEIN web applications. To make the results of both penetration tests comparable, we made sure that the same conditions and terms applied to both contractors.

Since the SEIN research funds were not intended for cybersecurity research, but only to ensure that required standards such as ISO 27001 were met, the sample size was limited to these two service providers. Both service providers are local companies that have ties to the university through graduates and lecturers. One provider was initially contracted to assist with the implementation of an Information Security Management System (ISMS), and penetration testing was already included in their proposal. The other service provider offered a free initial penetration test as a promotional activity.

A. General conditions

Both contractors were given four days to perform the penetration test, plus an additional day to create the final report. In addition, both parties have been provided with the same technical documentation, including a list of the systems to be tested with short descriptions, and a sequence diagram to illustrate the identification process. SEIN assured that no changes have been made during the penetration tests, so that the same conditions applied to both penetration tests.

The two service providers stated that the penetration tests would be performed by certified professionals. Further, they claimed that their methodologies are based on the BSI Penetration Testing Model and the OWASP Web Security Testing Guide.

The penetration tests were performed sequentially to ensure that the penetration testers did not interfere with each other. On completion of both penetration tests, the findings of the two reports were reviewed and compared.

B. Investigated web applications

Four web applications of the SEIN research project were examined. These included a business portal, the business portal API, a demo application, and the API of the SEIN backend server.

- **Business Portal**
  The Business Portal is a Javascript-based single-page application that is connected to the Business Portal API. Companies can register via the Business Portal to receive an API key for the use of the SEIN Backend API.
- **Business Portal API**
  The Business Portal API is based on Strapi, a headless content management system. Strapi does not provide its own web frontend, but solely provides a REST API that allows content to be retrieved or edited. Using this API the essential functions of the business portal are made available.
- **Demo Application**
  The demo application simulates a webshop where an identity check of customers is performed via SEIN as part of the ordering process. In the web store shopping cart view, users are asked to enter their personal data. The identification process then starts. For this purpose, the demo application communicates as a client with the SEIN backend via the API provided. After the verification is completed, the results are displayed in the demo application.
- **SEIN Backend**
  The SEIN backend provides a REST API that can be used to confirm a person's identity. After a client, such as the demo application, has sent the data to be verified to the API, the user is asked to select a bank. In the next step, the user logs into the selected bank's online banking portal and grants SEIN access to the account holder's personal data for verification purposes. The SEIN backend then queries the required information and performs a comparison with the previously provided data. Finally, the result of this data comparison is sent back to the client.

IV. Results

The penetration testing reports of both service providers were reviewed and the included findings were extracted. A comparison of the aggregated results of both penetration tests can be seen in Table I. The two right-hand columns indicate whether the respective finding was listed in the corresponding report of penetration test A or B.

Due to the fact that the contractors used similar approaches, the results show some overlap. However, the direct comparison illustrates that one service provider was able to identify significantly more vulnerabilities, especially more with high or medium criticality. Most of these are among the OWASP Top 10, a collection of the ten most common and critical vulnerabilities in web applications, which is maintained by OWASP to create awareness for web application security. The

TABLE I
COMPARISON OF THE IDENTIFIED VULNERABILITIES

Vulnerability	Risk	P.T. A	P.T. B
Stored Cross-Site-Scripting	High	✓	✗
Error-handling enables denial of service	High	✓	✗
Plain text transmission of authentication data	High	✓	✓
Support for TLS 1.0 and TLS 1.1 and cryptographically weak cipher suites	High	✓	✓
Use of outdated software	Medium	✓	✓
Missing attributes in HTTP headers	Medium	✓	✓
SSH service allows login by password	Medium	✓	✗
Incomplete implementation of two-factor authentication	Medium	✓	✗
Publicly available API documentation	Medium	✓	✗
Meaningful error messages allow user enumeration	Medium	✓	✓
Internal services exposed	Medium	✓	✓
Bypass of the reverse proxy possible	Medium	✓	✗
Use of self-signed certificates	Medium	✓	✗
Missing access control	Medium	✓	✗
Disclosure of software versions and components	Medium	✓	✓
Long-lived access tokens	Medium	✓	✓
No deactivation of access tokens after a user logout	Medium	✓	✗
Link to registration confirmation contains valid access token	Medium	✓	✗
Disclosure of internal error messages	Medium	✓	✓
Lack of rate limiting in the APIs	Medium	✓	✗
Sensitive data in URLs of the demo application and the backend API	Medium	✓	✗
Cross-Origin Resource Sharing for any origin	Medium	✓	✗
SSH weak MAC algorithms	Low	✗	✓
JSON Web Tokens use a symmetric algorithm for the signature	Info	✓	✗
Web server delivers default files	Info	✗	✓
Responding to ICMP timestamp requests	Info	✗	✓
Responding to TCP timestamp requests	Info	✗	✓

document provides information about these vulnerabilities and references other documents, such as specific OWASP Cheat Sheets, that can assist in their investigation and remediation.

A closer look reveals that a large number of the vulnerabilities, that have been overlooked by one of the contractors, are actually covered by the OWASP Web Security Testing Guide [2]. A variety of these are authentication and authorization based vulnerabilities, which the OWASP Testing Guide addresses in detail in the categories 'Identity Management Testing', 'Authentication Testing' and 'Session Management Testing'. Furthermore, the overlooked high-risk vulnerabilities are covered by the chapters 'Input Validation Testing' and 'Testing for Error Handling' [2]. By fully applying the OWASP Testing Guide and including the referenced Cheat Sheets, these should have also been found by the second service provider. Therefore, it is essential that the checks described in the guide are carried out without exception. The impact that skipping or forgetting individual checks can have on the results of a penetration test can be seen in Figure 2.

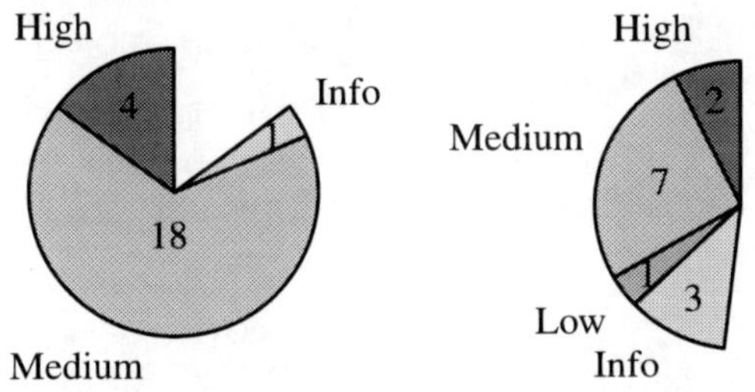

(a) Penetration Test A (b) Penetration Test B

Figure 2. Overall vulnerabilities identified by the contractors

Further, the comparison also shows some vulnerabilities that are not addressed by the OWASP Testing Guide. This indicates that both penetration testers performed checks beyond the OWASP Testing Guide as part of their individual approach. This may be due to the fact that the OWASP Testing Guide focuses primarily on the web application itself. Although the chapter 'Configuration and Deployment Management Testing' also covers the configuration of the webserver used, other services that could run on the same system are not considered here. Yet these could also be potential entry points for an attacker, which is why they are also checked for obvious vulnerabilities by some penetration testers. In that case, the individual approach determines which checks are performed beyond the OWASP Testing Guide to analyze these additional services. Since the focus of a web application penetration test lies on checking web applications, it must be decided where the line is drawn to an external IT infrastructure penetration test.

It appears that service provider B invested more effort into performing these additional checks. This enabled them to uncover a few minor misconfigurations, although they do not add much value for the customer. This work might have been better spent on processing the checks of the OWASP Testing Guide.

V. CONCLUSION

Overlooking vulnerabilities has a direct impact on the quality of the penetration test and thus on the client's security. To prevent this, penetration testers usually rely on standards that define which areas a penetration test should cover. However, a standard is no guarantee for a successful penetration test. As our studies have shown, the results of two penetration tests conducted in the same environment under identical conditions can still differ significantly despite the use of established standards. The decisive factor here was the human component, precisely the penetration testers themselves, as one of them was able to find considerably more vulnerabilities and, above all, more valuable ones in terms of risk.

As both were certified penetration testers, it is safe to assume they have similar hard skills. However, it appears the decisive factor was how they dealt with their creativity and intuition. While it may enable penetration testers to archive better results, it may also cause problems when they solely rely on intuition and do not stick to the chosen approach. It is important that all checks of this approach are performed without exceptions.

Furthermore, it could be observed that the penetration testers or their companies can add their own touch by using individual approaches that are an extension of established standards. This allows them to add value to the customer by performing additional checks on top of the predefined ones. Still, it is important not to lose focus on the actual objectives of the penetration test.

Future research could further investigate the interaction between hard skills and soft skills of penetration testers and their impact on penetration tests results. A larger sample size could provide insight into how often major discrepancies between penetration tests occur. This could also indicate whether it makes sense to always have penetration tests performed by several independent service providers in order to achieve better coverage. In addition, individual penetration testing approaches seem to be widely used but little researched. Further research could compare individual approaches with standardized ones in terms of their effectiveness. It could also be investigated whether combinations of standards are useful and which combinations work well together.

REFERENCES

[1] Bundeskriminalamt [in English: Federal Criminal Police Office], "Bundeslagebild Cybercrime 2020," Jul. 2021. [Online]. Available: https://www.bka.de/SharedDocs/Downloads/DE/Publikationen/JahresberichteUndLagebilder/Cybercrime/cybercrimeBundeslagebild2020.pdf?__blob=publicationFile&v=4 [retrieved: Aug, 2021].

[2] E. Saad and R. Mitchell, *OWASP Web Security Testing Guide Version 4.2*. OWASP Foundation, Dec. 2020.

[3] S. Alavi, N. Bessler, and M. Massoth, "A Comparative Evaluation of Automated Vulnerability Scans versus Manual Penetration Tests on False-negative Errors," in *CYBER 2018: The Third International Conference on Cyber-Technologies and Cyber-Systems*, 2018, pp. 1–6.

[4] P. Engebretson, *The basics of hacking and penetration testing: ethical hacking and penetration testing made easy*, 2nd ed. Amsterdam ; Boston: Syngress, an imprint of Elsevier, 2013.

[5] K. Scarfone, M. Souppaya, A. Cody, and A. Orebaugh, *Technical guide to information security testing and assessment.* National Institute of Standards & Technology, 2008.

[6] Federal Office for Information Security, "A Penetration Testing Model," 2003.

[7] J. Andress, *Foundations of information security: a straightforward introduction*, 1st ed. San Francisco: No Starch Press, 2019.

[8] H. C. A. v. Tilborg and S. Jajodia, Eds., *Encyclopedia of cryptography and security*, 2nd ed., ser. Springer reference. New York: Springer, 2011.

[9] K. M. Henry, *Penetration testing protecting networks and systems.* Ely, U.K: IT Governance Pub, 2012.

[10] P. Herzog, "OSSTMM 3-The Open Source Security Testing Methodology Manual: Contemporary Security Testing and Analysis," *ISECOM-Institute for Security and Open Methodologies*, 2010.

[11] C. Nickerson *et al.*, "The Penetration Testing Execution Standard," 2014. [Online]. Available: http://www.pentest-standard.org/index.php/Main_Page [retrieved: Aug, 2021].

[12] R. Baloch, *Ethical hacking and penetration testing guide.* Boca Raton: CRC Press, Taylor & Francis Group, 2015.

[13] T. P. Chiem, "A study of penetration testing tools and approaches," PhD Thesis, Auckland University of Technology, 2014.

[14] K. Cardwell, *Building Virtual Pentesting Labs for Advanced Penetration Testing*, 2nd ed. Birmingham: Packt Publishing, Limited, 2016, oCLC: 963293305.

[15] A. Shanley and M. Johnstone, "Selection of penetration testing methodologies: A comparison and evaluation," *13th Australian Information Security Management Conference*, pp. 65–72, 2015.

[16] OWASP Foundation, "OWASP - Main Page," 2021. [Online]. Available: https://www.owasp.org/index.php/Main_Page [retrieved: Aug, 2021].

[17] E. Rey, M. Thumann, and D. Baier, *Mehr IT-Sicherheit durch Pen-Tests.* Wiesbaden: Vieweg+Teubner Verlag, 2005.

[18] P. Herzog, "OSSTMM 2.2–Open Source Security Testing Methodology Manual," *ISECOM-Institute for Security and Open Methodologies*, 2006.

[19] D. Bhattacharyya, "Penetration Testing for Hire," *International Journal of Advanced Science and Technology*, vol. 8, pp. 1–8, 2009.

[20] M. Massoth and S. L. Ahier, "Fast Electronic Identification at Trust Substantial Level using the Personal Online Bank Account," in *CYBER 2020: The Fifth International Conference on Cyber-Technologies and Cyber-Systems*, 2020, pp. 94–99.

Performance Evaluation of Reconfigurable Lightweight Block Ciphers

Mostafa Hashempour Koshki
Faculty of Electrical and Computer Engineering
University of Tabriz
Tabriz, Iran
email: m.hashempour71@gmail.com

Reza Abdolee
Department of Computer Science
California State University, Channel Islands (CSUCI)
Camarillo, CA 93012, USA
email: reza.abdolee@csuci.edu

Behzad Mozaffari Tazekand
Faculty of Electrical and Computer Engineering
University of Tabriz
Tabriz, Iran
email: mozaffary@tabrizu.ac.ir

***Abstract*—The growing number of connected devices and massive data in the Internet of Things (IoT) cause information to encounter different types of attacks. One solution to the security problem of computationally intensive traditional cryptographic algorithms for IoT environments is stronger lightweight cryptography. This paper evaluates the security performance of reconfigurable lightweight block ciphers featuring round order and internal parameter randomization. We evaluate these lightweight block ciphers and compare their performance with that of conventional lightweight block ciphers in terms of execution time, energy consumption and throughput. The simulation results of reconfigured-based lightweight block ciphers show significant improvement in security performance with minor and negligible changes in energy-throughput performances.**

***Index Terms*—Security performance, Cybersecurity, Reconfigurable lightweight block ciphers, Round order randomization, Internet of Things (IoT).**

I. INTRODUCTION

Traditional cryptography algorithms have been designed for a network of computers with high processing power [1]. These algorithms are not suitable for communication devices with low computational power or storage spaces [2]. Alternatively, a new cryptography method called Lightweight Cryptography as a subset of cryptography was introduced [3]. A strong lightweight cryptography algorithm provides appropriate security level for resource-constrained devices. There are several categories in lightweight cryptography, including Lightweight Block Cipher (LWBC), Lightweight Stream Cipher (LWSC), and Lightweight Hash Function (LWHF) [4]. Block Ciphers (BC) are used in resource-constrained end-devices because they support keys and messages in varying sizes that can be adaptively changed. Lightweight block ciphers are defined based on the key size, block length, number of rounds, and key schedule structure that are smaller and simpler than conventional block ciphers.

Several types of LWBC have been proposed for IoT systems [5]. Some of the proposed LWBCs for resource-constrained devices have been derived from the optimization of conventional block ciphers, such as Welch-Gong cryptography (WG-8) [6] or Lighter algorithms from Advanced Encryption Standard (AES), Rivest Cipher-5 (RC-5), eXtended Tiny Encryption Algorithm (XTEA), and Data Encryption Standard (DES) [7]–[10]. In LWBC algorithms, smaller block/key sizes are considered for faster processing and consuming less resources. The PRESENT algorithm is provided with an 80-bit key [11] and the TWINE algorithm is presented with both 80-bit and 128-bit keys [12]. The number of rounds in this type of cryptography should be limited to save time to encrypt/decrypt the message. The Hummingbird [13] only has 4 rounds. A simple key schedule is used to produce subkeys such as converting a 128-bit key to 32-bit subkeys in the TEA block cipher by using a simple procedure [14]. Several LWBC algorithms are introduced as Generalized lightweight Feistel Network (GFN) categories for IoT systems such as PICCOLO, TWINE, and CLEFIA, with a trade-off between security and being lightweight [15] [16].

An attack on LWBC algorithms becomes more complicated by adding reconfigurability features and randomizing key parameters in their structures [17]. One way to do this is to use a Random Number Generator (RNG) to improve the security of the algorithm in exchange for small changes in the computational complexity and the consumption of resources and memory.

In this paper, we investigate the security performance of PICCOLO, TWINE, and PRESENT lightweight block ciphers via the round order randomization concept by using a pseudo-random number generator. In the Reconfigurable Hardware (RCH) method [18], only the order of the round keys in algorithms was reconfigured. However, in our proposed method, not only the order of the rounds is randomized, but also some internal parameters are randomized in key scheduling and data processing parts. For example, in PICCOLO algorithms, besides the order of round keys, the constant values of each round are also reconfigured separately. In fact, the initial table of constant values is shuffled. Additionally, in the 128-bit master key, which is initially divided into 8 subkeys (16-bit), randomization has been implemented. In this way, these subkeys are randomly selected to produce whitening keys and round keys. Even the number of rounds is reconfigured and randomly selected (11 to 41 for PICCOLO128 and 11 to 30 for PICCOLO80). In the key scheduling section of the TWINE algorithm, besides the order of rounds, the constant values of each round and the S-box are reconfigured separately and are randomly assigned to each round. In the data processing section, the table of $\pi[j]$ (Block indexes) values is randomized. In PRESENT algorithms, randomization of round orders and internal values such as S-box layer and P-layer is performed. In addition, the 64-bit algorithm key is randomly selected from the 80 or 128-bit master keys. In this algorithm, like PICCOLO, the number of rounds is considered variable between (20 to 35) for both key sizes of the PRESENT algorithm. We finally evaluate these round order and internal parameters of reconfigurable-based lightweight block ciphers and compare their performance with that of conventional lightweight block ciphers in terms of execution time, energy consumption, and throughput.

The paper is organized as follows. In Section II, we describe the proposed reconfigurable algorithms. Section III presents the performance analysis of LWBCs using round order and internal parameters randomization. Cryptanalysis of the randomized LWBCs is presented in Section IV. Finally, we conclude the paper in Section V.

II. RECONFIGURABLE LWBC ALGORITHMS

Using a RNG, the number of rounds of the algorithm, key scheduling part, and order of production of the round keys can be randomized. In this way, the key schedule becomes a pseudo-random function. If the algorithm is run successively for specific key and plaintext, different ciphers are produced. Therefore, a chosen-plaintext attack on the algorithm becomes impossible.

The steps of the randomization process are as follows. At first, a suitable range for the algorithm is defined and then by using an RNG, the number of rounds in the algorithm is determined. The randomization is also implemented in the key scheduling part with the same value generated by the RNG.

In this research, we introduce new reconfigurable-based algorithms for PICCOLO, TWINE, and PRESENT algorithms. They are, respectively, presented as Algorithms 1,2, and 3 in this paper. Algorithm 1 features different number of rounds and different order of round keys. In addition, it has a different key-table due to the randomizing order of master keys for the key scheduling part in each implementation. The RNG generates 30 and 41 random numbers for PICCOLO80 and PICCOLO128, respectively, that are indicated by $Random$ parameter in the algorithm. Therefore, the value of $fullround$ of the algorithm is the same as $Random$ parameter (30 and 41 for PICCOLO80 and PICCOLO128, respectively). In PICCOLO, each round has a constant value (con) that is computed by the number of each round. Roundkeys are reconfigured based on k and con, which are reconfigured based on n and

Algorithm 1: Proposed Reconfigurable PICCOLO128

```
Data: The master key k_j 0 ≤ j < n, n = 8,
  fullround = 41
Reconf (k_j, n) ◁ Reconfigure k based on n
Reconf (con_i, fullround) ◁ Reconfigure con based on
  fullround
Reconf (Roundkeys, k_j.con_i) ◁ Reconfigure Roundkeys
  based on con and n
i ← 0
for 0 ≤ i < fullround ◁ Store Random Index do
    Random ← RNG(seed)
    while i < n do
        rndi ← Random mod n
        knew[i] ← k[rndi] ◁ Reconfigure k based on n
    end
    r ← Random mod fullround
    newcon(2i, 2i + 1) ← con(2r, 2r + 1)
    if i=n+1 ◁ Reconfigure number of rounds then
        rndround ← r
        if rndround < 10 then
            rndround ← rndround + 13
            if rndround mod 2 = 0 then
                rndround ← rndround + 1
            end
        end
    end
end
Roundkeys ← keyschedule[con_i, knew]
G_r = Enc.Roundkeys_r
```

$fullround$, respectively. In addition, the whole algorithm is randomized based on the number of rounds when the value of i is equal to $n+1$. The number of rounds, order of round-keys, and key-table of the key scheduling part were reconfigured as shown in Algorithm 1. In this way, a temporary array is produced to store the random number 0 through $fullround$ where $fullround$ is the maximum value of PICCOLO rounds number. If reconfigurable hardware is used to control random values, randomization has minimal effect on the performance of algorithms. The memory requirements will be reduced when the hardware RNG creates random values. By using $rndi$, the order of key masters will be randomized and stored in a new table which is indicated by $knew$. The generated n^{th} random number is used to set the number of rounds in module $fullround$. Finally, we encrypt in r rounds and with a new table of master keys for the key scheduling section.

In the randomization of TWINE, both data processing and key scheduling sections have been reconfigured by randomized order of S-box as their internal elements. The order of a permutation of block indexes, which are indicated by $\pi[j]$ and $\pi^{-1}[j]$ for encryption and decryption in the data processing part, are randomized. In the key scheduling part, the order of constant value and order of round keys, along with S-box, are reconfigured. Because of the randomization of $\pi[j]$, the order of $\pi^{-1}[j]$ has changed. The RNG generates 36 random numbers for both key sizes of algorithms. The order of S-box, $\pi[j]$ and con_i were computed based on the number of rounds in the randomization of the TWINE algorithm. The original key is divided into 5 and 8 16-bit keys for TWINE80 and

Algorithm 2: Proposed Reconfigurable TWINE128

Data: The master key k_j $0 \leq j < n$, $n = 8$, $NbRound = 36$
Reconf (k_j, n) ◁ **Reconfigure** k based on n
Reconf $(con_i, NbRound)$ ◁ **Reconfigure** con based on $NbRound$
Reconf $((\pi[j]$ & $\pi^{-1}[j], 16))$ ◁ **Reconfigure** $\pi[j]$ and $\pi^{-1}[j]$ based on 16
Reconf $(S(x), 16)$ ◁ **Reconfigure** S based on 16
Reconf $(Roundkeys, k_j.con_i.S(x))$
$i \leftarrow 0$
for $0 \leq i < NbRound$ ◁ ***Store Random Index*** **do**
  $Random \leftarrow RNG(seed)$
  while $i < n$ **do**
    $rndi \leftarrow Random$ mod n
    $knew[i] \leftarrow k[rndi]$ ◁ **Reconfigure** k based on n
  end
  $r \leftarrow Random$ mod $NbRound$
  $newcon(i) \leftarrow con(r)$
  while $i < 16$ ◁ ***Reconfigure*** *number of rounds* **do**
    $rndi \leftarrow Random$ mod 16
    $Snew[i] \leftarrow S[rndi]$
    $\pi[i] \leftarrow \pi[rndi]$
    $\pi^{-1}[\pi[i]] \leftarrow i$
  end
end
$Roundkeys \leftarrow keyschedule[newcon_i, knew, S_i]$
$Enc \leftarrow Encryption[S_i, \pi[i]]$
$Dec \leftarrow Decryption[S_i, \pi^{-1}[i]]$
$G_r = Enc.Roundkeys_r$
$G_r^{-1} = Dec.Roundkeys_r$

TWINE128, respectively. As seen, an RNG is seeded with a primary value in the randomizing path. A temporary array is generated to store the random number 0 through $NbRound$ which is 36 in both the TWINE80 and TWINE128 algorithms. By randomizing the con, k, and S, the order of round keys has changed. The entire encryption and decryption process has been reconfigured by randomizing the S_i, $\pi[j]$, and $\pi^{-1}[j]$.

Finally, for the PRESENT, some parameters have been considered for reconfiguring the algorithm. Like PICCOLO algorithm, PRESENT is reconfigured by randomizing the number of rounds (between 20 and 32). The S-box and P-layer have also been randomized to reconfigure both the key scheduling and data processing parts of the PRESENT algorithm. Another change is in the selection of a 64-bit algorithm key from an 80-bit or 128-bit master-key. In the original cipher, the most significant 64 bits of the master-key are selected as the algorithm key, while in the proposed method, the mentioned key is obtained randomly from the 80-bit or 128-bit key. The order of the round keys is also randomized. The RNG generates 64 random numbers for the PRESENT algorithm with both of the key sizes (80 and 128). Since S-box, P-layer, and master key are reconfigured, the order of round keys is reconfigured based on them and $NbRound$. The computations of the parameters which are involved in the algorithm randomization are indicated in Algorithm 3.

In our implementation, we use the STM32F401RE, which is an STM32 (ARM Cortex M4) microcontroller. Its ARMv7E-M architecture with 3 stage pipelining results in ideal average Clocks Per Instruction (CPI) of 1.67 [19]. The performance metrics parameters such as energy consumption, execution time, memory efficiency, and throughput of the proposed algorithms were analyzed for PICCOLO, TWINE, and PRESENT with a pseudo-random number generator. For randomized PICCOLO, the number of rounds, order of subkeys, and constant value of each round are reconfigured. The possible number of rounds is 17 and 28 for PICCOLO80 and PICCOLO128, respectively. In other words, the total possible combination for PICCOLO80 and PICCOLO128, respectively, is $17 \times r! \times con!$ and $28 \times r! \times con!$ where $r!$ is the permutations of the subkeys and $con!$ is the permutations of each round's constant values. The order of internal keys, S-boxes, diffusion of round indexes, and constant value of rounds are randomized in TWINE algorithms implementation. The permutation of the internal keys with $n!$ (n=5 for TWINE80 and n=8 for TWINE128), $con!$ with $NbRound!$, S and $\pi[j]$ with 16! has made the entire possible combination of both TWINE algorithms, so the permutation of algorithms is $n! \times NbRound! \times 16!$. The proposed PRESENT algorithms have the same permutation for both key sizes. The number of rounds, algorithm key, order of round keys, S-box, and P-layer have 12, 64!, 32!, 16!, and 64! possibilities. Therefore, the total permutation of the PRESENT algorithms is $12 \times 64! \times 32! \times 16! \times 64!$.

Algorithm 3: Proposed Reconfigurable PRESENT128

Data: The master key K_128, Round Key rk Bits of algorithm's key k_i $0 \leq i < ksize$, $ksize = 64$, Maximum of $NbRound$ is 32
Reconf $(k_i, ksize)$ ◁ **Reconfigure** k based on $ksize$
Reconf $(rk, NbRound, k_i, Sbox, Player)$ ◁ **Reconfigure** rk based on $NbRound$, k_i, $Sbox$, and $Player$
Reconf $(Sbox, 16)$ ◁ **Reconfigure** $Sbox$ based on 16
Reconf $(Player, 64)$ ◁ **Reconfigure** $Player$ based on 64
$i \leftarrow 0$
for $0 \leq i < 64$ ◁ ***Store Random Index*** **do**
  $Random \leftarrow RNG(seed)$
  if *i=0* ◁ ***Reconfigure*** *number of rounds* **then**
    $NbRound \leftarrow Random$ mod 12 + 20
  end
  $r \leftarrow Random$ mod 64
  $Player[i] \leftarrow Player[r]$
  while $i < NbRound$ **do**
    $r \leftarrow Random$ mod $NbRound$
    $rk[i] \leftarrow rk[r]$
  end
  while $i < 16$ **do**
    $r \leftarrow Random$ mod 16
    $Sbox[i] \leftarrow Sbox[r]$
  end
end
$rk \leftarrow keyschedule[k_i, NbRound, Sbox, Player]$
$G_r = Enc.rk$

III. Performance Analysis

In our analysis, we investigate execution time, memory consumption, energy consumption, and throughput for PICCOLO, TWINE, and PRESENT.

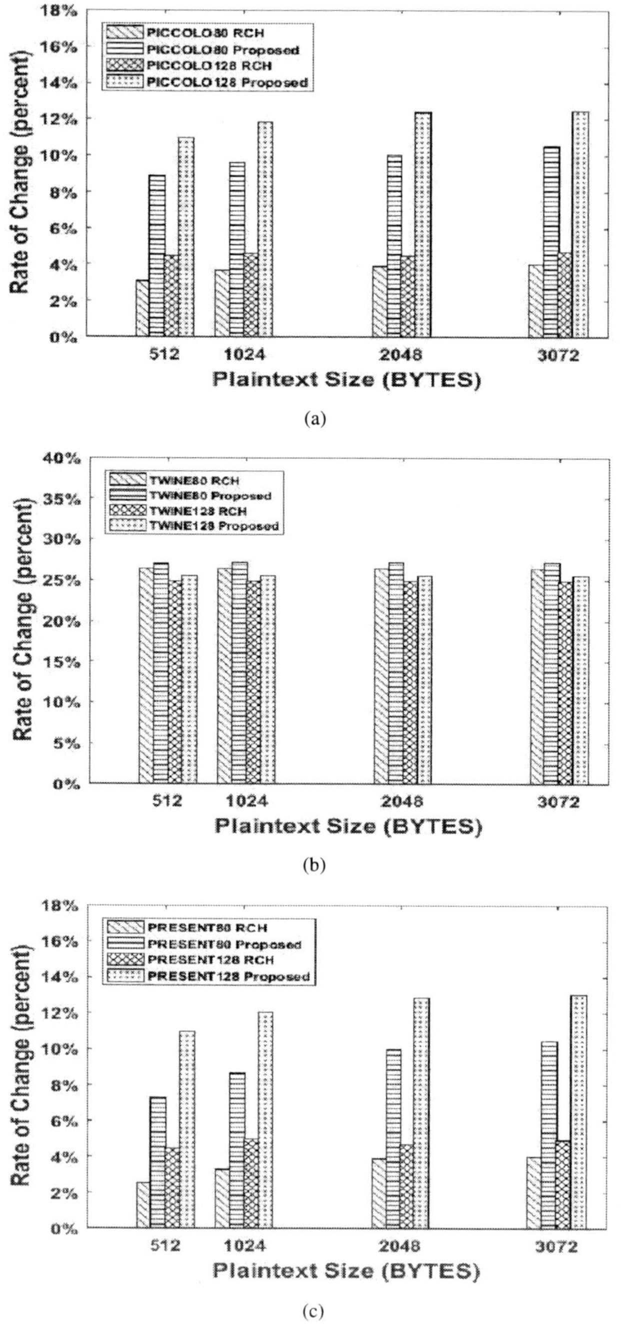

Fig. 1. Comparison of the execution time of original ciphers, the RCH simulations and the round order and internal parameters of algorithms randomization based ciphers in terms of the 80-bit and 128-bit keys for (a) PICCOLO, (b) TWINE and (c) PRESENT.

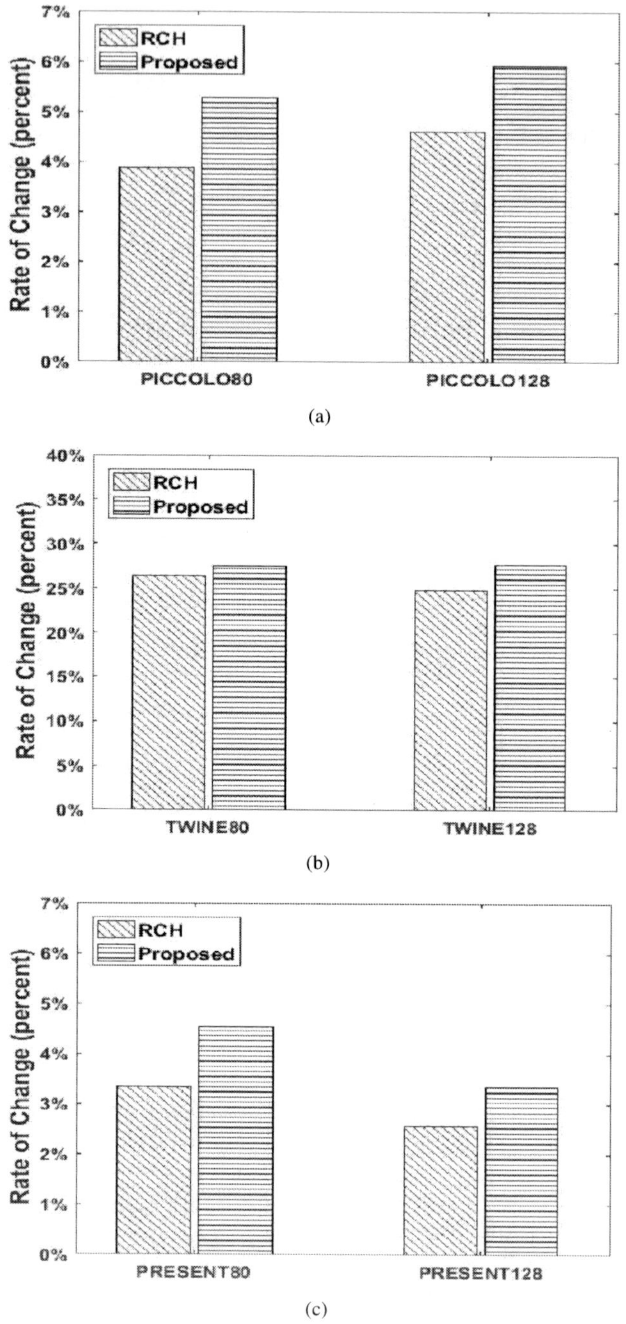

Fig. 2. Comparison of the energy consumption of original ciphers with the RCH method and the round order and internal parameters of algorithms randomization based ciphers in terms of the 80-bit and 128-bit keys for (a) PICCOLO, (b) TWINE and (c) PRESENT.

In Figure 1, a comparison is made between the execution time of the original ciphers, the Reconfigurable Hardware (RCH) [18], and the proposed block ciphers. We consider 80-bit and 128-bit keys for PICCOLO, TWINE, and PRESENT algorithms for these different cases. As seen for PICCOLO with an 80-bit key, the differences in execution time between the original cipher and RCH for plaintext of 512, 1024, 2048, and 3072 are 3.11%, 3.69%, 3.89%, and 4.02% while those differences between our proposed ciphers and the original cipher are 8.87%,9.64%, 10.06%, and 10.51%.

Furthermore, for 128-bit of PICCOLO the increases in time for 512, 1024, 2048, 3072 bit plaintexts are 4.51% 4.63%,

4.51%, and 4.70%, respectively, whereas the increases in time for our method against the original cipher are 10.98%, 11.82%, 12.35%, and 12.48%. The results of the same comparison between the original ciphers and the RCH method for TWINE80 with plaintext 512, 1024, 2048 and 3072 are 26.35%, 26.39%, 26.38%, and 26.38% while the results for our methods are 27.05%, 27.10% ,27.10%, and 27.11% for the same plaintext. For TWINE128 the rates of change from original cipher in RCH mode for 512, 1024, 2048, and 3072 plaintexts are 24.81%, 24.82%, 24.83%, and 24.83%, in the meantime, those measurements for our method are 25.53%, 25.55%, 25.56%, and 25.57%. The similar results were obtained for PRESENT algorithms. The differences in execution time for PRESENT80 and PRESENT128 are shown in Figure 1(c). It should be noted that the differences between the proposed block ciphers and the RCH method are similar to previous results between the original ciphers and the RCH results.

One of the several approaches to compute energy consumption is using the CPU's operating voltage and the average current dragged by each cycle, which can be as [20]:

$$E = I \times N \times \tau \times V \quad (1)$$

where, I, N, τ, and V are the average current, the number of clock cycles, the clock period, and the voltage, respectively. Figure 2 compares the energy consumption of PICCOLO, TWINE, and PRESENT block ciphers. The supply voltage and average current of Cortex-M4 microcontrollers are 3.6 V and 0.0155 A, respectively. Its operating frequency is 84 MHz. Since the voltage, average current, and clock period are constant, the number of clock cycles for each encryption round should be calculated and compared, which are provided by Data Watchpoint and Trace (DWT) [15]. As can be seen, the differences of average clock cycles of PICCOLO80 and PICCOLO128 between the original cipher and the RCH method are 3.86% and 4.61%, respectively. On the other hand, the increases of PICCOLO's average clock cipher compared with our round order and internal values randomization-based ciphers are only 5.27% and 5.92%, respectively. In the same way, the increases in average clock cycles for RCH are 26.38% and 24.82% for TWINE80 and TWINE128, respectively. In PRESENT80 and PRESENT128, the change rates of average clock cycles for reconfigurable hardware (RCH) are 3.33% and 2.57%. In the meantime, those increment rates for our method are 4.54% and 3.35%. The same increases are shown in our results when compared with previous results. The amount of processed data in a period of time can be measured by throughput, which determines that lightweight block cipher has the best performance in an IoT environment [15]. First, we divide the number of cycles by the block size of each algorithm. The total encryption cycles per bit for each algorithm is obtained as [15]:

$$Encryption(cycles/bit) = \frac{Numberofcycles}{Blocksize} \quad (2)$$

Since MCU operates under 84MHz, it can execute 84,000,000 cycles in each second. Therefore, the throughput of each block

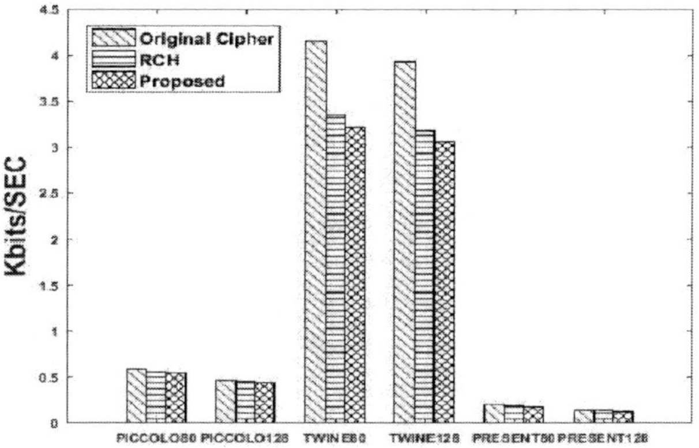

Fig. 3. Throughput comparison of original ciphers, the RCH simulations and the round order and internal parameters of algorithms randomization based ciphers in terms of the 80-bit and 128-bit keys for PICCOLO, TWINE, and PRESENT.

cipher can be expressed as follows [15]:

$$Throughput = \frac{CPUspeed}{Enc(cycles/bit)} \quad (3)$$

In Figure 3, a comparison is made between the throughput of original ciphers, the RCH simulations, and the round order and internal parameters of algorithms randomization-based ciphers in terms of the 80-bit and 128-bit keys for PICCOLO, TWINE, and PRESENT. As can be seen, all throughput values are close together for each cipher.

IV. Cryptanalysis of the Proposed Reconfigurable LWBCs

Most security analysis has been considered for proposed randomization algorithms against critical attacks such as the differential attack, boomerang attack, and Meet In The Middle attack (MITM). The differential attack is a chosen-plaintext attack that analyzes how the difference of input evolves through the several rounds of the cipher. To be exact, the probability of observing the difference of output (δ_{out}) that gives an input difference (δ_{in}) is as follows [21]:

$$\Pr[f(x \oplus \delta_{in}) \oplus f(x) = \delta_{out}] \quad (4)$$

In the following, a block cipher (E) reduced to t rounds will be denoted by E^t, as shown in Figure 4(a). As a result, $Pr[\delta_0 \to \delta_t]$ represents the probability of a differential $\delta_0 \to \delta_t$:

$$\Pr[\delta_0 \to \delta_t] = \Pr_{X,K}[E_K^t(X) \oplus E_K^t(X \oplus \delta_0)] \quad (5)$$

where $Pr_{X,K}$ is the probability computed on all possible input plaintext (X) and all possible keys (K). This probability can be calculated as:

$$\begin{aligned} Pr_{X,K}[E_K^t(X) \oplus E_K^t(X \oplus \delta_0)] &= Pr_{X,K}[C \oplus (C \oplus \delta_t)] \\ &= Pr_{X,K}[\delta_t] \end{aligned} \quad (6)$$

For the proposed reconfigurable block ciphers, the second time it will be a different block cipher with a different key after the

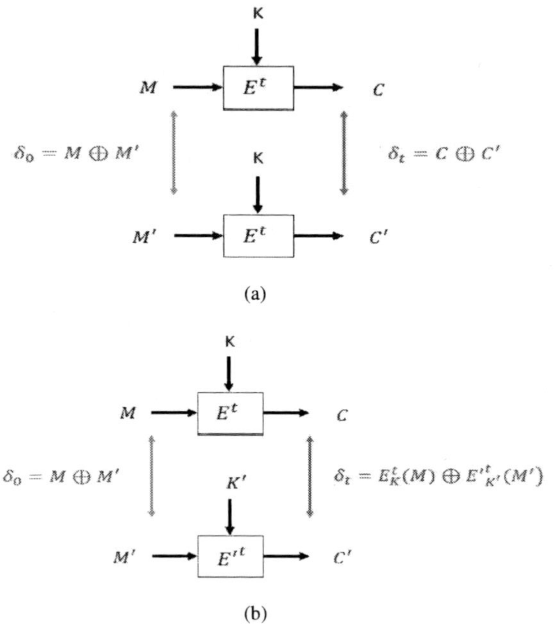

Fig. 4. A differential on t rounds of (a) cipher E and (b) our round order and internal parameters randomization based ciphers.

block cipher is run for r rounds. In this way, the probability of all possible input plaintexts X and key K is as follows:

$$Pr_{X,K}[E^t_K(X) \oplus E'^{\,t}_{K'}(X \oplus \delta_0)] = \Pr_{X,K}[C \oplus (C' \oplus \delta_t)] \neq \Pr_{X,K}[\delta_t] \quad (7)$$

The difference between outputs and inputs for block ciphers is depicted in Figure 4(b). The boomerang attack is a chosen-plaintext and cipher text attack which maximizes the probability of breakage by combining sets of four messages of M_0, M_1, M_2 and M_3. This attack uses differentials like a differential attack for examined algorithms [22] [23]. We implement this method for one of the messages, the result is the same for the other ones. Since the equation of probability is not equal to the difference of messages (α), our method has high safety against this attack as follows:

$$\begin{aligned} &E^{-1}(E(M_0) \oplus \delta) \oplus E'^{-1}(E'(M_0 \oplus \alpha) \oplus \delta) \\ &\Rightarrow [M_0 \oplus E^{-1}(\delta)] \oplus [M_0 \oplus \alpha \oplus E'^{-1}(\delta)] \\ &\Rightarrow E^{-1}(\delta) \oplus E'^{-1}(\delta) \oplus \alpha \neq \alpha \end{aligned} \quad (8)$$

The newest method of attack for this category is the three-subset Meet In The Middle (MITM) attack, which has good results on lightweight block ciphers [24] [25]. In PICCOLO algorithms, the number of rounds is considered variable. Therefore PICCOLO80 and PICCOLO128 have 10 and 16 possible number of rounds. The MITM attacks have two sides. The right side starts encryption operation partially from the beginning and the left side performs decryption partly from the ending. For PICCOLO algorithms, the right and left sides equations are performed for each guess of the subkeys, respectively, as follows:

$$v = \lambda_{1,i}(p) = k_{1,i} \oplus CON_{1,i} \quad (9)$$

$$u = \lambda^{-1}_{i+1,r}(c) = k_{i+1,r} \oplus CON_{i+1,r} \quad (10)$$

where $\lambda_{i,j}$ describes the operation of an r-round block cipher encryption (from round i to round j) with a fixed key and $\lambda_{i,j-1}$ describes the decryption in the same circumstances. The key schedule and constant value of rounds are indicated by $k_{i,j}$ and $CON_{i,j}$. The computational complexity which is indicated by $\varsigma_{comp\ origind}$ will be reduced with respect to the MITM attack. In our algorithms, due to the randomization of key scheduling part and constant value of rounds, the computational complexity is increased. For 80-bit and 128-bit keys, the complexity is computed as follows:

$$\varsigma_{compP80} = 10 \times 5! \times 30! \times \varsigma_{comporiginal} \quad (11)$$

$$\varsigma_{compP128} = 16 \times 8! \times 41! \times \varsigma_{comporiginal} \quad (12)$$

For TWINE algorithms, the right and left sides of the MITM attack are performed for each guess of subkeys as follows:

$$v = \lambda_{1,i}(p) = k_{1,i} \oplus S_{1,j} \oplus CON_{1,i} \oplus \pi_{1,j} \quad (13)$$

$$u = \lambda^{-1}_{i+1,r}(c) = k_{i+1,r} \oplus S_{i+1,r} \oplus CON_{i+1,r} \oplus \pi^{-1}_{i+1,r} \quad (14)$$

where $k_{i,j}$, $S_{i,j}$, $CON_{i,j}$, $\pi_{i,j}$ and $\pi^{-1}_{i,j}$ are key schedule, S-box, constant value of rounds, and diffusion of block indexes for encryption and decryption, respectively. In proposed algorithms for TWINE, because of randomizing the key scheduling part, S-box, constant value of rounds and diffusion of block indexes for encryption or decryption, the computational complexity is increased. For the proposed TWINE with 80 and 128 bits keys this can be calculated as:

$$\varsigma_{compT80} = 5! \times 16! \times 36! \times 16! \times \varsigma_{comporiginal} \quad (15)$$

$$\varsigma_{compT128} = 8! \times 16! \times 36! \times 16! \times \varsigma_{comporiginal} \quad (16)$$

The mentioned MITM equations for PRESENT algorithms are as follows:

$$v = \lambda_{1,i}(p) = k_{1,i} \oplus Sbox_{1,j} \oplus Player_{1,i} \quad (17)$$

$$u = \lambda^{-1}_{i+1,r}(c) = k_{i+1,r} \oplus Sbox_{j+1,r} \oplus Player_{i+1,r} \quad (18)$$

where $k_{i,j}$, $S_{i,j}$, and $P - layer_{i,j}$ are key scheduling part, S-box layer, and the P-layer. In the proposed randomization algorithms for PRESENT, the increase in complexity for both key sizes is the same and it is computed as follows:

$$\varsigma_{compPRESENT} = 12 \times 64! \times 32! \times 16! \times 64! \times \varsigma_{comporiginal} \quad (19)$$

V. Conclusion

In this paper, the security performance of lightweight block ciphers including the PICCOLO, TWINE, and PRESENT, using randomization round order and internal parameters of algorithms are presented for IoT environments. Our results indicate that the proposed reconfigurable-based block ciphers exhibit significant improvements in security performance with minor and negligible changes in energy-throughput performances. In other words, the round order and internal parameters randomizations have minimal effect on the complexity of the lightweight block ciphers, but they significantly decrease an attacker's ability to guess keys.

References

[1] M. Maroufi, R. Abdolee, and B. M. Tazekand, "On the convergence of blockchain and internet of things (IoT) technologies," *Journal of Strategic Innovation and Sustainability (JSIS), vol. 14*, pp. 1–11, 2019.

[2] M. N. Bhuiyan, M. M. Rahman, M. M. Billah, and D. Saha, "Internet of things (IoT): A review of its enabling technologies in healthcare applications, standards protocols, security and market opportunities," *IEEE Internet of Things Journal*, 2021.

[3] J. Yogi, U. S. Chauhan, A. Raj, M. Gupta, and S. S. Sudan, "Modeling simulation and performance analysis of lightweight cryptography for IoT-security," in *2018 3rd International Conference and Workshops on Recent Advances and Innovations in Engineering (ICRAIE)*. IEEE, 2018, pp. 1–5.

[4] K. McKay, L. Bassham, M. Sönmez Turan, and N. Mouha, "Report on lightweight cryptography," National Institute of Standards and Technology, Tech. Rep., 2016.

[5] U. du Luxembour. Lightweight block ciphers. [Online]. Available: https://www.cryptolux.org/index.php/Lightweight-Block-Ciphers

[6] X. Fan, K. Mandal, and G. Gong, "WG-8: A lightweight stream cipher for resource-constrained smart devices," in *International Conference on Heterogeneous Networking for Quality, Reliability, Security and Robustness*. Springer, 2013, pp. 617–632.

[7] K. Iokibe, K. Maeshima, H. Kagotani, Y. Nogami, Y. Toyota, and T. Watanabe, "Analysis on equivalent current source of AES-128 circuit for HD power model verification," in *2014 International Symposium on Electromagnetic Compatibility, Tokyo*. IEEE, 2014, pp. 302–305.

[8] R. L. Rivest, "The RC5 encryption algorithm," in *International Workshop on Fast Software Encryption*. Springer, 1994, pp. 86–96.

[9] J. Yu, G. Khan, and F. Yuan, "XTEA encryption based novel RFID security protocol," in *2011 24th Canadian Conference on Electrical and Computer Engineering (CCECE)*. IEEE, 2011, pp. 000 058–000 062.

[10] G. Leander, C. Paar, A. Poschmann, and K. Schramm, "New lightweight DES variants," in *International Workshop on Fast Software Encryption*. Springer, 2007, pp. 196–210.

[11] A. Bogdanov, L. R. Knudsen, G. Leander, C. Paar, A. Poschmann, M. J. Robshaw, Y. Seurin, and C. Vikkelsoe, "PRESENT: An ultra-lightweight block cipher," in *International workshop on cryptographic hardware and embedded systems*. Springer, 2007, pp. 450–466.

[12] J. Hosseinzadeh and M. Hosseinzadeh, "A comprehensive survey on evaluation of lightweight symmetric ciphers: hardware and software implementation," *Advances in Computer Science: an International Journal*, vol. 5, no. 4, pp. 31–41, 2016.

[13] B. J. Mohd, T. Hayajneh, and A. V. Vasilakos, "A survey on lightweight block ciphers for low-resource devices: Comparative study and open issues," *Journal of Network and Computer Applications*, vol. 58, pp. 73–93, 2015.

[14] D. J. Wheeler and R. M. Needham, "TEA, a tiny encryption algorithm," in *International workshop on fast software encryption*. Springer, 1994, pp. 363–366.

[15] L. Ertaul and S. K. Rajegowda, "Performance analysis of CLEFIA, PICCOLO, TWINE lightweight block ciphers in IoT environment," in *Proceedings of the International Conference on Security and Management (SAM)*. The Steering Committee of The World Congress in Computer Science, Computer Engineering and Applied Computing (WorldComp), 2017, pp. 25–31.

[16] K. Shibutani, T. Isobe, H. Hiwatari, A. Mitsuda, T. Akishita, and T. Shirai, "PICCOLO: An ultra-lightweight blockcipher," in *International workshop on cryptographic hardware and embedded systems*. Springer, 2011, pp. 342–357.

[17] R. Abdolee and V. Vakilian, "Reconfigurable security hardware and methods for internet of things (IoT) systems," Oct. 29 2020, US Patent App. 16/859,478.

[18] S. A. Kahan, R. Abdolee, E. Argueta, and V. Vakilian, "Security performance improvement of lightweight block ciphers via round order randomization," in *International Conference on Communication and Signal Proccessing (ICCSP), Tehran*. IEEE, 2018, pp. 1–99.

[19] Systemy RT I embedded. [Online]. Available: http://www.ue.pwr.wroc.pl/systemy-rt/RTE6.pdf

[20] D. Salama, H. A. Kader, and M. Hadhoud, "Studying the effects of most common encryption algorithms," *International Arab Journal of e-Technology*, vol. 2, no. 1, pp. 1–10, 2011.

[21] E. Biham and A. Shamir, *Differential cryptanalysis of the data encryption standard*. Springer Science & Business Media, 2012.

[22] D. Wagner, "The Boomerang attack," in *International Workshop on Fast Software Encryption*. Springer, 1999, pp. 156–170.

[23] J. Kelsey, T. Kohno, and B. Schneier, "Amplified Boomerang attacks against reduced-round MARS and Serpent," in *International Workshop on Fast Software Encryption*. Springer, 2000, pp. 75–93.

[24] K. Aoki and Y. Sasaki, "Meet-In-The-Middle preimage attacks against reduced SHA-0 and SHA-1," in *Annual International Cryptology Conference*. Springer, 2009, pp. 70–89.

[25] A. Bogdanov and C. Rechberger, "A 3-subset Meet-In-The-Middle attack: cryptanalysis of the lightweight block cipher KTANTAN," in *International Workshop on Selected Areas in Cryptography*. Springer, 2010, pp. 229–240.

Relevance of GRC in Expanding the Enterprise Risk Management Capabilities

Alina Andronache
Affiliation during research: Brunel Business School, Brunel University, current affiliation: University of the West of Scotland, London, UK, email: alina.andronache@partner.uws.ac.uk

Abraham Althonayan
Brunel Business School, Brunel University, London, UK, email: Abraham.Althonayan@brunel.ac.uk

Seyedeh Mandana Matin
Affiliation during research: Brunel Business School, Brunel University, current affiliation: University of the West of Scotland, London, UK, email: mandana.matin@partner.uws.ac.uk

***Abstract*—This research explored the need for enhancing the Enterprise Risk Management concept. Thus, delved into challenges and drawbacks to acknowledge levels of maturity. In addition, it studied the reasoning for a paradigm shift, which aggregates "GRC" (Governance, Risk and Compliance) under its umbrella to increase concept capabilities to not only align or comply but to foresee, adapt, and create future-oriented risk strategies. Overall, the key findings from 15 qualitative interviews indicated that Enterprise Risk Management maturity has yet to achieve its full potential. It was found that in practice Enterprise Risk Management no longer suffice to an organisation's needs. Stakes and risk-return have consequently become considerably higher and broader in scope so the need to orchestrate the disjointed risk functions is higher. Given the significant drawbacks identified, this article suggests a value proposition of integrating GRC into Enterprise Risk Management to increase organisational risk capabilities. The joint approach is suggested to reinforce the effects of Enterprise Risk Management, and last but not least, enable maturity of the concept.**

Keywords—Enterprise Risk Management, GRC, align, risk compliance, maturity.

I. INTRODUCTION

Given the increase in the number of organisational failures, previous studies have reported that managing risk has become essential for an organisation's success [1][2]. Additionally, globalisation, uncertainties in the business environment, hyper-competition within industries, political risks, increased demand for compliance and governance, and heightened stakeholders' expectations have articulated the necessity for strengthening a cross-dimensional risk function [2]-[4].

Risks are continually evolving, and the ramifications of these changes have increased organisations' interest in shifting from the traditional silo perspective that comes with conventional Risk Management (RM) towards the holistic approach of Enterprise Risk Management (ERM) in order to deal with risk in a more all-encompassing way [4]-[6]. Intrinsically desirable, ERM has been recognised as an integrative risk oversight approach that helps organisations manage an extensive range of risks in a coordinated and comprehensive manner. Even though risk governance efficiency has been improved in recent years, attaining enterprise-wide risk governance remains a complex challenge for many scholars. ERM has a long history stemming from its capability to shift into aligning various organisational functions in a multi-strategy approach [7][8]. Likewise, successful ERM is driven by the alignment of risk oversight with strategic planning, respectively organisation strategy [5][8]-[10].

ERM concentrates on 'risk oversight' value, articulating and embedding due diligence within an organisation's strategy to establish a risk mindset across the organization [11]. Research on risk oversight has been growing, and there is clear evidence that the siloed practice of RM is being abandoned as an effect of the post-global financial crisis of 2008 [12]-[14].

Overall, the paradigm shift towards ERM supports a change in emphasis from tactical to strategic [1]. Moreover, the concept provides organisational effectiveness and preserves shareholder value on a continual basis [1][7]. The output of such a trend in recent years reinforces the value of a holistic approach delivered by ERM. Thus, this paper investigates the aptness of strategic planning and effectiveness of managerial risk control for improving resiliency, customised to an organisation's specific needs and objectives rather than being a mere compliance burden or serving the tick-box approach.

The benefits of ERM have been thoroughly discussed by many researchers [15]-[24]. However, questions regarding how mature/effective ERM implementation is, and how successful ERM has been in yielding its proactive capacity/maturity entirely, remain valid [9][10]. In spite of the ERM implementation, prior research has thoroughly investigated ERM adoption, implementation, and measurement. Nonetheless, little research has been conducted to show the limitations and challenges of ERM as encountered by organisations. A majority of prior researchers have failed to evaluate and identify ERM maturity, future direction, and potential solutions [21].

Despite substantial theoretical legacy, ERM is still in a developmental stage in terms of alignment to an organisation's strategic planning. Thus, several studies such as [6][8][9][14][24]-[26] have advocated a call for improvements in the designing and implementation processes due to a lack of strategic alignment, a lack of understanding of ERM benefits, an inappropriate understanding of risk, inadequate ways to report risks, an undeveloped risk culture, a lack of an ERM framework fit with organisations' needs, a lack of accurate and unbiased data on corporate risk management activities, a lack of a constantly updated and reliable risk control system, a lack of constant environmental scanning, a lack of compliance with numerous and changing regulations, and an inability to capture risks holistically.

While ERM has been a growing field over recent years [14][27], studies concerning why ERM remains immature are few. Surprisingly, there are only a few articles (e.g., [7][9][28]) that, apart from identifying the limitations of ERM, also open a debate to discuss whether ERM is sufficient to support an organisation's vision and mission. For instance, [28] emphasises that the main success factors in implementing ERM are human factors, clearer guidance, the proper definition of risk appetite, proper performance metrics, and adaptability to challenging environments [29]; all of which contribute towards beneficial risk governance practices [25][28]. Additionally, some potential solutions have been suggested by [30], focusing on communication, articulated objectives, and understanding of potential impact and probability in order to render risk governance optimisation and risk functions prioritisation [30]. Moreover, [8] discusses that setting up a reliable risk control system along with continuous environmental scanning helps for more effective ERM implementation [8]. Similarly, it has been argued by [10] that organisations' competitive advantage is contingent upon having their risk management integrated with a robust risk control system. Indeed, organisations with reliable risk control systems are more able to deal with today's uncertainties [10].

Consequently, this paper investigates challenges among ERM practices. Despite its effectiveness, ERM remains immature in implementation (e.g., repeatability, processes, effectiveness, sophistication) [31]-[33]. Additionally, the immaturity of ERM encourages an extension of its principles and broadens further to GRC that incorporates ERM principles under its umbrella [24][34] along with additional functions of 'risk governance'. There is scarce evidence in terms of ERM and GRC similarities [32]. ERM maturity has previously been analysed through the lens of practicality and not much attention has been paid to the ERM paradigm's maturity conceptually [3]. Most existing literature has been based on descriptive and prescriptive aspects of how and why implementation should be achieved [20][35]. Whether ERM is theoretically mature is a question addressed in this paper.

Based on the points presented so far, this paper argues that understanding ERM's current conceptual maturity helps authors to enrich further their theory and better understand the dynamic capability of the new school of thought regarding 'risk control', 'risk oversight', and 'risk governance', in other words, the industry trend towards GRC. This paper corroborates ERM's drawbacks to justify the necessity of ERM maturity for assuring the fulfilment of organisation strategy and objectives [32]. In this regard, this paper aims to explore the challenges and drawbacks of ERM, consciously acknowledge current maturity as well as exploring the justification rationality for a paradigm shift towards GRC. In the next section, a thorough analysis of the research background is provided. We will then delve into the research methodology and research findings. Lastly, we will contextualize the research results and discuss their implication and future work.

II. BACKGROUND

ERM's increased importance and popularity have ensued due to the Global Financial Crisis (GFC), 2008-2009, when organisations realised that business operations were becoming more complex and the number of risks in business markets were, and indeed still are, increasing.

Moreover, numerous corporate fraud and financial scandals leading up to the GFC pressured institutional investors, rating agencies, legislators, and regulators into pushing organisations towards advancing their commitment to ERM and taking a more effective approach for dealing with risks that affect performance [3][4][8][36]. Accordingly, the catastrophes of the GFC have highlighted that silo RM needs to move towards a more holistic ERM [4][14][32]. The economic environment encounters rapid internal and external changes due to globalisation and increasing complexity of risks that can positively or negatively affect the achievement of an organisation's strategic objectives [3][37]-[39]. The highly volatile post-crisis period revealed the ineffectiveness of past RM approaches and proved that relying on a traditional approach of RM is no longer appropriate [3][8]. As a result, regulators, institutional investors, and rating agencies demanded organisations to evaluate their RM approaches and focus on more transparent and effective RM practices [8][30][40]. A more holistic approach of RM was encouraged to enhance effectiveness across organisations. Thus, over time, old practices of silo RM advanced to modern ERM practices, considered more accurate and multi-faceted [29]. Moreover, ERM has developed as an approach that incorporates existing strategies, resources, technology, and knowledge in order to evaluate and manage uncertainties that many organisations encounter [14][41][42]. The central focus of ERM is to identify, measure, mitigate, and manage risks that would otherwise hinder the achievement of organisational objectives [14][41][43].

Most researchers in the field agree that the implementation of ERM is driven by various determinants (i.e., internal and external, mandatory or discretionary) such as an organisation's own willingness to improve its risk oversight, pressure from regulators, rating agencies and organisation executives, academic research, industry norms, stakeholders' encouragement, technology shifts, and marketing competition [30][44][45]. Consequently, several studies have focused on the factors associated with effective ERM implementation. For instance, [15] proposes a framework of ERM and performance and reports that successful ERM implementation is conditioned by several internal and external factors such as business environment uncertainty, competition in the business area, organisation complexity, organisation size, and monitoring by senior managers and directors. The research presented in [46] in a financial firm that used S&P's risk management rating found that having a reliable risk control system leads to effective organisational risk management. Likewise, [47] emphasises that the organisations where their Chief Executive Officers (CEO) pay more attention to the importance of risk and have an inclination towards effective risk management are more likely to employ Chief Risk Officers (CRO) and develop appropriate risk governance. Nonetheless, [48] outline factors such as an organisation's size, type of ownership, income and profitability, leverage, and CRO employment as significant determinants that influence effective ERM implementation. Similarly, [49] argues that CRO appointment is a prerequisite of effective ERM implementation.

Although the concept of ERM has evolved significantly over recent years a review of existing subject literature reveals the ineffectiveness of current ERM practices in protecting enterprise value. Existing literature on ERM includes some studies that have focused on different dimensions of ERM. For instance, several research works, such as [14][38][47][50], explore the factors that lead organisations to decide to implement ERM. Others, such as [10][49][51], evaluate the approaches of ERM implementation. Moreover, researchers such as [3][8][15], [17][33][38][50] evaluate the effect of ERM implementation on organisations' value. Most of these researchers agree that ERM is stuck at its development stage and moving forward from this stage to become the driving force of organisational value and effectiveness requires more research and understanding. In fact, though the importance of ERM and its strategic role in organisations' objective achievement has been admitted by previous researchers, the question of how the implementation of ERM can yield to organisations' sustainability and increased value, still needs more attention. For instance, research carried out by [4] found a positive relation between ERM adoption and organisational value through empirical investigation in 649 firms from 2004 to 2013, however, in this investigation, ERM is mostly considered as a close internal control activity rather than a risk management practice.

COSO [52], as one of the most common ERM practices, positions ERM in the context of strategy by emphasising that ERM needs to be "applied in [a] strategy setting" in order to "provide reasonable assurance regarding the achievement of entity objectives". Indeed, COSO highlights that ERM needs to be integrated into organisations' strategic initiatives [10]. Risks are changing continually, and this brings both challenges and opportunities for organisations regarding the achievement of their strategic objectives [53][54]. Therefore, a continuous risk oversight is required as an evolving process for a critical assessment to provide updated information regarding emerging risks that might be considered as opportunities or threats towards an organisation in accomplishing its strategic objectives and ultimate goals. Hence, the output of an organisation's ERM process should be used as an input for its strategic planning [53][55]. Despite this view, survey-based studies show that focus on strategic risks in organisations' ERM process has been narrow and limited. For instance, a study by Gates [44], which is now over a decade old, concludes that only 16% of organisations under investigation have aligned ERM and strategic planning.

Moreover, [51] carried out a survey that concluded 36% of surveyed organisations do not have any process for monitoring and identifying strategic risks. [51] have come to understand from a large sample of participants (who are seniors and executives) that ERM's strategic role is more effective when an organisation has a risk management committee, regular risk management training, a centrally updated risk system, and link among risk management and executive compensation. Research done by [20] focuses on high-level participants working in financial reporting process of 11 organisations. Based on [2] findings, Chief Financial Officers (CFOs) and members of audit committees pay much more attention to strategic risk management than do auditors. It was concluded that this is due to responsibilities being taken by seniors and directors versus auditors. Much progress has been made in managing risk, however, intervention to date has only moderated the siloed and reactive practice of managing risks and draws fundamental criticism. In the same vein, previous literature indicated limitations.

While adoption of ERM is an approach to lower risk or to exploit opportunities, practice shows that one does not always leverage the expected results (unfit for purpose) [24][49]. Henceforth, it is believed that currently, ERM does not suffice an organisation's needs. Consequently, the stakes and risk-return have become considerably higher and broader in scope. Recent years have shown that organisations are more and more concerned about finding a catalyst for risk foresight, thus exerting higher pressure to create holistic risk governance to predict risks [56]. Attaining enterprise-wide risk governance is a complex issue requiring the alignment of multiple functions and ramifications of an organisation. The problem is that the relational mechanism that manages risks and aligns with the business is missing or is partially applied/decentralised, and thus the risk is managed reactively and randomly, and most often it omits to correlate all functions.

Even though risk governance efficiency has been improved recently, in many financial organisations, the benefits derived from ERM are not fully gained. This represents a mismanagement of risk, a siloed approach, duplication of risk management outlay, misuse of resources, duplication of effort and time, and/or inefficient capital allocation.

Indeed, it is concluded from literature that organisations acknowledge the importance of ERM alignment with business strategy. However, the implementation of this alignment has remained a challenge for senior managers. The factors and challenges of failure of this alignment have not been investigated in depth. Additionally, existing researchers do not provide ERM champions' insight that can help to better understand the efforts required to be able to align ERM with strategy.

Moreover, the immaturity of ERM has encouraged an extension and incorporation of its principles and GRC [24]. GRC compounds different disciplines (governance, risk and compliance), which were initially adopted to deal with IS/IT management [57] and later evolved to 'incorporate' GRC. Perceived as an advancement of an organisation's risk capability, with the aim of synchronising strategy, processes, technology, and people to enable organisations to function more efficiently [34][58]. GRC not only supports achieving an organisation's objective, but also addresses uncertainty and integrity at a strategic level [26][59]. A lot of available evidence highlights that GRC is driven by principles of (G) 'directing, controlling and evaluating', (R) 'managing processes and resource', and (C) 'proving fulfilment of requirements' [24][59][60].

Evidence shows that GRC emerged within industry practices because specific software systems were adopted. Besides, laws and guidelines such Sarbanes Oxley Act (SOX) and Basel II, among others, recommend adoption [61][62] and proliferation of systems vendors and thus innovation and propulsion of the domain. The term was initially proposed by PricewaterhouseCoopers in 2004 [61] as an automated solution. Moreover, frameworks such as OCEG Capability Model further promote GRC practices.

The discussion above enables an understanding of risk practices evolution in terms of strategic approaches. Furthermore, Figure 1 compares the risk philosophy and the centrality of each approach towards risk mitigation and resiliency.

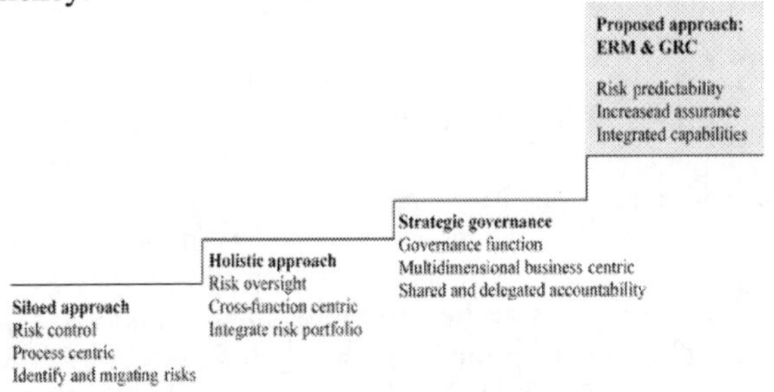

Figure 1. Conceptual risk mitigation evolution

As Figure 1 above illustrates, the approaches dealing with risks and threats have evolved in terms of practice. Both ERM and GRC disciplines are recognised within industry practices [63]. Even though ERM has been extensively researched both theoretically and empirically, GRC shows signs of being significantly adopted by practitioners [61], [64].

Confusion in terms of what ERM and GRC can offer to organisations has been highlighted since early 2013 by the empirical findings of the Institute of Internal Auditors Research Foundation (IIARF) [63]. It has been found that 60% of respondents perceive GRC as an umbrella for ERM, while the other 40% was unable to differentiate between the concepts. Referring to GRC as an umbrella function, Von [64] states that GRC sets the tone through its normative basis (rules, principles, conventions, roles). ERM applies the descriptive normative basis of GRC model in process and structure to address the mitigation response directly, cohesively, and holistically. In this regard, it explores why ERM encounter challenges and drawbacks in practice given that there is significant theory in place. This shall be done through the lens of interviews with ERM managers, discussed in Section 4, to complement the existing open debate found within literature and to explore ERM's immaturity.

III. METHODOLOGY

The research approach is qualitative and aims to explore challenges and drawbacks of ERM, whilst exploring the paradigm shift towards GRC.

Evaluating prior research allowed the authors of this paper to create a list of main concepts relevant to the research questions. Exploration of the phenomenon was driven by the need to understand the current state of ERM, challenges of ERM and strategy alignment, and key factors for enterprise-wide implementation. Data was obtained from 15 upper management individuals from UK small-medium enterprises organisations, who either were involved in the adoption or implementation process with ERM. Also, another important aspect in sample selection was the respondents' years of experience.

The primary data was analyzed through Nvivo software and thematic analysis.

IV. RESEARCH FINDINGS

The research findings are grouped to respond to the three main questions below:

(1) - What is the state of ERM and business strategy alignment?
(2) - What are the challenges of ERM and strategy alignment?
(3) - What are the organisational factors/initiatives critical for this alignment?

The following subsections illustrate the key findings of the research.

A. *Maturity of ERM Alignment with Strategy*

The majority of the interviewed participants stated that their ERM alignment with strategic planning is limited and that ERM needs to be considered as a bigger part of an organisation's strategic planning. Others agreed on the limitation of ERM alignment with strategy, but they mentioned signs of recent growth.

Few participants stated that ERM is not properly aligned with strategic management as those in strategic planning sectors do not pay enough attention to insights provided by those in the ERM process even though they should. They stated that if organisations would like to achieve their ultimate objectives, they need to consider the result of ERM process in their strategic planning. Indeed, organisations need to employ the outcomes of their ERM process as input for their strategic planning.

It was discussed by a few participants that different organisational departments mostly seek ERM when making decisions related to compliance matters. Indeed, the fact that ERM can support organisational strategic decisions and yield to value creation is admitted yet ignored in practice. Few others stated that ERM and strategy are still being dealt with separately and in silos. Organisations' seniors claim that they align ERM with strategic planning but in practice these two are not integrated and risks are managed in silos. This is because seniors do not know how to align ERM with the organisation's strategy in practice. Three participants mentioned that ERM was recently aligned in the process of strategic planning, and then the outcomes of ERM are considered in strategic planning in a way that risk reports written by ERM committee affect the strategic decisions of their organisation.

Key Findings

Most of the participants discussed that, in theory, ERM is considered an important part of their organisation's strategic planning, but alignment is not strong enough. In fact, organisations adopt ERM mostly to respond to policies insisted upon by regulators and rating agencies. It seems that senior managers also struggle to understand the concept of ERM and the benefits of ERM alignment with organisational strategies and to find appropriate techniques for effective ERM alignment within the context of business strategy in practice. In some organisations, ERM might be considered more as an initiative of compliance than strategy.

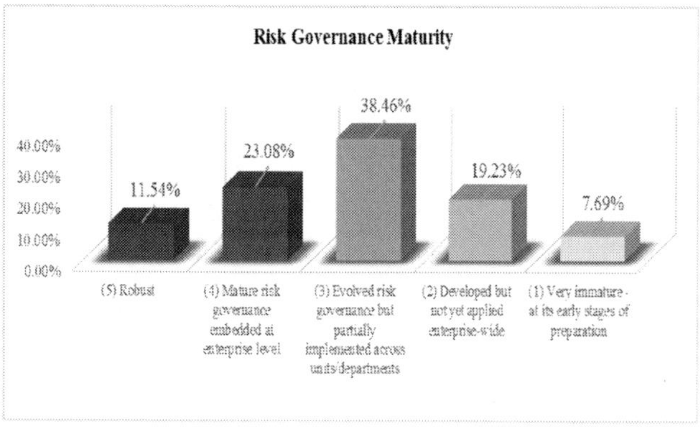

Figure 2. ERM maturity

As shown in Figure 2, 38.46% of respondents consider that risk governance is evolved but, partially implemented across units/departments (3). 23.08% state that mature risk governance is embedded at an enterprise level (4). 19.23% of respondents define maturity as developed, but not yet applied enterprise-wide (2), whilst only 11.54% declared themselves to be robust (5).

The next section segregates findings into two paths, A) challenges of ERM and strategy alignment and B) critical factors in ERM and strategy alignment.

A) Challenges of ERM and Strategy Alignment

While almost all the research participants agreed on the benefits of ERM implementation and its alignment with business strategy, most of them stated that their organisations are struggling with challenges associated with effective ERM implementation and its successful alignment with strategic planning.

Senior Managers' Support

Most of the interviewees considered the lack of senior managers' proper understanding of ERM concepts and benefits as well as appropriate knowledge of right principles as two challenging issues.

Interviewees stated that implementation and success of any new managerial process need strong backing of boards and senior managers. Nonetheless, they argued that their seniors do not support this alignment strongly enough due to poor understanding of ERM benefits and inadequate knowledge regarding approaches of ERM and strategy alignment.

Organisation Culture

The existence of a silo risk mindset was also stated by the vast majority of participants as a challenge of this alignment. Interviewees discussed that though ERM is progressively finding its place in organisations, a silo mindset of risk management remains a challenge for effective ERM implementation in organisations. Participants argued that, if a new process or function is being applied in the organisation, that function's culture also needs to be integrated along with the process itself. Seniors in many organisations still believe that risks are confidential and should not be communicated among different organisational layers because of security issues.

Another cultural issue mentioned by few participants was that people who hold top-level responsibility for specific tasks do not normally like to share their weaknesses and seek help. One reason might be the fear of losing power and position if others realize that they are not able to solve the upcoming problems.

Centralised Framework for ERM

Another issue discussed by one particular research participant was the lack of an appropriate, centralised and formal ERM approach that should be followed by organisations' C suites. Moreover, other participants mentioned the lack of extensive training regarding the benefits of ERM implementation and its influence on the achievement of business objectives. Interviewees discussed those organisations mostly take an informal approach to implement ERM, and they do not appoint a wide range of training on appropriate ERM implementation and the ultimate benefit it could yield. This prevents the effectiveness of ERM and hinders understanding of the necessity of ERM alignment with business strategy.

Fit of ERM into Organisation Structure

It was discussed by the interviewees that choosing the right ERM process to effectively fit into an organisation's current structure has been one of the challenges faced by ERM champions. They argued that when their organisations are called by regulators or rating agencies for ERM adoption, senior managers just rush to respond as fast as possible. Many organisations adopt one of the common existing ERM approaches/standards without examining its applicability in that specific organisation's structure. This leads to choosing and implementing a process used by other organisations without considering the difference in terms of many issues such as context, size, structure, etc. Indeed, it was believed by the participants that picking the right ERM process to fit an organisation's situation is the foundation of its efficiency yet is often overlooked.

Reluctance and Resistance to Change

The unwillingness to change in different business managerial sections was considered challenging by more than two-thirds of interviewees. Several interviews showed that top managers who are responsible for business strategic planning are not willing to let ERM oversight affect their process. ERM champions consider this process as strategic, but other initiatives view ERM as compliance-focused. This hinders the effective alignment of ERM and strategy.

Some others commented that sometimes managers are reluctant to accept and move towards change due to their weak understanding of new concepts. On the other hand, employees would not like to do more tasks than the ones they already do. This is because they do not consider themselves a part of the business and its success. Consequently, they prefer to apply minimum effort.

Risk Centralisation

Lack of appropriate ERM structure along with reliable and unbiased risk data among entire organisations' layers was another challenge mentioned by almost half of the participants. Interviewees argued that in order to have effective ERM implementation, organisations need to build a proper ERM committee that continually updates the system with reliable risks reports. Unfortunately, many organisations do not have a centralised risk system, which in turn makes it difficult to identify and manage organisational risks in time. It was evidenced that an accurate risk data system in an organisation is a crucial factor to understand the overall risk profile.

Participants further discussed that, for effective ERM and strategy alignment, organisations need to create (and continually update) a systematic list of key risk drivers identified by ERM processes based on the organisation's strategic objectives.

Real-world Alignment Guidance

A lack of practical guidance on how to align ERM and strategic planning was discussed by most of the participants. Indeed, several interviewees stated that having a practical guidance on how to align ERM process with their organisation strategic planning is a challenge and needs to be viewed accordingly. In fact, C suites need guidelines on how to shift from alignment theories (explored through several pieces of research) to practice. There is a need for a step-by-step implementation guide to enable the organisation to implement this alignment effectively.

B) Critical Factors in ERM and Strategy Alignment

After discussing the challenges of effective ERM alignment with strategy, research participants were asked to discuss the critical elements influencing the maturity of this alignment. A vast majority of interviewees considered strong support of senior management as a critical factor for effective ERM and strategy alignment. Almost all of the participants stated that if ERM does not receive strong support from senior managers, it becomes a risky process itself, losing its sustainability over time. This research revealed a lack of senior management involvement in organisations' effective ERM development due to a poor understanding of ERM's benefits pertaining to an organisation's sustainability and lack of sufficient knowledge regarding the effective implementation of ERM. Senior managers of many organisations do not have the necessary knowledge of risk management. They might be able to take basic steps of ERM implementation through using available universal risk management frameworks/standards, however, when it comes to critical stages of the process, there is severe need for an expert team with related skills and experience appears.

Therefore, in addition to the strong support needed from board directors, delegating a Chief Risk Officer (CRO) is also one of the most important factors of ERM and strategic alignment. The CRO is the most appropriate person and with relevant knowledge, skills, and experience to take responsibility of tackling these challenges; respectively, to execute, monitor, and ensure the effectiveness of organisational ERM process.

Another critical factor identified by the research participants is their organisation's culture. It is recognised that ERM awareness has been increasing over the years. However, in practice, organisations are still following their old ways of dealing with organisational risks. In order to have successful ERM and effectively align it with business strategy, organisations need to change their risk management culture proactively. The findings suggest that alignment of all managerial functions shall ensure holistic and collaborative oversight across business units, avoiding silos, as well as understanding at the enterprise level which areas need improvements.

Furthermore, participants considered 'ERM Bases' and 'Knowledge Management' as critical factors for overcoming the lack of ERM structure and lack of systematic reliable risk data. Participants explained that to have a successful ERM implementation, organisations first require 'ERM Bases'. This means developing organisational effective risk structures, policies and procedures, and a business continuity plan in order to enhance risk management capabilities. Secondly, it is necessary to have good 'Knowledge Management' to increase the understanding of businesses' emerging risks and thus support organisations' risk decision making. Other research works, such as [54][55][65]-[67], also demonstrate that 'ERM Bases' and 'Knowledge Management' are considered a strategic resource, increasing the success and sustainability of organisational risk management. 'ERM Base' helps C suites to build robust ERM infrastructure, leading to advance risk oversight, risk identification, and risk mitigation. 'Knowledge Management' adds value to organisations by achieving positive outcomes through systematically coordinating organisations' structure, people, technology, and the process. Individual's judgement can fail to foresee and recognise emerging risks as uncertainty is created. Knowledge sharing has an important influence on avoiding emerging risks and enables C suites to recognise risks associated with their strategic business objectives.

Literature has identified that much progress has been made in managing risk. However, intervention to date has only moderated the siloed and reactive practice of managing risk and draws fundamental criticism. Whilst it highlights the role of ERM, key benefits, and critical success factors, it continues to recommend a unified risk oversight. Nonetheless, within the applicability of ERM, the interview respondents stated that senior managers fail to understand ERM benefits. Nevertheless, literature also shows drawbacks in implementation (e.g., people expertise, training, culture, etc.), thus highlighting the rationale of practitioners that already adopt the GRC principles. Findings from both the empirical evidence (semi-structured interviews) and the literature review articulate that risk demands organisations to protect themselves proactively from greater risks. When GRC is adopted, the traditional ERM approach is integrated not only to ensure protection, but also to ensure performance and compliance assurance [59].

This research explored how ERM is perceived and what renders adoption and implementation, both in theory and practice. Table 1 below summarizes key findings from interviews and demonstrates that ERM has strategic, cultural and technical implications.

TABLE 1. SUMMARY OF KEY FINDINGS

What is the state of ERM and business strategy alignment?	Alignment is not strong enough
What are the challenges of ERM and strategy alignment?	Senior Managers' Support Organisation Culture Centralised Framework for ERM Fit of ERM into Organisation Structure Reluctance and Resistance to Change Risk Centralisation Real-world Alignment Guidance
What are the organisational factors/initiatives critical for this alignment?	Strong support of senior management Delegating a chief risk officer (CRO) Organisation's culture 'ERM Bases' and 'Knowledge Management' Knowledge sharing

As emphasized above, the governance, management, and assurance functions of GRC seem not only appropriate, but also imperative for enhancing an organisation' long-term resiliency and viability.

V. CONCLUSION AND FUTURE WORK

This paper demonstrates that ERM maturity has yet to achieve its maximum. It presents evidence on deviations and the way in which organisations align risk functions remains a current challenge. Risks are continually evolving and the interrelated ramifications are thus increasing. Therefore, this research presents convincing arguments and contributes to the understanding of why the value proposition of ERM was not achieved due to various impediments in implementation, such as senior managers' support, organisational culture, centralised framework/ERM approaches and training, the appropriate fit of ERM into the organisation's structure, reluctance and resistance to change, appropriate ERM structure, central reliable risk data system and practical alignment guidance.

Additionally, this paper explores the ambiguity regarding ERM's successful factors, as investigated through the literature review and semi-structured interviews. The findings suggest that ERM needs to be consciously acknowledged in terms of its current level of maturity because there is evidence that organisations struggle with challenges associated with effective ERM implementation. As a result, the integrated approach of ERM is insufficient in today's business context. Therefore, in light of drawbacks regarding ERM implementation, the GRC paradigm is understood to cover an organisation's needs more efficiently. Despite the substantial focus on ERM value proposition and control, the extended risk oversight of GRC challenges the effectiveness of the ERM school of thought. As an all-encompassing strategic function, GRC plays a supervisory role (governance) that integrates both RM function and risk compliance function (audit). This undeniably better positions an organisation for ensuring improved performance, viability, and resiliency.

In conclusion, this research contributes to academia and the industry by shedding a contemporary light on the current state of literature and practice while suggesting an update to the body of knowledge that incorporates the lens of ERM and GRC. As such, GRC can play an important role in addressing the issue and ensuring maximisation in achieving organisational strategy, vision, and mission as well as helping to reduce/prevent the deficiencies of siloed controls, thus strengthening an organisation's security posture and building enterprise-wide risk resiliency and foresight of risks.

However, despite such advancement, more research is needed to determine the practicality of the alignment of ERM with GRC as a solution for risk complexity and challenges encountered by organisations.

REFERENCES

[1] I. J. Dabari, S. F. Kwaji and M. Z. Ghazali, "Aligning Corporate Governance with Enterprise Risk Management Adoption in the Nigerian Deposit Money Banks", *Indian-Pacific Journal of Accounting and Finance*, 1(2), pp. 4-14, 2017.

[2] J. Cohen, G. Krishnamoorthy and A.Wright, "Enterprise risk management and the financial reporting process: The experiences of audit committee members, CFOs, and external

auditors", *Contemporary Accounting Research*, 34(2), pp. 1178-1209, 2017.

[3] M. K. Shad, F. Lai, C. L. Fatt, J. J. Klemeš, and A. Bokhari, "Integrating sustainability reporting into enterprise risk management and its relationship with business performance: A conceptual framework", *Journal of Cleaner Production*, 2008, pp. 415-425, 2019.

[4] J. R. Silva, A. F. D. Silva, and B. L. Chan, "Enterprise Risk Management and Firm Value: Evidence from Brazil", *Emerging Markets Finance and Trade*, 55(3), pp. 687-703, 2019.

[5] A. Althonayan, J. Keith and A. Misiura, "Aligning enterprise risk management with business strategy and information systems", *in European, Mediterranean & Middle Eastern Conference on Information Systems 2011*, Athens, Greece p. 109-129, 2011.

[6] G. Mensah and W. Gottwald, "Enterprise Risk Management: factors associated with effective implementation", *Risk Governance and Control: Financial Markets & Institutions*, 6(4), 2016.

[7] M. Majdalawieh and J. Gammack, "An Integrated Approach to Enterprise Risk: Building a Multidimensional Risk Management Strategy for the Enterprise", *International Journal of Scientific Research and Innovative Technology*, 4(2), pp.95-114, 2017.

[8] J. Sax and T. J. Andersen, "Making Risk Management Strategic: Integrating Enterprise Risk Management with Strategic Planning*", European Management Review*, 2018.

[9] T. R. Viscelli, D. R. Hermanson and M.S. Beasley, "The integration of ERM and strategy: implications for corporate governance", *American Accounting Association*, 31 (2), pp. 69-82. doi: 10.2308/acch-51692, 2017.

[10] S. P. Saeidi, S. Sofian, M. Nilashi, and A Mardani, "The impact of enterprise risk management on competitive advantage by moderating role of information technology", *Computer Standards & Interfaces*, 63, pp. 67-82, 2019.

[11] N. Andrén and S. Lundqvist, "Incentive Based Dimensions of Enterprise Risk Management", *SSRN Electronic Journal*, pp. 1-48, 2017.

[12] V. Stein and A. Wiedemann, "Risk governance: conceptualization, tasks, and research agenda", *Journal of Business Economics*, 86(8), pp.813-836, 2016.

[13] G. Mensah and W. Gottwald, *Enterprise Risk Management: Effective Implementatio*n, 2016.

[14] J. Ogutu, M. R. Bennett and R. Olawoyin, "Closing the Gap: Between Traditional and Enterprise Risk Management Systems", *Professional Safety*, 63(04), pp. 42-47, 2018.

[15] L.A. Gordon, M. P. Loeb, and C. Tseng, "Enterprise risk management and firm performance: A contingency perspective", *Journal of Accounting and Public Policy*, 28(4), pp. 301-327, 2009.

[16] A. Fox and M. S. Epstein, "Why Is Enterprise Risk Management (ERM) Important for Preparedness?", *Risk and Insurance Management Society*, 2010.

[17] R. E. Hoyt and A. P. Liebenberg, "The value of enterprise risk management", *Journal of Risk and Insurance*, 78(4), pp. 795-822 2011.

[18] J. DeLoach (2012) "Integrate the ERM Process With What Matters. Corporate Compliance Insights".[Online]. Available: http://www.corporatecomplianceinsights.com/integrate-the-erm-process-with-what-matters

[19] J. DeLoach, (2013), "10 Questions You Should Ask About Risk Management. Corporate Compliance Insights".[Online]. Available at: http://www.corporatecomplianceinsights.com/ten-questions-you-should-ask-about-risk-management/

[20] J. L. Keith, "Enterprise risk management: developing a strategic ERM alignment framework-Finance sector." PhD diss., Brunel University London, 2014.

[21] P. Bromiley, M. McShane, A. Nair and E. Rustambekov, "Enterprise risk management: review, critique, and research directions", *Long Range Planning Journal*, 48(4), pp. 265-276. doi: 10.1016/j.lrp.2014.07.005, 2015.

[22] C. Florio and G. Leoni, "Enterprise risk management and firm performance: The Italian case2, *The British Accounting Review*, 49(1), pp. 56-74, 2017.

[23] M. Matin, "Alignment of ERM with performance management: the case study of automotive industry". PhD diss., Brunel University London, 2017.

[24] R. Agarwal and J. Ansell, "Strategic Change in Enterprise Risk Management", *Strategic Change*, 25(4), pp.427-439, 2016.

[25] American Institute of Certified Public Accountants (AICPA), "2017 the state of risk oversight: an overview of enterprise risk management practices". [Online]. Available: http://www.aicpa.org/InterestAreas/BusinessIndustryAndGovernment/Resources/ERM/DownloadableDocuments/AICPA_ERM_Research_Study_2017.pdf, 2017.

[26] J. Ai, V. Bajtelsmit, and T. Wang, "The combined effect of enterprise risk management and diversification on property and casualty insurer performance", *Journal of Risk and Insurance*, 85(2), pp. 513-543, 2018.

[27] K. K. Alawattegama, "The Impact of Enterprise Risk Management on Firm Performance: Evidence from Sri Lankan Banking and Finance Industry", *International Journal of Business and Management*, 13(1), pp. 225, 2017.

[28] K. Dornberger, S. Oberlehner ans N. Zadrazil, "Challenges in implementing enterprise risk management". *ACRN Journal of Finance and Risk Perspectives*, 3(3), pp. 1-14, 2014.

[29] I. Jonek-Kowalska, "Efficiency of Enterprise Risk Management (ERM) systems. Comparative analysis in the fuel sector and energy sector on the basis of Central-European companies listed on the Warsaw Stock Exchange", *Resources Policy*, 62, pp.405-415, 2009.

[30] F. Fraser and B. Simkins, "The challenges of and solutions for implementing enterprise risk management", *Business Horizons*, 59(6), pp. 689-698. doi: 10.1016/j.bushor.2016.06.007, 2016.

[31] M. Beasley, B. Branson, and B. Hancock, "Current State of Enterprise Risk Oversight and Market Perceptions of COSO's ERM Framework". [Online]. Available: https://www.coso.org/Documents/COSO-Survey-Report-FULL-Web-R6-FINAL-for-WEB-POSTING-111710.pdf, 2010.

[32] D. Kerstin, O. Simone and Z. Nicole, "Challenges in implementing enterprise risk management", *ACRN Journal of Finance and Risk Perspectives*, 3(3), pp. 1-14, 2014.

[33] G. Aras, N. Tezcan, and O. K Furtuna, "Multidimensional comprehensive corporate sustainability performance evaluation model: Evidence from an emerging market banking sector", *Journal of Cleaner Production*, 185, pp. 600-609, 2018.

[34] R. Gupta, "Efficient operation of GRC processing platforms", 2008.

[35] M. Matin, "Alignment of ERM with performance management: the case study of automotive industry". PhD diss., Brunel University London, 2017.

[36] S. A. Lundqvist, "Why firms implement risk governance – Stepping beyond traditional risk management to enterprise risk management", *Journal of Accounting and Public Policy*, 34(5), pp.441-466, 2015.

[37] A. Althonayan, J. Keith, and A. Misiura, "Aligning ERM with Corporate and Business Strategies". Birmingham: British Academy of Management, 2011b.

[38] M. S. Beasley, R. Clune and D. R. Hermanson, "Enterprise risk management: An empirical analysis of factors associated with the extent of implementation", *Journal of Accounting and Public Policy*, 24(6), pp. 521-531, 2005.

[39] İ. Kaya, "Perspectives on Internal Control and Enterprise Risk Management", in Eurasian Business Perspectives. Springer, pp. 379-389, 2018.

[40] T. Aven, Risk management and governance. Heidelberg: Springer, 2010.

[41] M. A., Hofmann, "Interest in enterprise risk management is growing", *Business Insurance*, 43(18), pp. 14-16, 2009.

[42] P. Burnaby and S. Hass, "Ten steps to enterprise-wide risk management", *Corporate Governance*: The international journal of business in society, 9(5), pp. 539-550, 2009.

[43] S. Francis and T. Richards, "Why ERM matters and how to accelerate progress", *Risk Management*, pp. 28, 2007.

[44] S. Gates, "Incorporating strategic risk into enterprise risk management: a survey of current corporate practice", *Journal of Applied Corporate Finance*, 18(4), pp. 81-90. doi: 10.1111/j.1745-6622.2006.00114.x, 2006.

[45] P. Bromiley, M. McShane, A. Nair and E. Rustambekov, "Enterprise risk management: review, critique, and research directions", *Long Range Planning Journal*, 48(4), pp. 265-276. doi: 10.1016/j.lrp.2014.07.005, 2015.

[46] M. K. McShane, A Nair, and E. Rustambekov, "Does enterprise risk management increase firm value?", *Journal of Accounting, Auditing and Finance*, 26(4), pp. 641–658. doi: 10.1177/0148558x11409160, 2011.

[47] D. Pagach and R. Warr, "The characteristics of firms that hire chief risk officers", *The Journal of Risk and Insurance*, 78(1), pp.185-211, 2011.

[48] A. R. Razali, A. S. Yazid, and I. M. Tahir, "The determinants of enterprise risk management (ERM) practices in Malaysian public listed companies", *Journal of Social and Development Sciences*, 1(5), pp. 202-207, 2011.

[49] J. Ai, P.L. Brockett and T. Wang, "Optimal enterprise risk management and decision making with shared and dependent risks", *Journal of Risk and Insurance*, 84(4), pp. 1127-1169, 2017.

[50] R. Baxter, J. C. Bedard, R. Hoitash, and A.Yezegel, "Enterprise risk management program quality: Determinants, value relevance, and the financial crisis", *Contemporary Accounting Research*, 30(4), pp. 1264-1295, 2013.

[51] M. Beasley, B. Branson, and D. Pagach, "An analysis of the maturity and strategic impact of investments in ERM", *Journal of Accounting and Public Policy*, 34 (1), pp. 219-243, 2015.

[52] Committee on National Security Systems, Enterprise Risk Management (COSO)—Integrated Framework 92014).[Online].Available: https://www.coso.org/documents/coso-erm-executive-summary.pdf

[53] T. R. Viscelli, D. R. Hermanson, and M.S. Beasley, "The integration of ERM and strategy: implications for corporate governance", *American Accounting Association*, 31 (2), pp. 69-82. doi: 10.2308/acch-51692, 2017.

[54] N. Manab, S. Othman and I. Kassim, "Enterprise-wide risk management best practices: The critical success factors", 2012.

[55] N. Manab and N. Aziz, "Integrating knowledge management in sustainability risk management practices for company survival", *Management Science Letters*, 9(4), pp. 585-594, 2019.

[56] B. L. Handoko, I. E. Riantono and E. Gani, "Importance and Benefit of Application of Governance Risk and Compliance Principle", *Systematic Reviews in Pharmacy*, 11(9), pp.510-513, 2020.

[57] N. Mayer and D. De Smet, "Systematic Literature Review and ISO Standards analysis to Integrate IT Governance and Security Risk Management", *International Journal for Infonomics*, 10(1), pp.1255-1263, 2017.

[58] N. Racz, E. Weippl, and A. Seufert, "A frame of reference for research of integrated governance, risk and compliance (GRC)". In IFIP International Conference on Communications and Multimedia Security (pp. 106-117). Springer, Berlin, Heidelberg, 2010.

[59] Open Compliance and Ethics Group (OCEG) "GRC capability model: version 3.0". [Online].Available: https://go.oceg.org/grc-capability-model-red-book, 2013.

[60] K. Oliveira, M. Méxas, M. Meiriño and G. Drumond, "Critical success factors associated with the implementation of enterprise risk management", *Journal of Risk Research*, pp.1-16, 2018.

[61] A. Papazafeiropoulou and K. Spanaki, "Understanding governance, risk and compliance information systems (GRC IS): The experts view", *Information Systems Frontiers*, 18(6), pp.1251-1263, 2015.

[62] G. Miller, The Law of Governance, Risk Management, and Compliance.New York: Wolters Kluwer, 2017.

[63] The Institute of Internal Auditors Research Foundation (IIARF) "Contrasting GRC and ERM: perceptions and practices among internal auditors", 2013.

[64] M. van Asselt and O. Renn "Risk governance", *Journal of Risk Research*, 14(4), 431-449, doi: 10.1080/13669877.2011.553730, 2011.

[65] P. Massingham, "Knowledge risk management: a framework", *Journal of knowledge management*, 14(3), pp. 464-485, 2010.

[66] A. Mikes and R. S. Kaplan, "When one size doesn't fit all: Evolving directions in the research and practice of enterprise risk management", *Journal of Applied Corporate Finance*, 27(1), pp. 37-40, 2015.

[67] T. Palermo, M. Power and S. Ashby, "Navigating institutional complexity: The production of risk culture in the financial sector", *Journal of Management Studies*, 54(2), pp. 154-181, 2017.

A High-Performance Solution for Data Security and Traceability in Civil Production and Value Networks through Blockchain

Erik Neumann
Faculty Applied Computer Sciences and Biosciences
University of Applied Sciences Mittweida
Mittweida, Germany
e-mail: neumann3@hs-mittweida.de

Kilian Armin Nölscher
Department Digitalization in Production
Fraunhofer IWU
Chemnitz, Germany
e-mail: kilian.noelscher@iwu.fraunhofer.de

Gordon Lemme
Department Digital Production Twin
Fraunhofer IWU
Dresden, Germany
e-mail: gordon.lemme@iwu.fraunhofer.de

Adrian Singer
Department Digitalization in Production
Fraunhofer IWU
Chemnitz, Germany
e-mail: adrian.singer@iwu.fraunhofer.de

***Abstract*—This paper presents a blockchain-based solution for secure distribution of product, process and machine data across value networks. The data is stored in a high-performance private blockchain, which is a self-development as part of the federal funded project "safe-UR-chain". The infrastructure is secured by design through distributed ledger with a selectable consensus mechanism. In addition to the architectural overview of the concept, a system evaluation follows based on machine tool data.**

Keywords—Private Blockchain; Data Security; Traceability; Value Chain.

I. Introduction

Both, vertical and horizontal value chains have been increasingly threatened by cybercrime, sabotage and industrial espionage in recent years. The German Federal Criminal Police Office identified a total of 82,649 cases of cybercrime in the narrower sense (+80.5% compared to the previous year) in Germany. Studies by the digital association Bitkom and the Federal Office for the Protection of the Constitution (BfV) estimate an annual damage of 55 billion Euros for the German economy due to cybercrime, its consequences and defense measures. Of around 1,000 companies surveyed in Germany, 53% said they had been affected by cybercrime in the last two years, with the proportion of affected companies increasing steadily with company size (60% for 500+ employees) [1]. The origin of these crimes ranges from own or former employees, competitors to organized crime. Due to the general drive towards digitalization, this trend will continue in the future, posing an enormous threat to the civil infrastructure. As a countermeasure to this development, simply improving IT security step by step, e.g., by "hardening" software, is not enough. The project "safe-UR-chain" [2] researches new solutions for the described challenges.

A. Motivation

The basic protection objectives for digital communication include confidentiality, integrity, and availability [3]. There are numerous approaches to guaranteeing these, but in the past it has not been possible to implement these objectives with appropriate solutions in such a holistic way that they are applied across the board in operational practice. Communication between networked systems can be protected, e.g., by means of "end-to-end encryption". Production-specific data can also be encrypted to ensure confidentiality. This already poses an increasing dilemma when it comes to designing data-transparent value creation networks across company boundaries. Companies, especially Small and Medium-sized Enterprises (SMEs), are also increasingly having to make use of cloud solutions to maintain availability, as these guarantee high availability, which would only be possible as an in-house solution with cost-intensive effort. This service provided by third-party providers is in competition with real-time requirements and confidentiality aspects. What is not taken into account here is data integrity, i.e., ensuring that stored data is correct. This goes hand in hand with a less strong protection goal of so-called non-repudiation (bindingness). Here, it is important to design communications in such a way that they are indisputable to a third party in retrospect.

This means that value networks consisting of production and logistics lack a practical, encrypted, traceable and tamper-proof solution for storing production-related data. Currently, production-relevant data is stored by various network nodes in a central database. Due to the already high and increasingly growing data density in the manufacturing industry, with simultaneous necessary data distribution and conditional data disclosure in distributed value chains, this approach appears to be increasingly disproportionate and impractical, especially for SMEs and with a lack of trust among the companies. Furthermore, future systems (machines, plants) will consist of a number of individual systems (control, measuring system, etc.), which is why new approaches are needed to save and synchronize the data recorded by the subsystems and, if necessary, to make it available to other applications within or outside the company.

In the field of transparent and tamper-proof data exchange and data storage, blockchain technology, as a representative of distributed ledger technologies, has become an increasingly relevant tool. By its very nature, a blockchain is a distributed stored linked list with the unique property that the addition of new data packets (blocks) is decided by a pseudo-democratic consensus process. The current main applications of blockchain technology are digital payment systems (e.g., Bitcoin [4]) and project financing. Due to their decentralized architecture and the consensus mechanisms used, these so-called public blockchains fulfill the requirements for availability and bindingness of the stored data. However, due to their lack of bandwidth, high costs and the fact that they are public, these public blockchains are unsuitable for practical use as storage locations for large and sensitive data volumes. Therefore, the use of so-called private blockchains, such as Hyperledger [5], is emerging in the enterprise environment. These differ in that access to them can be restricted. Furthermore, provided that the participating entities trust each other, a costly consensus algorithm for transaction verification can be avoided, thus significantly increasing bandwidth. The security properties of such a private blockchain (depending on the number of network nodes involved) is significantly lower compared to public blockchains [6].

B. Objectives

This motivation gave rise to the mentioned project "safe-UR-chain", whose backbone is a private blockchain with inherent protection mechanisms. This paper provides the description, design and testing of the same. The primary goal was to increase IT security beyond the current state of the art, while consuming few resources and providing a transferable concept for a wide range of applications. In the subsequent evaluation, the deployment in a value network will be considered. The result is thus the provision of a blockchain-based architecture for the traceable and tamper-proof storage of selected data in the private blockchain, without being bound to data models. In particular, the following data is relevant:

- relevant master data of both companies,
- process and sensor data of the plant,
- movement and quality data of the products along the production and
- product-related data for end customers.

After the presentation of motivation and objectives in the Section I, the further structure of the work is as follows: After Section II "Architectural overview" presents the blockchain system and explains how it is implemented, the Section III "Setup of the example scenario" follows, which provides a testbed for the overall system in an industrial environment that is as close to reality as possible. The insights gained from this are presented and evaluated in the Section IV "Evaluation", after which the Section V "Conclusion and Future Work" completes the paper.

II. Architectural overview

The primary purpose of the system is to store data in such a way that the integrity of individual records can be verified at a later date. To achieve this, the participating companies each use private blockchain networks that store both local records and block hashes from the blockchains of the other networks.

Each record goes through the same process until its existence at a certain point in time can be verified by all participating companies:

- intake of the data set
- distribution over the network
- inclusion into the blockchain
- "countersigning" by the other parties

This process is carried out on different layers of the system, these layers are the focus of this section.

A. Nodes

Nodes form the backbone of each local blockchain network. All of them perform basic tasks such as verifying cryptographic signatures and forwarding network messages - these essential tasks do not place high demands on the hardware. However, other tasks require either computational power or mass storage and are therefore implemented in a way that allows their use to be configurable. The node software is divided into several modules, as shown in Figure 1.

The **Ingest** module provides multiple interfaces for feeding data into the system. The simplest of which is a file ingest that watches a particular directory and reads the contents of all files that match the intake criteria (such as file name or type). This interface can be easily included into most existing systems since it only involves writing data to files. Other ingest interfaces can be added to this module, e.g., proprietary network based protocols that may already be used in some companies (see Section II-E). Within the ingest module, records are also extended with metadata and signed with the node's private key. All nodes are assigned a public/private key pair, which they use to sign data within the system. By using private/public key cryptography, each node gets a unique, verifiable identity. This signature can later be used to trace records back to their origin. This signed bundle of data is generally referred to as a transaction. It is passed on to the **Processing** module where a configurable amount of worker threads perform a multitude of parallelizable tasks that are relevant for the node's operation. These tasks include the creation and queuing of network messages, as well as the processing of incoming messages. The messages are sent and received by the **Networking** module. This module maintains a list of nodes in the network and establishes keep-alive connections to some of them over which data is sent to the network through the use of a flooding protocol [7]. Received and local transactions are bundled up

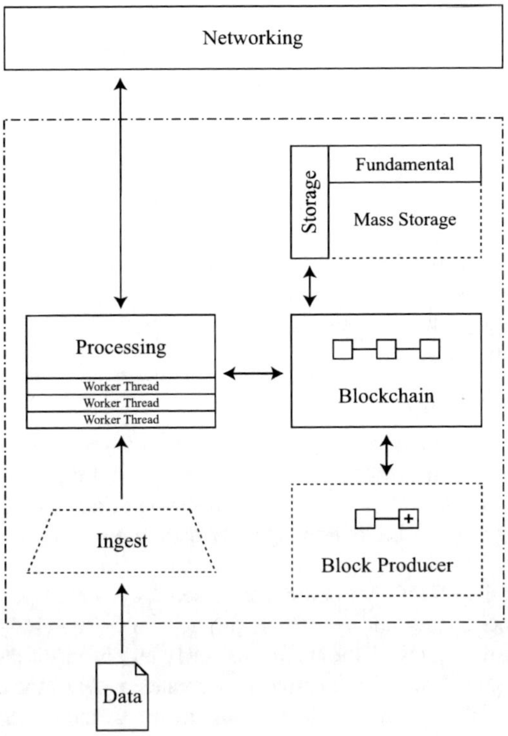

Figure 1. Software modules of a node; dashed lines indicate optional modules; the dash-dotted border signifies the system boundaries to other nodes and external data sources.

into blocks by nodes that have the **Block Producer** module enabled. The production of new blocks and their inclusion into the blockchain is governed by a generic interface that defines block validity and block work, which is used to decide upon the canonical (i.e., the "correct"/"longest" chain). Newly created blocks are then broadcast to the network and included in all nodes' blockchains. The transactions within these new blocks, are not necessarily stored on all nodes since this could use up the available storage on some of them. Instead, each node stores only the data that is absolutely necessary to verify the integrity of received data (i.e., block headers) and discards all other data based on a configurable filter. This way, the nodes' mass storage is only used for data that is relevant to their operation. Nodes that store *all* transaction data, can be used as archives within the network and can make this data quickly accessible to any program that consumes the node's API, e.g., GraphQL. By enabling only certain modules, four main node types can be created (see Table I). Using these types, the system can be integrated into existing infrastructures. E.g., in factories thin nodes can be used to ingest data from machine tools, Block Producers to add data into the blockchain and archive nodes for long term storage.

B. Blockchain

Within the system, each company uses a separate blockchain to store their own records, as well as data, which can later be used to verify the existence of remote records. Data is stored

TABLE I
NODE TYPES

	Networking & Blockchain	Block Creation	Mass Storage
Thin Node	yes	no	no
Block Producer	yes	yes	no
Archive	yes	no	yes
Full Node	yes	yes	yes

in a block by grouping transactions together into a merkle tree, by using this data structure the inclusion of single records in the blockchain can be proven by providing the block header, the merkle path, and the record itself [8]. This means that any future proof will only reveal the data in question, also proofs of this nature are efficient size wise, even if many records are stored in a particular block.

The `Block` structure itself only contains the fields `header` and `data` (see Figure 2), its hash is not included and will be calculated on each node individually. The hash is calculated by serializing and then hashing the block header, which includes the the root of the merkle tree.

```
struct Block {
header: BlockHeader,
data: MerkleTree,
}
```

Figure 2. Block data structure.

The block header (see Figure 3) contains all fields that are necessary to verify a block and place it in the blockchain. Additionally, it contains fields that can be used by the generic interface that governs block validity and block work (therefore the consensus mechanism), e.g., the `nonce` field can be used to manipulate what hash the block has in proof of work and derivative mechanisms. And the `signatures` field can be used for protocols in which blocks become valid only when a certain amount of validators sign them. The fields in this data structure were chosen to facilitate many different consensus algorithms, so the system could potentially even be used in a non-private blockchain network.

```
struct BlockHeader {
timestamp: u128,
previous_digest: Vec<u8>,
difficulty: Difficulty,
nonce: Vec<u128>,
height: usize,
merkle_root: Vec<u8>,
signatures: Vec<SignedData>,
}
```

Figure 3. Block header data.

Further, transactions can be *stripped*, such transactions loose their payload and only retain a signed hash, as well as some metadata. These transactions allow for the construction of selectively stripped blocks (see Figure 4), which are used on most non-archive nodes to save space while keeping enough data to know what transaction to ask the network for, if additional information is ever needed.

Blocks themselves are stored in a tree like data structure (see Figure 5), which uses whatever consensus protocol was defined to create the canonical chain. It also keeps track of orphaned blocks and resolves them whenever possible. This `Block Tree` also contains a generic interface for storing block headers, merkle trees and transactions, each company can either use the supplied file system database or integrate their own storage solution into the system. The current implementation allows lookups in near constant time.

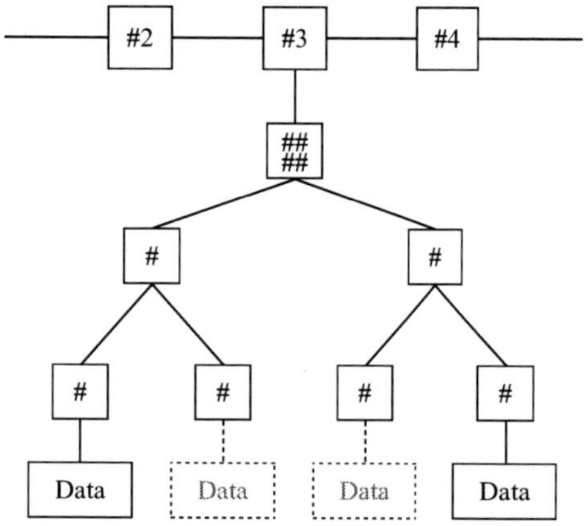

Figure 4. Blockchain (top) with the merkle tree shown for block No. 3, transactions (bottom) with a dotted outline are *stripped*.

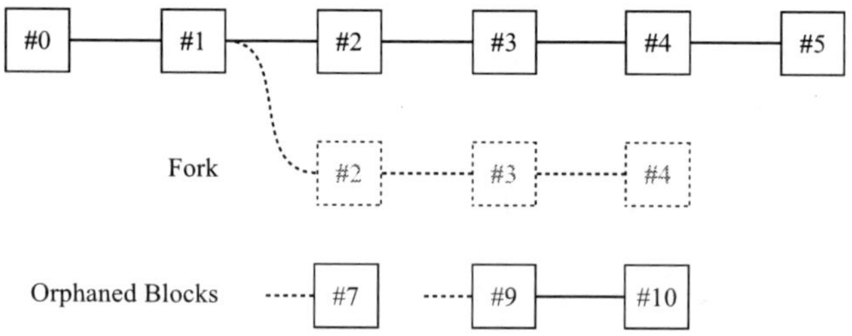

Figure 5. Block tree structure with the canonical chain (top), a fork (center) and orphaned blocks (bottom).

C. Local Network

A peer-to-peer network protocol is used to facilitate communications between nodes. It is constructed in a way that reduces manual maintenance by implementing automated bootstrapping and self repairing capabilities. The bootstrapping process uses so called "seed" nodes, which are nodes that have a high availability within the network (i.e., archive nodes). If at least one seed node is online, new nodes within the network will obtain information about the other peers and in turn request even more information from them. This method of bootstrapping as chosen to allow for automatic bootstrapping in networks which do not allow broadcast messages to be sent.

All nodes will try to maintain a complete list of all nodes, which are currently online in the network but only communicate to some of them. If any node goes offline, the list can be used to immediately increase the number of active connections to the desired amount. This behavior in addition to the use of a flooding protocol ensure the delivery of messages to wide parts of the network.

D. Global Network

Companies regularly share block hashes from their respective blockchains, these hashes are included into the other companies' blockchains, which removes the possibility for one company to retroactively change any data and recompute their local blockchain (some consensus protocols would allow this). This has the effect, that companies essentially "entangle" their local blockchains and in effect, provide an acknowledgment that they now possess the means to verify any proof of data up to this point. Example: company A creates a new block #1A and sends the block's hash to company B. Company B then includes a transaction with the remote block hash in block #2B. When the hash of #2B (or of any successor block) is sent to company A and included in their blockchain, all data from both blockchains is linked up to the shared block hashes. Since all companies on the global network do this, no peer will be able to change their blockchain and therefore be fully accountable for any records included in it. Figure 6 visualizes this concept.

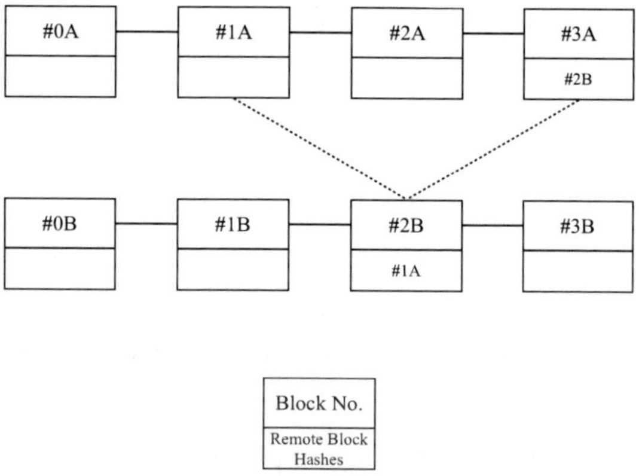

Figure 6. Two blockchains, both include block hashes from the other.

The exchange of these hashes is made possible by the use of an HTTPs message broker. This broker runs on a server that is accessible by certain nodes on all of the participants' networks. HTTPs was chosen as connections via this protocol are usually allowed by the firewalls used within an industry setting. All data sent to this broker is network-to-network encrypted, making it impossible to read messages even if an attacker were to gain access to the broker.

E. Extensibility

The nodes also provide an Application Programming Interface (API) to ingest any kind of data as new record into the blockchain. This API implements a transparent protocol called "Profichain" (Production and Factory Information over Blockchain). The Profichain protocol may be implemented in any kind of programming language, in order to ensure the highest compatibility to factory specific environments. The data is transmitted over the Transmission Control Protocol (TCP). The reference implementation also takes place within the evaluation and demonstrates that any process data of machinery or files are ingested safely. The protocol implements a 2-tier encryption with the Advanced Encryption Standard (AES). All tiers are optional and can be configured on clientside. The first tier represents an end-to-end encryption between the clientside and the node. The second tier provides a private encryption of the data that none of the network participants is able to decrypt except the original sender. The 2-tier encryption enables participants to work with strictly confidential data within the overall blockchain networks.

III. Setup of the Example Scenario

For the testbed, the complex construct of modern value chains is reduced to a minimal example and the delivery to a customer is simulated. This results in four stations, along which critical data is generated, see Figure 7. The raw material is turned into a semi-finished product (1), which is then further processed (2). This is followed by the assembly of the semifinished product with supplier components (3) and a final quality control (4). Transport takes place between each of the stations. During all steps, the product is clearly identifiable by an applied code. All data is assigned to this code, which enables the purchaser of the product in the event of an audit to seamlessly track product manufacture in retrospect.

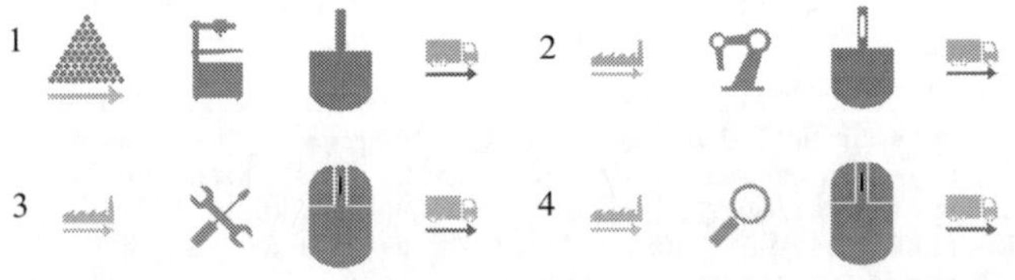

Figure 7. A simple value chain as a test scenario.

Physically, the value chain is represented for this research as follows: The origin of semifinished parts production lies in a 3D printer. By means of additive manufacturing, this generates a structure that is roughly similar to the final product. The background to this is increased productivity of the overall process, since a more finely finished structure must also be reworked to achieve high-precision requirements, but this entails a significantly longer printing time. Thus, the first data sets with relevance for storage in the blockchain result in information about the filament from source material, the 3D CAD model, or the converted machine code, as well as production data dropped during the process. The code for identifying the component is generated during printing and applied to a surface of the component that does not require any processing. This code is also stored in the blockchain. For the transport between the stations, an Automated Guided Vehicle (AGV) is used, which, equipped with a scanning unit and mobile blockchain nodes, can acknowledge the transport. Subsequently, iterative machining and comparison of actual to target geometry is used to evaluate the part accordingly. Depending on the number of iterations, a lot of data is generated here, which is stored in the blockchain. Subsequently, the assembly to the finished product takes place. Supplier parts, which consequently cannot show any data history in the blockchain, are identified via batch or part numbers. Finally, the quality inspection follows - its result and an inspection report are the last data records for the blockchain.

In order to be independent of different manufacturers of machine and automation controllers, data sources are transferred to OPC UA (Open Platform Communications Unified Architecture) servers: OPC UA is a standardized data exchange protocol for machine-to-machine communication [9]. Here, the data can be stored using suitable logger applications before being made available to the ingester.

As listed in Table I, the blockchain is based on different types of nodes. To create an executable instance of the blockchain, a Full Node is built into the network and thin nodes are built on each of the machines in the value chain. The physical component for the full node is a server with 8 cores and 32 GB RAM, as well as SSD mass storage, and for each of the thin nodes a single-board computer with 4 cores (x86), 8 GB RAM and SSD mass storage. Ubuntu 20.4 LTS is used as the operating system on all IT devices.

IV. Evaluation

A. Proceeding

The following system evaluation is to be seen as a first test of the fusion of blockchain system and testbed, while further and more extended investigations are ongoing. Therefore, the following evaluation was primarily limited to the basic questions regarding the performance of the blockchain system in conjunction with OPC UA data sources. The following questions had to be answered:

- Do packets get lost, especially during high transaction loads?
- What is the effect of varying the payload of a transaction?
- How big is the latency between transaction and block creation?

In advance, the blockchain system was tested in an isolated manner. For this, random transactions with a payload of 1kByte were generated and passed to the Ingester. The block time here, as in the following runs, was 15 seconds, and the experimental duration was 660 seconds, or 44 blocks.

For the test with real-world components, a data handler was written in Python3, which, as an OPC UA client, retrieves data from the OPC UA servers assigned to it, transfers it to a file and passes it on to the ingester. On each of the thin nodes such a data handler is running.

For this purpose, several test runs with different configurations were performed in a semi-automated way. The difference in the configuration refers to the size of the payload: 100Byte, 10x 100Byte, 100x 100Byte and 1000x 100Byte. This means that either a record of the machine with 100Byte was passed to the ingester immediately, or multiples were collected first and then passed as one transaction. In addition, each transaction that was passed to the ingester was also stored locally. This makes it possible to find possible packet losses. Before each launch, all existing data regarding the blockchain was deleted, so that a new blockchain was used each time.

B. Results

During the simulated tests of the blockchain system, up to 100 transactions per second could be processed. This is thus considered by us to be the limit of what is possible, determined by the load test.

The tests under the machine shop conditions delivered an average time between two data packets of $22.1\,\mathrm{ms} \pm 0.4\,\mathrm{ms}$ based on the thin node, with hardly any deviations occurring in the different configurations and no correlation between low and high payload could be found. At this point, the authors refer to the higher overhead for data retrieval between OPC UA server and client than for data storage. The delay between the times of transaction and block creation, on the other hand, is at least one block, i.e., 15 seconds, and depends on the number of transactions in the transaction pool and thus on the size of the payload. When few transactions with large payloads were created, they could usually be found within the next block. Many smaller transactions however were included within two blocks.

Finally, it should be noted that no packet was lost during the entire evaluation, which means that all data was transferred to the blockchain without errors.

V. Conclusion and Future Work

The connectivity of blockchain technology, has significant potential across all major value-added industries. These include, but are not limited to:

- automotive industry,
- machinery and plant engineering,
- aerospace industry,
- medical technology and the medical sector.

All of the industries mentioned are already characterized by a value chain in which upstream and downstream processes are linked via sensitive data processing. Due to the practicable and highly flexible implementation, the developed overall system is suitable for future integrations into existing production facilities, as it was developed independently of specifications regarding the data structure of the payload. Thus, the blockchain network is estimated to be easily transferable.

During operation, a stable sampling rate could be proven within the scope of the naturally occurring deviations due to the network communication of the OPC UA protocol. For high-frequency data acquisition, the Profichain API mentioned under Section II-E must be used. An evaluation of this is pending.

The described realization of the target system makes an important contribution to securing civil production and value creation networks, since faulty or manipulated product data are detected before products can cause damage in further processing or pose a threat to civil security at the end consumer in the public. Particularly noteworthy compared to other solutions is the combination of slimness, flexibility and high performance.

However, the mere safeguarding of data alone does not yet qualify it for use as a functional tool in the manufacturing industry. As global value networks grow ever closer together, the companies involved need tamper-proof and transparent production data with changing contractual partners. To increase trust in the authenticity of the data stored in the blockchain, hash values of blocks from the private blockchain are to be stored cyclically in a public blockchain. In this way, the advantages of both solutions (high performance for the private, high trustworthiness for the public) can be combined in a target-oriented manner.

As further work, on the one hand, a procedure is to be described to authenticate domain-specific data across locations and to distribute it in a tamper-proof manner. Furthermore, the exchange of relevant data between two sites or companies in a horizontal value chain is necessary. On the other hand, a detailed investigation must be carried out to gain knowledge regarding the possible attack vectors on the estimated system.

Acknowledgment

The project is funded by the German Federal Ministry of Education and Research within the framework of the announcement "Civil Security - Critical Structures and Processes in Production and Logistics" under the funding codes 13N15150 to 13N15153.

References

[1] R. Klatt, "Danger from cyber attacks has increased sharply in Germany." [Online]. Available from: https://www.forschung-undwissen.de/nachrichten/oekonomie/gefahr-durch-cyberangriffe-hat-indeutschland-stark-zugenommen-13375090, June 2021.

[2] Fraunhofer IWU, "safe-UR-chain Webpage." [Online]. Available from: https://safe-ur-chain.de, August 2021.

[3] G. Lemme, D. Lemme, K. A. Nölscher, and S. Ihlenfeldt, "Towards safe service ecosystems for production for value networks and manufacturing monitoring," in Journal of Machine Engineering, Vol. 20 No. 1, March 2020, pp. 4–5.

[4] S. Nakamoto, "Bitcoin: A Peer-to-Peer Electronic Cash System." [Online]. Available from: https://bitcoin.org/bitcoin.pdf August 2021.

[5] "An Introduction to Hyperledger." [Online]. Available from: https://www.hyperledger.org/wp-content/uploads/2018/07/HL_Whitepaper_IntroductiontoHyperledger.pdf August 2021.

[6] G. Lemme, K. A. Nölscher, E. Bei, C. Hermeling, and S. Ihlenfeldt, "Secure data storage and service automation for cyber physical production systems through distributed ledger technologies," in Journal of Machine Engineering, Vol. 21 No. 1, March 2021, p. 4.

[7] A. S. Tanenbaum and D. J. Wetherall, "Computer Networks (5th ed.)," Pearson Education, 2010, p. 368.

[8] R. Merkle, "Protocols for Public Key Cryptosystems," IEEE Symposium on Security and Privacy, 1980, pp. 125–127.

[9] OPC Foundation, "OPC 10000-1: OPC Unified Architecture - Part 1: Overview and Concepts." [Online]. Available from: https://opcfoundation.org/about/opc-technologies/opc-ua/, July 2021.

An Automated Reverse Engineering Cyber Module for 5G/B5G/6G

ML-Facilitated Pre-"ret" Discernment Module for Industrial Process Programmable Logic Controllers

Steve Chan
Decision Engineering Analysis Laboratory, VT
San Diego, USA
e-mail: schan@dengineering.org

***Abstract*—Industrial Control System (ICS) components have been subject to heightened cyber risk as hardware/software supply chain vulnerabilities have been illuminated and cyberattacks have become increasingly sophisticated. At the center of this ICS cyber maelstrom is the Programmable Logic Controller (PLC), a key component of Industry 4.0, as it is a main controller for physical processes (e.g., the control of an actuator). Many PLCs were designed for another era; they are resource-constrained, non-optimized, and beset with a variety of legacy facets (e.g., compiler, programming language, etc). This described sub-optimal paradigm also exists within the rubric of standards that specify the time interval between signal ingestion and actuation (e.g., IEEE 1547 specifies 2 seconds) for the operating environment. Hence, the designing/architecting/implementing of a light computational footprint continuous Monitoring/Detecting/Mitigating Module (MDMM) is non-trivial. This paper investigates a specific scenario of an ICS PLC operating within a 5G Ultra-Reliable Low-Latency Communications (URLLC) inter-PLC context and posits a viable MDMM construct that can operate within the paradigm. Central to its viability, the MDMM leverages apriori scan cycle traffic, utilizes Machine Learning (ML)-facilitated PLC logic/code optimization, and endeavors to undertake mitigation via a bespoke Automated Reverse Engineering (ARE) mechanism. The introduced MDMM requires further quantitative benchmarking, but the initial experimental results show promise.**

Keywords-cybersecurity; industrial control system; programmable logic controller; Industry 4.0; Industrial Internet of Things; smart manufacturing; smart grid; 5G; machine learning; artificial intelligence; automated reverse engineering.

I. INTRODUCTION

The benefits of ARE for PLC binaries to reduce the investigation time needed by those in the specialized cybersecurity functional sub-field of Digital Forensics and Incident Response (DFIR) is well documented in the literature [1][2]. Time is of the essence for these DFIR teams, as their task is to quickly comprehend the involved attack vector objective(s) (e.g., PLC exploitation) and effectuate countermeasures post-exploitation analysis. The need to reduce the time needed for exploitation analysis was illuminated by, among other examples, the ICS Stuxnet case study (wherein the PLCs at the involved nuclear facility were targeted). The prolonged non-automated, manual labor-intensive paradigm of that particular reverse engineering process greatly delayed the forensic investigation and articulated the need for an ARE mechanism as well as the need of a digital mirror for supporting such a mechanism.

Yet, ARE, if not properly architected, can also constitute a vulnerability, if it is somehow exploited by attackers. Just as the advisories made available by the National Vulnerability Database (NVD) and Sentient Hyper Optimized Data Access Network (SHODAN) can be used by cyber defenders as early warning indicators, they can also be leveraged by cyber attackers for exploitation opportunities and as attack accelerants [3]. This phenomenon should be of no surprise, as historically, malicious entities have engaged in reverse engineering on two fronts: Hardware Reverse Engineering (HRE) and Software Reverse Engineering (SRE). HRE has long been used by attackers to discern the inner workings of Integrated Circuits (ICs) [4]; indeed, tools, such as HAL – The Hardware Analyzer, have facilitated HRE [5]. On the SRE side, tools include IDA Pro, Radare2, Ghidra (open-sourced by the National Security Agency or NSA), Hopper, and others. When the aforementioned HRE/SRE tools, among others, are utilized as attack accelerants, defending security teams have witnessed the might of reverse engineering attacks, and the detection of these types of attacks has posed an ongoing challenge.

Despite the dilemma and distinct possibility of being utilized as an attack accelerant, the efficacy of ARE constitutes a key capability for forensic investigations. As can be seen by the SolarWinds incident (wherein malicious code was injected into the company's software, which in turn was widely distributed and utilized by client companies for a plethora of Information Technology (IT) management and remote monitoring needs), vulnerable software was quickly propagated throughout an ecosystem of mission-critical organizations. The Time to Response (TTR) was recognized as critical, but non-automated, manual labor-intensive reverse engineering intrinsically has a low TTR. Given the double-edged sword aspect of ARE, the notion of such a mechanism for mission-critical Critical Infrastructure (CI) controllers, such as ICS PLC binaries, has remained an open issue/challenge.

This paper endeavors to respond to that challenge by positing an ARE Cyber Module (ARECM), which is less prone to being utilized as an attack accelerant. Central to the requisite "less prone" protective element is an ML-facilitated Discernment Module (MLDM), which strives to detect that an attack is occurring/has occurred and timely employs (potentially), time-permitting and if still feasible, a bounded active defense mechanism to mitigate against the attack (the mitigation element is beyond the scope of this paper). Central to this discernment element is yet another module, which also utilizes ML facilitation so as to perform PLC logic/code optimization (a.k.a., ML-facilitated Logic/Code Optimization Module or MLLCOM). The paper utilizes a variety of acronyms, and some of the key ones are provided for the reader's convenience in Table 1 below.

TABLE I. KEY TERMS AND THEIR ACRONYMS

Term	*Acronym*
Anomalous Sample Detection	ASD
Architecture Event Trace	AET
Automated Reverse Engineering	ARE
ARE Cyber Module	ARECM
Branch Trace Store	BTS
Instruction Translation Lookaside Buffer	ITLB
Last Branch Record	LBR
Machine Learning	ML
ML-facilitated "Pre-'ret'" Discernment Module	MLPRDM
ML-facilitated Discernment Module	MLDM
ML-facilitated Logic/Code Optimization Module	MLLCOM
Monitoring/Detecting/Mitigating Module	MDMM
Performance Monitoring Unit	PerMU
PLC Program Execution Context	PLCPEC
Precise Event Base Sampling	PEBS
Prior to the Return	(Pre-Ret)
Return-Oriented Programming	ROP
Return-to-Libc	Ret2Libc
Time to Response	TTR
Translation Lookaside Buffer	TLB

The key components — ARECM, MLDM, and MLLCOM — are delineated within the context of the MDMM Amalgam, as shown in Figure 1 below. The MDMM Amalgam is comprised of three sections: "Monitor," "Detect," and "Mitigate." ARECM is situated in the second dotted box under the "Detect" section. MLDM is also situated in the second dotted box under the "Detect" section. MLLCOM is situated in the first dotted box under the "Detect" section. The MLLCOM helper is situated under the "Monitor" section.

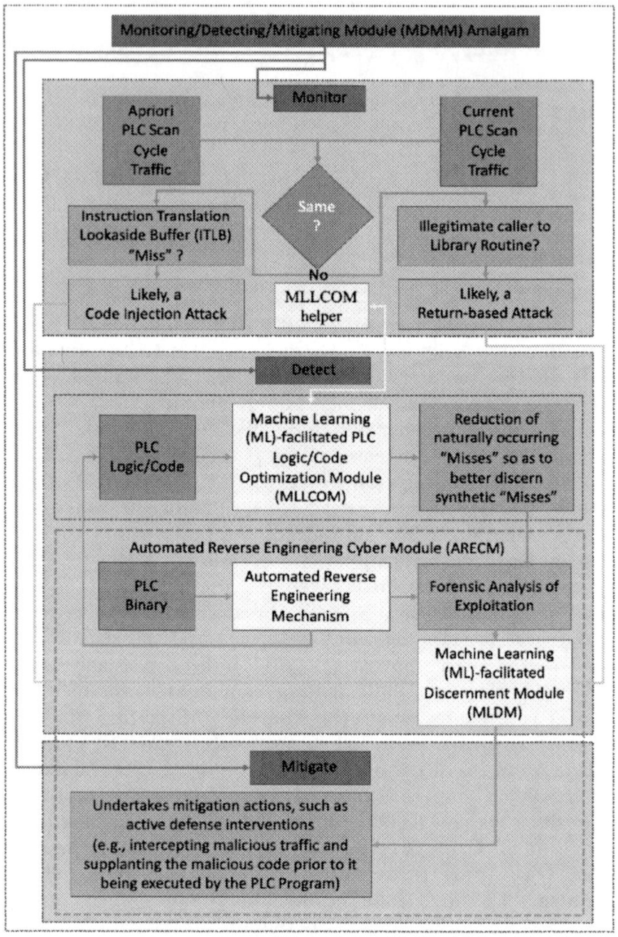

Figure 1. Monitoring/Detecting/Mitigating Module (MDMM) Amalgam: Automated Reverse Engineering Cyber Module (ARECM) with an ML-facilitated Discernment Module (MLDM) and ML-facilitated [PLC] Logic/Code Optimization Module (MLLCOM)

This section introduces the problem space. Section II presents background information and discusses the operating environment and the state of the challenge. Section III delineates the referenced ARE challenge and presents some experimental findings derived from scrutinizing a particular ICS architectural stack module, which centers upon edge PLCs engaged in inter-PLC communications, via 5G URLLC links; it also posits a prospective pathway for effectuating a viable ARECM. Section IV concludes with some observations, puts forth envisioned future work, and the acknowledgements close the paper.

II. Background Information

Fundamentally, ICS are systems that interconnect, monitor, and control physical processes within industrial settings [6]. A plethora of sectors (e.g., energy, manufacturing, etc.) rely upon ICS for their ongoing operations. Supervisory Control and Data Acquisition (SCADA) systems are an example of ICS, and these also constitute CI/Strategic Infrastructure (SI) (a.k.a., CI/SI).

These CI/SI have been heavily scrutinized for security vulnerabilities, and communications is, among others, an affected area.

A. Operating Environment

With regards to the current operating environment, communications/connectivity has become a backbone of the Industrial Internet of Things (IIoT), wherein devices are interconnected so as to collect, exchange, analyze, and actuate upon data. A commonly used term that captures this paradigm is Machine to Machine (M2M) communications, and in the 5G, Beyond 5G (B5G), and 6G communications context, the envisioned service paradigm is that of massive Machine-Type Communications (mMTC) and URLLC.

As IIoT has advanced, such as within the energy and manufacturing sectors, the attack surface area for communications/connectivity has increased. This has been demonstrated by the SHODAN Internet of Things (IoT) search engine, which returns publicly accessible information regarding IoT devices (e.g., sensitive information related to internet-connected ICS devices) [3]. Many of the SHODAN-illuminated devices do not yet have the firmware updates to mitigate against the Common Vulnerabilities and Exposures (CVE) delineated by the NVD and/or U.S. Computer Emergency Response Team (CERT)- Cybersecurity and Infrastructure Security Agency (CISA) portals, and this incongruity remains an ongoing issue.

The digital transformation advances being effectuated by IIoT are encompassed within what is referred to as Industry 4.0. By way of example, "Smart Grid," a subset of Industry 4.0, is defined by the National Institute of Standards and Technology (NIST) as "modernizing the electric power grid so that it incorporates information technology to deliver electricity efficiently, reliably, sustainably, and securely… a modernized grid enables all participants to benefit from the new introduction of new technologies, from distributed resources to *advanced communications and controls*." "Smart Manufacturing," another subset of Industry 4.0, is defined by NIST as being "fully-integrated, collaborative manufacturing systems that respond in real time to meet changing demands and conditions in the factory, in the supply network, and in customer needs;" roughly speaking, this translates to the fact that, "in the factories of the future, *smart communications* will become increasingly critical in all aspects of the operation," and a smart factory involves physical production processes being combined with digital technology (i.e., *control*) [7].

For both of these industrial subsets of Industry 4.0, communications is paramount, and a key counterpoised element is the PLC. Among other tasks, the PLC acquires data from sensory machines/devices, applies certain logic/mathematical functions, and outputs computationally-derived values (to establish thresholds, etc). Within both the Smart Grid and Smart Manufacturing sectors, while SCADA systems supervise, the PLCs perform the actual operations; they are typically installed on the machines/devices they control. In the spirit of the communications/connectivity envisioned under Industry 4.0/mMTC/M2M, etc, increasingly, PLCs are engaging in inter-PLC communications. Accordingly, interoperability specifications are addressed by reference architectures, such as the Industrial Internet Reference Architecture (IIRA) of the Industrial Internet Consortium (IIC), Reference Architectural Model of Industry 4.0 (RAMI 4.0), and others; IIRA adheres to International Organization for Standardization (ISO)/International Electrotechnical Commission (IEC)/Institute of Electrical and Electronics Engineers (IEEE) 42010:2011 "Systems and Software Engineering – Architecture Description," and RAMI 4.0 showcases various standards, such as IEC 62264 (a standard built upon the American National Standards Institute or ANSI/International Society of Automation or ISA-95 to facilitate information flow across Enterprise Resource Planning or ERP, Manufacturing Execution System or MES, and SCADA systems).

As the PLC is a principal controller for Industry 4.0, it has become a key target for cyber attackers. The ICS section of the CERT-CISA portal, as of 25 July 2021, lists 1730 advisories (69 pages of 25 advisories per page plus 5 advisories on page 70) [8]. While prior thinking held that the PLC was not subject to attack, as it was, theoretically, fully isolated from the publicly-facing external network, case studies, such as Stuxnet, have demonstrated the potential speciousness of this notion [9]. Common communications congestion attack vectors, in the form of Denial-of-Service (DoS) and Distributed Denial of Service (DDoS), are well-known. More recent studies have shown that degradation of ICS can readily be effectuated by communications degradation in the form of delay and/or loss of data packets. Among other methods, PLC output can be mutated and re-written to the PLC (this delay/loss of data has been achieved within the communications channel of ICS, such as from Phasor Measurement Units or PMUs to Phasor Data Concentrators or PDCs [10]).

To conduct PLC exploitation (e.g., malware) analysis, it is necessary to examine the PLC binary. By way of background, hopefully, the involved PLC subscribes to the standards, as delineated by IEC 61131-3, which pertain to PLC architectures, programming languages, data types, variable attributes, etc. If so, the PLC logic/code is usually developed via an IEC 61131-3-compliant Integrated Development Environment (IDE) and then compiled into a PLC binary via some compiler. The resultant PLC binary logic/code then, in effect, controls the involved PLC. The reverse engineering of this PLC binary is not straightforward, as the Tactics, Techniques, and Procedures (TTPs), via available tools/frameworks, do not directly translate between the Operational Technology (OT) arena (wherein the PLC resides) and IT arena [11]. For example, in the OT arena, there are a plethora of proprietary compilers used in generating PLC binaries, and axiomatically, these PLC binaries may not be readily accessible to commonly used IT tools (e.g., Interactive Disassembler or IDA, IDA Pro). If the PLC binary is indeed IEC 61131-3 compliant via one of the major platforms for ICS (e.g., CODESYS), then the reverse engineering process is more straightforward; however, in many situations, this is not the case.

To address this complexity, the notion of ARE has long been discussed [12]. Indeed, the notion of reverse engineering has become a cornerstone of software supply chain verification/integrity, particularly given the recent surge in issued directives, such as the "Improving the Nation's Cybersecurity" (Executive Order 14028, which was issued on 12 May 2021 and proceeded to direct NIST to enhance software supply chain security guidelines). The ability to uncover software supply chain vulnerabilities is essential for enhancing cyber resiliency, and ARE has been shown to effectively contribute by not only discerning vulnerabilities, but also facilitating the re-engineering of legacy software to supplant deprecated components and/or streamline for better performance. In fact, reverse engineering (and its examination and review of the design/components/build) is often used to redesign (as well as aid in source code recovery and binary code reuse [13]), enhance the involved system/product, and facilitate innovation; it is also often coupled with forward engineering, which aims to innovate and develop a new system/product. The amalgam of reverse/forward engineering is more advantageous than just forward engineering, which (in isolation) can lead to recalls/callbacks if actuated without the benefit of a Janusian perspective (i.e., leveraging lessons learned, project retrospectives, after action reviews, etc). Hence, the state of the challenge now resides in successfully counterpoising between the two (reverse/forward engineering).

B. State of the Challenge

The open challenge of ARE centers upon the point that while it can indeed accelerate the forensic work of a cyber defender, it also represents a potential exploitation point/accelerant for a cyber attacker. Architecting an ARE cyber module (in a reverse/forward engineering fashion), which favors the defender, has been an elusive, non-trivial feat. However, the literature does present several contributions to this area, and specifically, this paper posits a ML-facilitated "Pre-'ret'" Discernment Module (MLPRDM), which shows some promise; in particular, the MLPRDM focuses upon recognizing the set of legitimate instruction calls prior to the return or "ret" (or "Pre-'ret'") instruction contained within the subroutines of the PLC Program. Legitimate instruction calls proceed accordingly while MLPRDM-recognized illegitimate instruction calls may experience intervention (time-permitting and if practical). The MLPRDM gleans patterns from the work of the MLLCOM and is the key engine for the MLDM. The MLPRDM is delineated within the context of the MDMM Amalgam, as shown in Figure 2 below. The MLPRDM is situated in the "Detect" section and straddles the PLCPEC dotted box (which is located within the ASD dotted box) and the ARECM dotted box.

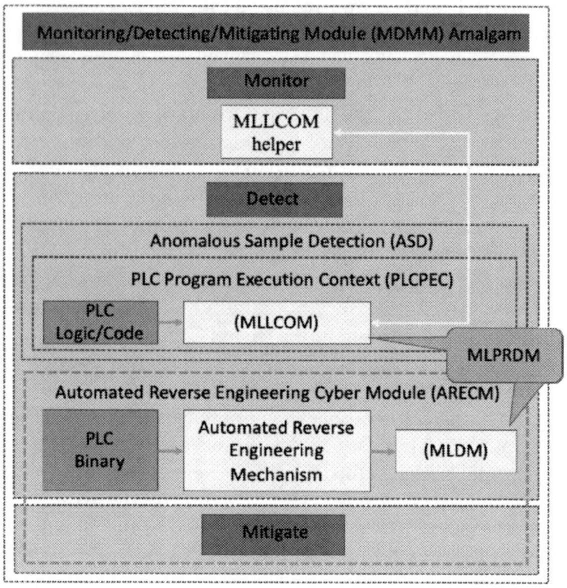

Figure 2. MLPRDM depicted within the context of the MDMM Amalgam

To clarify the value-added proposition of the MLPRDM, some background information is required. Broadly speaking, there are three methods for PLC exploitation: Firmware Modification Attacks (FMA), Control-flow Attacks (CFA), and Configuration Manipulation Attacks (CMA); these attack vector categories had been delineated at the BlackHat European Conference in 2016, and combinatorial attacks involving an amalgam, from among these categories (i.e., FMA, CFA, and CMA), are particularly potent; others classify PLC exploitation by security defects: firmware security defects, program security defects, and operation security defects [14]. Operation security defects can be further sub-divided into: (1) attack on protocol defects (e.g., since most communications protocols are not encrypted, packets can be captured and/or the data store of the registers can be read, and replay attacks [legitimate data is repeated and/or delayed], etc. can then be effectuated), (2) tampering attack at the Input/Output (I/O) interface (e.g., since modifying the I/O pin configuration does not necessarily issue an alarm, a tampering attack can be covertly effectuated), (3a) injection attack to affect the program flow control instructions or operational control flow (e.g., as operational control flow is dictated by PLC code blocks, intermediate code instrumentation and/or malicious code execution can exploit this facet), and (3b) return-oriented attack to affect the operational control flow (e.g., by leveraging exploits, wherein legitimate instructions are overwritten, malicious instructions can be indirectly executed [14]. The latter sub-divisions (3a, 3b) are the focus of MLPRDM.

C. Formal Verification of PLC Logic/Code

There are numerous pathways to undertake verification of PLC Programs. One pathway involves formal verification of PLC Programs; this is typically achieved by translating the PLC Program into a formal model, which in turn can serve as input into a model checker (e.g., SMV Symbolic Model Checker, NuSMV [a re-implementation and extension of SMV], UPPAAL [a portmanteau of Uppsala University and Aalborg University], etc.) [15][16]. Yet, the macro vantage point might not necessarily discern the more micro matters. For example, various software security studies have declared that simple micro-errors (intentional and/or unintentional) can readily disrupt the availability and integrity of a target PLC [17]. To aggravate this matter, in many cases where errors do exist, the code will still compile and run on the PLC; hence, no warning is necessarily issued. Suffice it to say, mitigation of these PLC errors or code defects (e.g., buffer overflows/ overruns, stack overruns, etc) is difficult, as these defects are difficult to discern, and fuzz testing (a.k.a., fuzzing) has met with limited success; furthermore, as the PLC often has numerous constituent programming languages, the requirements for the fuzzing schema tend to be quite elaborate so as to undertake the challenge of the associated semantic complexity, and the efficacy of even state-of-the-art fuzzers has been sub-optimal [18][19].

D. General Detection within the PLC Program

The notion of installing a general detection module aboard the PLC has, to date, met with limited appeal; due to the already limited computational resources onboard the PLC, installing an additional program (with its additional computational load requirements) aboard the already resource-constrained PLC, so as to examine the PLC Program, has met with various heuristical challenges. For example, for real-time operations, the task of detection has a lower priority than that of a control task, particularly given the mission-critical nature of a PLC [20]. This de-prioritization sets the stage for detection misses, so the potential efficacy is already in question.

E. Anomalous Sample Detection within the PLC Program

The challenge then becomes one of designing a specialized detection module, which has both minimal impact on the computational load of the already resource-constrained PLC as well as a minimal footprint given the higher priority control tasks at hand. It turns out that this approach vector is somewhat feasible in the form of Anomalous Sample Detection (ASD), which demonstrates some promise with regards to code-injection and Return-Oriented Attacks (ROAs).

As a generalization, a code-injection attack (a.k.a., Remote Code Execution or RCE) refers to the exploitation of code defect or bug (e.g., buffer overflow/overrun, dangling pointer, etc) that processes the externally injected malicious code and alters the course of instruction execution (i.e., operational control flow). In the case of a buffer overflow/overrun, the legitimate return address is overwritten, and the operational control flow is diverted to the location specified by the new return address. In contrast, a ROA does not inject malicious code; rather, it attains control of the call stack and leverages the internally resident pre-existing code. ROAs are further sub-divided into Return-to-Libc (Ret2Libc) attacks (which causes the PLC Program to jump to some code block, such as that for various functions — system(), execve(), etc. — within the standard library, say, for the C programming language or libc, which is already loaded into memory) and Return-Oriented Programming (ROP) attacks (which manipulate the call stack to indirectly execute specific instructions or groups of instructions immediately prior to the "ret" instruction contained within the subroutines of the PLC Program). This is shown in Figure 3 below.

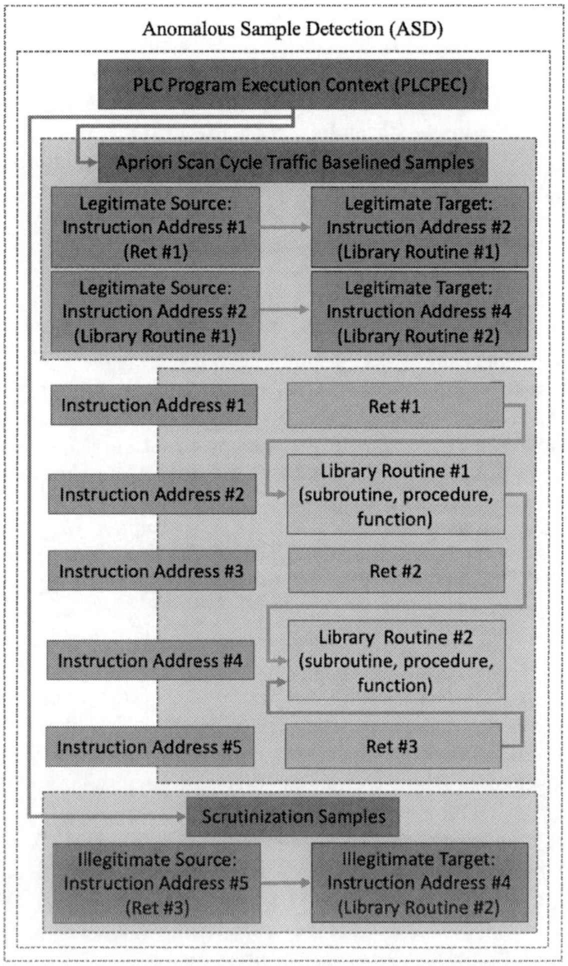

Figure 3. PLC Program Execution Context (PLCPEC) in the context of Anomalous Sample Detection (ASD)

Regardless of the attack vector (e.g., code-injection attack, ROA), the anomalous aspect can be discerned when comparing the examined *scrutinization samples* (a.k.a., performance samples) against *apriori baselined samples*. For example, a Translation Lookaside Buffer (TLB) or Instruction Translation Lookaside Buffer (ITLB) "miss" could indicate a code injection attack (wherein the operational control flow is transferred to the injected malicious code, and hence, the "miss" for legitimate code). As another example, an examination of the legitimate callers of the various library routines (a code block — subroutine, procedure, function, etc — used for recurring tasks) should be instructive as to whether an illegitimate caller executed a ROA. As anomalies can indeed be discerned, regardless of the attack vector utilized (e.g., code-injection attack, ROA, etc), via these scrutinization samples, the described approach is loosely considered to be operation security defect agnostic (bounded within the scope of either code injection attacks or ROAs). This ASD approach correlates events with the ongoing PLC Program Execution Context (PLCPEC). This PLCPEC is in the form of baselined instruction addresses and callers of library routines, such as shown in Figure 3 above. It can be ascertained, via examining Figures 2 and 3, that the ASD approach is predicated upon the MLPRDM (shown in Figure 2), and this particular module is further explained in the experimentation section.

III. EXPERIMENTATION FINDINGS

The experimentation involved a particular ICS architectural stack module, which centers upon [edge] PLCs focused upon inter-PLC communications, via 5G URLLC links, within an ICS context. As should be axiomatic, a key aspect of the 5G/B5G/6G ecosystem is that hardware is principally supplanted with software so that future upgrades will be software-centric. However, this increased utilization of Software-Defined Networking (SDN) within the network core also expands the attack surface opportunities [21]. For this particular case, the 5G-related PLCs were the targets. Given the comparable nature of the involved PLCs, only one PLC was examined.

In accordance with the acknowledged deterministic behavior of the underlying engineering software for the PLC Program (e.g., the same set of request messages are utilized), a specific heuristic was utilized; given the scan cycle traffic of prior sessions, a pattern among the request messages could be ascertained; this particular heuristic is supported within the literature [22]. Accordingly, to operationalize the posited ASD approach, several facets were baselined apriori by pre-processing the PLC binary and recording the following: (1) legitimate callers of the library, (2) legitimate callers for each library routine, and (3) legitimate callers for various consecutive call patterns for the library routines. Furthermore, the instructions occurring prior to any "ret" instruction were recorded, and a relative weighting was assigned to each instruction depending upon their distance to their associated "ret."

These operationalization actions spawned other complexities. For example, while using dedicated processor commands, such as Branch Trace Store (BTS) can be quite effective for recording (e.g., memorializing the last executed branches), the computational overhead can also be quite high; there are also comparable processor commands (e.g., Last Branch Record or LBR, Architecture Event Trace or AET, etc.). For these cases, a substantive portion of the overhead can be attributed to the large number of *performance samples* (derived from the Performance Monitoring Unit or PerMU of the involved processor), which include various control transfer events (e.g., calls [to subroutines], returns or "rets" [wherein control flow continues with the instruction following the call], exceptions/interrupts [wherein unexpected events disrupt instruction execution/control flow]) and their associated control transfer information (e.g., source address, target address, and various other properties, etc.) [23].

The standard recordings of PerMUs can include TLB/ITLB misses, cache misses [wherein the processor must retrieve the data from main memory], branch prediction misses or branch mispredictions [a misprediction in the next instruction to process], etc. Typically, the computational overhead associated with tabulating these events is compounded by the ensuing interrupts (spawned when the pre-defined memory is saturated). However, Precise Event Base Sampling (PEBS) or comparable approaches can process these recordings of events into pre-defined memory sectors, such as when the event occurrences exceed a particular threshold, rather than spawn an interrupt. Hence, the "tighter" the threshold, the more quickly and more likely it is for, let us say, TLB/ITLB *synthetic misses* (i.e., indicative of a code-injection attack) to be detected. However, to decrease the likelihood of false positives, it is necessary to decrease the likelihood of *naturalistic misses*, and this is achieved via the PLC logic/code [performance] optimization performed by the MLLCOM (e.g., an enhancement of code layout, such as by re-positioning code blocks within a procedure to decrease branch misses). After all, if the control flow frequently traverses several distinct and disparate pathways throughout the code region, it is more likely to experience misses.

Experimentation has shown that the use of certain algorithmic approaches (e.g., Code Tiling-like), particularly for code layout optimization, achieves better performance (e.g., call frequency grouping) within the allotted time span than other algorithms (e.g., Pettis-Hansen); the algorithms are known to have $O(n*(n+n^2))=O(n^3)$ as the worst-case asymptotic complexity, but the difference in approach — the utilization of various approximations — underpin the performance differences [24]. Moreover, with the MLLCOM engaging in code layout optimization and gleaning the apriori consecutive call patterns, it is able to facilitate a reduction in the number of false positives by better distinguishing between legitimate and illegitimate control flow behavior. Preliminary experimentation with MLLCOM has also noted that its profiling (via its MLLCOM helper) at the Monitor level and trace processing at the Detect level well serves to facilitate better optimizing basic blocks within a procedure (i.e., procedure splitting) via the notion of hot blocks (executed frequently) and cold blocks (i.e., executed infrequently). This helps to decrease branch misses.

Overall, these types of optimizations, among others, are central to the discernment equation. Due to "real-time execution deadlines" and Quality of Service (QoS) stipulations, "compilers for PLC binaries typically only undertake very conservative optimizations, if any" [13]. Yet, there are several opportunities to optimize PLC binaries. As previously discussed, the paradigm of sub-optimal instruction locality can adversely impact the PLC Program performance, via, by way of example, TLB/ITLB misses, which can induce memory stalls (cycles for which the processor is stalled while awaiting memory access) [24]. However, a paradigm of optimized instruction locality (e.g., pre-positioning callers in close proximity to their callees) can dramatically improve performance [24][25].

From an architectural perspective, the overall MDMM amalgam is able to monitor/detect units of work that are in conformance with the PLC scan cycle. By way of background, non-PLC languages (and their associated binaries) typically adhere to sequential units of work as part of their execution model. In contrast, PLC binaries adhere to an execution model that conforms to the continuously executing scan cycle. Due to the continuous nature of the execution scan cycle, dynamic analyses of the PLC binary is non-trivial. The MDMM architecture lends to overcoming this challenge, via the positioning of its various constituent modules. In particular, the ARECM is nicely operationalized within the ASD of the MDMM by way of the interplay between the MLDM and MLLCOM, via the MLPRDM, such as previously shown in Figure 2 and summarized in Figure 4 below. With the enhanced context from the MLLCOM (given the optimization work) and the insights from the MLDM (e.g., comparison of the current scan cycle traffic with apriori scan cycle traffic) serving as accelerants for the ARECM, the MDMM architecture and underpinning MLPRDM provide enhanced discernment.

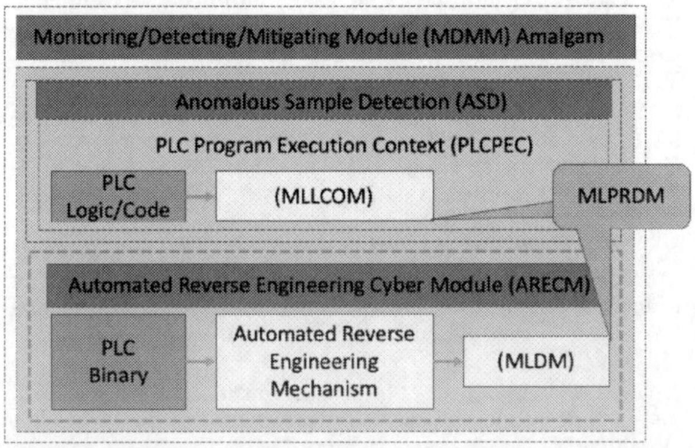

Figure 4. Automated Reverse Engineering Cyber Module (ARECM) in the context of the Monitoring/Detecting/Mitigating Module (MDMM) Amalgam's Anomalous Sample Detection (ASD)

As previously shown in Figures 2, 3, and 4, the methodological approach centers upon the fact that the MLPRDM discerns the set of legitimate instruction calls prior to the return or "ret" (or "Pre-'ret'") instruction contained within the subroutines of the PLC Program. Legitimate instruction calls are permitted to proceed while MLPRDM-recognized illegitimate instruction calls may experience intervention (time-permitting and if practical). The MLPRDM discerns patterns from the work of the MLLCOM and is, in effect, the key engine for the MDMM, which directly addresses the ARE open issue/challenge.

IV. Conclusion

While ICS were originally designed to operate in isolated environments, the convergence of OT and IT have increased the attack surface area within this ecosystem, particularly for key devices, such as PLCs. Several attack vectors, within the rubric of Denial of Engineering Operations (DEO), have emerged to target, among other devices, PLCs [26]. Unfortunately, the cyber defense and resiliency capabilities in the OT sector greatly differ from that of the IT sector, such that the TTPs, which can be brought to bear in support of PLCs, have been limited thus far. Furthermore, the PLCs operating within the OT environment have had a high availability onus (of controlling real-world physical processes), but are often limited by their resource-constrained, legacy (and possibly proprietary) environs.

It has been shown that PLCs have been vulnerable to DEO attacks, wherein the legitimate instruction in a control logic is replaced with noise data (e.g., a sequence of 0xFF bytes) to cause the PLC to malfunction, and/or the PLC may have had legitimate instructions relaced with malicious instructions. In either case, the operational control flow has been compromised. Two synergistic pathways for mitigation are evident. First, detection is ideal; to the degree that this can be achieved with enough time to take mitigation action, then it would be ideal to effectuate an active defense (e.g., ironically, a man-in-the-middle counter-attack) by intercepting the malicious traffic and supplanting the malicious code prior to that code being executed by the PLC Program. Whether or not this detection/active defense can be achieved, a forensic analysis to comprehend the extent of the control flow manipulation is required. Consequently, second, ARE is required; to the degree that it can occur in real-time for a robust diagnosis of the attack, such that active countermeasures can be readily deployed, then the intent for which MLPRDM was designed would be operationalized.

Key to its success, the MLPDRM goals of profiling and trace processing are critical; its actions will, among other effects, minimize the number of naturally occurring ITLB misses so that synthetically occurring ITLB misses will be more illuminated. The posited MLPRDM, set amidst the MDMM architecture, requires further quantitative benchmarking, but the initial architectural techniques (for a lower overhead, minimally intrusive approach vector, and more accurate monitoring/detection paradigm) and preliminary experimental results show promise. The significance of this potential is that the approach addresses the Industry 4.0 cyber-physical security open issue/challenge surrounding ARE for PLCs; in essence, the posited ARE cyber module, which leverages the various described ML facilities to aid in the ARE task, is less prone to be utilized as an attack accelerant. The author hopes to focus on substantive quantitative benchmarking as part of future work, as the preliminary results are quite promising.

ACKNOWLEDGMENT

This research is supported by the Decision Engineering Analysis Laboratory (DEAL), an Underwatch initiative. This is part of a VT white paper series on 5G-enabled defense applications, via proxy use cases, to help inform Project Enabler.

REFERENCES

[1] R. Awad, S. Beztchi, J. Smith, B. Lyles, and S. Prowell, "Tools, Techniques, and Methodologies: A Survey of Digital Forensics for SCADA Systems," Annual Computer Security Applications Conference, 2018, pp. 1-8.

[2] T. Wu and J. Nurse, "Exploring the Use of PLC Debugging Tools For Digital Forensic Investigations on SCADA Systems," The Journal of Digital Forensics, Security and Law, vol. 10, 2015, pp. 79-96, https://doi.org/10.15394/jdfsl.2015.1213

[3] S. Chan, "Prototype Orchestration Framework as a High Exposure Dimension Cyber Defense Accelerant Amidst Ever-Increasing Cycles of Adaptation by Attackers: A Modified Deep Belief Network Accelerated by a Stacked Generative Adversarial Network for Enhanced Event Correlation," The Third Conference on Cyber-Technologies and Cyber-Systems (CYBER 2018) IARIA, 2018, pp. 28-38, ISSN: 2519-8599, ISBN: 978-1-61208-683-5.

[4] S. Becker, C. Wiesen, and N. Albartus, "An Exploratory Study of Hardware Reverse Engineering – Technical and Cognitive Processes," Proceedings of the Sixteenth Symposium on Usable Privacy and Security, 2020, pp. 1-17.

[5] M. Fybrbiak et al., "HAL – The Missing Piece of the Puzzle for Hardware Reverse Engineering, Trojan Detection and Insertion," IEEE Transactions on Dependable and Secure Computing, 2018, pp. 498-510.

[6] "Industrial Control Systems Security," Accessed on: Aug 27, 2021. [Online]. Available: https://wp.nyu.edu/momalab/industrial-control-systems-security/

[7] S. Bagchi, "Smart Communication: Factory of the Future – Critical Connections," Accessed on: Aug 27, 2021. [Online]. Available: https://www.automation.com/en-us/articles/2015-2/smart-communication-factory-of-the-future-critical

[8] "ICS-CERT Advisories," Accessed on: Aug 27, 2021. [Online]. Available: "https://us-cert.cisa.gov/ics/advisories?items_per_page=25&page=0

[9] S. Gallagher, "Vulnerable industrial controls directly connected to Internet? Why not?," Accessed on: Jul 23, 2021. [Online]. Available: https://arstechnica.com/information-technology/2018/01/the-internet-of-omg-vulnerable-factory-and-power-grid-controls-on-internet/

[10] Y. Wang et al., "Access Control Attacks on PLC Vulnerabilities," Journal of Computer and Commpunications, Vol. 6, pp. 311-325, 2018, doi: 10.4236/jcc.2018.611028.

[11] "2020 Gartner OT Security Best Practices," Accessed on: Jul 23, 2021. [Online]. Available: https://www.armis.com/analyst-reports/2020-gartner-ot-security-best-practices/

[12] S. Zonouz, J. Rrushi, and S. McLaughlin, "Detecting Industrial Control Malware Using Automated PLC Code Analytics," IEEE Security & Privacy, vol. 12, pp. 40-47, 2014, doi: 10.1109/MSP.2014.113.

[13] A. Keliris and M. Maniatakos, "ICSREF: A Framework for Automated Reverse Engineering of Industrial Control Systems Binaries," 2018, pp. 1-15, doi: 10.14722/ndss.2019.23271.

[14] H. Wu, Y. Geng, K Liu, and Wenwen Liu, "Research on Programmable Logic Controller Security," IOP Conf Series: Materials Science and Engineering, vol. 569, pp. 1-13, 2019, doi: 10.1088/1757-899X/569/4/042031.

[15] J. Bengtsson, K. Larsen, F. Larson, P. Pettersson, and W. Yi, "UP-PAAL – a Tool Suite for Automatic Verification of Real-Time Systems," Proc Workshop Hybrid Systems III: Verification and Control, vol. 1066, 1996, pp. 232-243.

[16] V. Gourcuff, O. Smet, and J. Faure, "Efficient Representation for Formal Verification of PLC Programs," 2006 8th International Workshop on Discrete Event Systems, 2006, pp. 182-187, doi: 10.1109/WODES.2006.1678428.

[17] S. Valentine and C. Farkas, "Software security: Application-level vulnerabilities in SCADA systems," 2011 IEEE International Conference on Information Reuse & Integration, 2011, pp. 498-499, doi: 10.1109/IRI.2011.6009603.

[18] C. Lemieux and K. Sen, "Fairfuzz: A Targeted Mutation Strategy for Increasing Greybox Fuzz Testing Coverage," 33rd ACM/IEEE International Conference on Automated Software Engineering, 2018, pp. 475-485.

[19] L. Simon and A. Verma, "Improving Fuzzing through Controlled Compilation," 2020 IEEE European Symposium on Security and Privacy (EuroS&P), 2020, pp. 34-52, doi: 10.1109/EuroSP48549.2020.00011.

[20] S. Kottler, M. Khayamy, S. Hasan, and O. Elkeelany, "Formal Verification of Ladder Logic Programs using NuSMV," IEEE Southeastcon, 2017, pp. 1–5, doi: 10.1109/SECON.2017.7925390.

[21] K. Fysarakis et al., "A Reactive Security Framework for operational wind parks using Service Function Chaining,"2017 IEEE Symposium on Computers and Communications (ISCC), 2017, pp. 663-668, doi: 10.1109/ISCC.2017.8024604.

[22] S. Qasim, J. Lopez, and I. Ahmed, "Automated Reconstruction of Control Logic for Programmable Logic Controller Forensics," Springer International Publishing, 2018, pp. 1-21.

[23] L. Yuan, W. Xing, H. Chen, B. Zang, "Security Breaches as PMU Deviation: Detecting and Identifying Securing Attacks Using Performance Counters," The 2nd ACM SIGOPS Asia-Pacific Workshop on Systems (APSys), 2011, pp. 1-6, doi: 10.1145/2103799.2103807.

[24] X. Huang, B. Lewis, K. McKinley, "Dynamic Code Management: Improving Whole Program Code Locality in Managed Runtimes," Proc. of the Intl. Conf. on Virtual Execution Environments (VEE), 2006, pp. 1-11, doi: 10.1145/1134760.1134779.

[25] J. Chen and B. Leupen, "Improving instruction locality with just-in-time code layout," Proceedings of the USENIX Windows NT Workshop, 1997, pp. 25-32.

[26] S. Senthivel, S. Dhungana, H. Yoo, I. Ahmed, and V. Roussev, "Denial of Engineering Operations Attacks in Industrial Control Systems," Proceedings of the Eighth ACM Conference on Data and Application Security and Privacy, 2018, pp. 319-329, https://doi.org/10.1145/3176258.3176319.

Interference Testing on Radio Frequency Polarization Fingerprinting

Page Heller
Endpoint Security Inc.
College Station, Texas, USA
email: heller@endpointsecurityinc.com

Abstract— **As nation state actors become more active in cyber-attacks on infrastructure, they also become more sophisticated, choosing to target product quality over a plant shutdown, thus making it harder to detect an intrusion. To make cyber-attacks harder to initiate, naturally-occurring polarization in radio frequency signals is being explored as a means of authentication that doesn't require digital data. By means of polarization mode dispersion, it is possible to protect the wireless channel (the path from sensor to access point) by identifying hostile actors who attempt to imitate authenticated devices to gain entry into a wireless network. In this article, recent test results are examined for their impact on the resilience of this type of wireless security. Specifically, performance in the case of low received-signal-strength is analyzed. Also, troublesome presence of electrical interference from a microwave oven and fans is studied.**

Keywords-cybersecurity; authentication; wireless intrusion detection; radio frequency fingerprinting; interference.

I. INTRODUCTION

As nation state actors become more active in cyber-attacks on infrastructure, they also become more sophisticated [1]. Rather than shutting down a plant, for instance, they might target product quality, which is harder to detect. Rather than using dictionary attacks, they might employ man-in-the-middle attacks or implement rogue access points because they are also harder to detect [2]. To stay out in front of the attackers requires a proactive approach that includes new systems of security for wireless edge devices.

A new form of Wireless Intrusion Detection System (WIDS) has been developed that detects wireless intruders by the signal they send, rather than simply relying upon the data that the signal contains [3] [4]. By using polarization mode dispersion, it is possible to protect a wireless channel (that is, the path from sensor to access point) by identifying hostile actors who attempt to imitate authenticated devices to gain entry into a wireless network.

In this article, recent test results are examined for their impact on the resilience of this type of wireless security. Specifically, performance in the case of low received signal strength is analyzed. Also, presence of electrical interference from a microwave oven and from fans is studied.

The remainder of this paper is organized as follows. Section II describes the test setup, including a description of a prototype device under test, and further describes a set of fixed transmitting devices emulating industrial sensors, the general environment in which tests are conducted and the condition under test, which may involve introducing a tertiary device. Section III describes the test performed with signals received that are characterized by low relative signal strength. Section IV addresses tests performed with different types of electric fans producing electrical interference near the transmitting devices. Section V covers a test performed with a microwave oven in operation near the transmitting devices and Section VI provides concluding remarks on the tests. The paper closes with references cited.

II. TEST SETUP

A prototype system (Figure 1) was previously developed and is employed here to monitor wireless signals and identify unique edge devices by a naturally occurring fingerprint comprised of polarization characteristics in the wireless analog signals they transmit. This fingerprint is quite unique and very stable for each fixed wireless device. When a set of devices are authenticated based on their fingerprints, a new device entering the area can be identified as an unknown device, even if the perpetrator is using the MAC address and password of an authenticated device to attempt connection with a network. In addition, devices of the same make and model will yield very different fingerprints, making the authentication device specific.

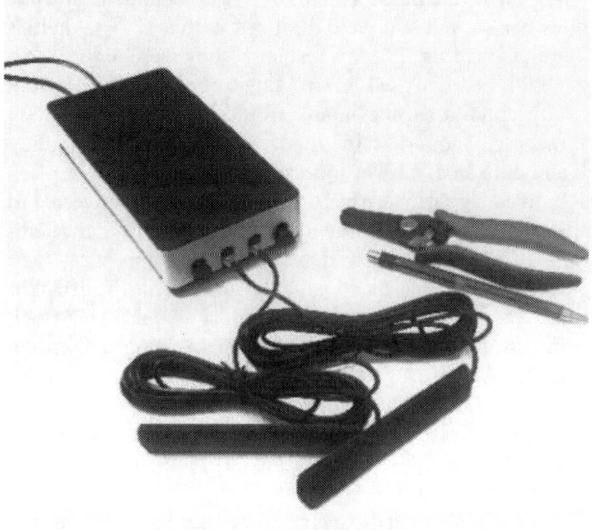

Figure 1. Device under test: a prototype wireless intrusion detection system

Since the fingerprints are naturally occurring, this method of identifying wireless intrusion works with legacy devices, which may have little or no security measures embedded. It also works with any protocol and with any standard for communications, thus making it a potentially desirable mechanism to employ in sensitive industrial environments. However, most industries are electrically noisy and any new security system must be able to operate in an environment with high electrical interference. Thus, a study is needed to ensure its viability for industrial applications.

Electrical interference can raise the noise floor of a received wireless signal. This may result in an otherwise satisfactory signal strength arriving with a low Signal-to-Noise Ratio (SNR), causing problems for some receivers. In addition, electrical interference can result in sporadic increases in energy received, which may appear as new signals, or which may obfuscate desired signals.

To test the prototype under these conditions, a 40-foot by 80-foot metal warehouse was used to simulate a plant environment. It was set up with four sensors each based on the same make and model of microcontroller; in this case, Raspberry Pi 4Bs. The sensors alternately each sent a pair of wireless signals containing data.

Two identical prototypes, each with a unique pair of antennas, were set up to monitor the incoming signals from the sensors for comparison of antenna types. Twelve tests were run using different signal gains and interference sources in varying forms of electrical noise within the field of the transmitting sensors.

The wireless signals were received by each of the prototypes using orthogonally-polarized antennas; one set of RF Elements OARDSBX244 Omni Directional 2.4 GHz, 4dBi antennas and one set of Bestkong Omni WiFi Booster 2.4 GHz 5dBi antennas. The signals were sampled at 20M samples per second and were digitized with a 12-bit Analog-to-Digital Converter. For this test case, they were recorded so they could be analyzed in off-line processing. In actual operating conditions, the inputs would be analyzed as they were received and a decision made as to whether or not they were authenticated, known sources.

Received signals were band-pass filtered and converted to complex baseband in the Universal Software Radio Peripheral [5]. A proprietary pulse detection algorithm was then employed on the baseband signals, and a block of 4096 samples was formed upon detection of a signal. The block was transformed to the frequency domain using a Discrete Fourier Transform (DFT). Further processing, including an algorithm for finding the main spectrum lobe [6], was used to derive a polarization mode dispersion profile across the spectrum of the DFT, eliminating artifacts derived from spectral leakage.

By averaging energy over many symbols within the received packet, one is able to mitigate concerns of incipient deviations, scalloping, unbalanced spectra and other fading phenomena which might influence the calculation of polarization mode dispersion. This computation produces a frequency-dependent fingerprint based on polarization mode dispersion across the signal bandwidth that is quite unique for each sensor. The fingerprint is compared to a bank of collected fingerprints to determine if the received input has been identified previously. This is done through a correlation process, concluding with a number between 0 and 1 that indicates the degree of confidence for each case where the fingerprint of the incoming signal is compared to each known source.

III. Low Relative Signal Strength

A. Setup

In this series of experiments, three of the signals received from sensors each had an SNR of 20 dB and a fourth received signal had a 14 dB SNR. These signal strength levels are undesirable in communications and often reflect conditions where the bit-error rates increase to the point where packets fail and must be re-transmitted. Figure 2 depicts a dial which reflects, on average, when wireless communications are good and when they begin to fail. It should be noted that the range from 15 dB to 25 dB is referenced as "poor," indicating that re-transmissions are frequent. Three of the sensors are transmitting signals that are received in this range. The fourth sensor resides in the range below that, denoted as minimum SNR, 10-15 dB. In this range, data may get through only

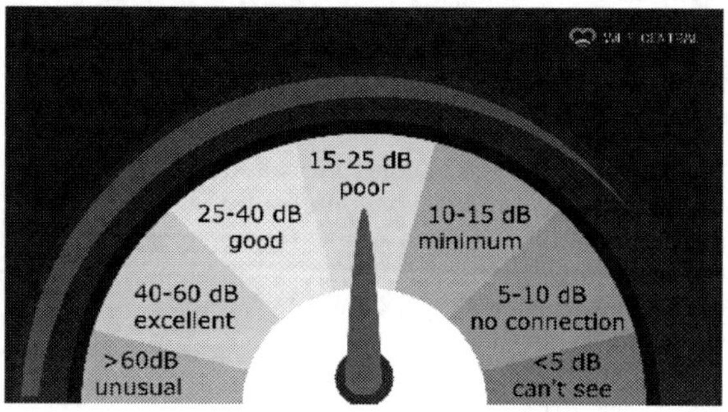

Figure 2. A dial indicating how SNR impacts quality of signal

periodically. The degradation is clearly evident in the actual recorded signal spectrum, shown in Figure 3, where the intensity across the spectrum is indicated with a relative intensity, in Volts, on the vertical axis for each frequency bin number on the horizontal axis.

Typically, one would expect the average spectrum to be approximately symmetric around the center of the chart. Frequency-selectivity due to multipath in the propagation channel can result in signal levels that depend on the frequency, leading to an unbalanced spectrum.

B. Results

While this phenomenon and other frequency-selective fading can reduce signal levels and even cause bit-error rates to increase, the effect is not significant enough to negatively impact the ability to correctly match the fingerprint of a received signal with one of a set of known sources. Because the polarization dispersion measurement is averaged over multiple symbols within the packet, transient effects are minimized and an integration gain is achieved.

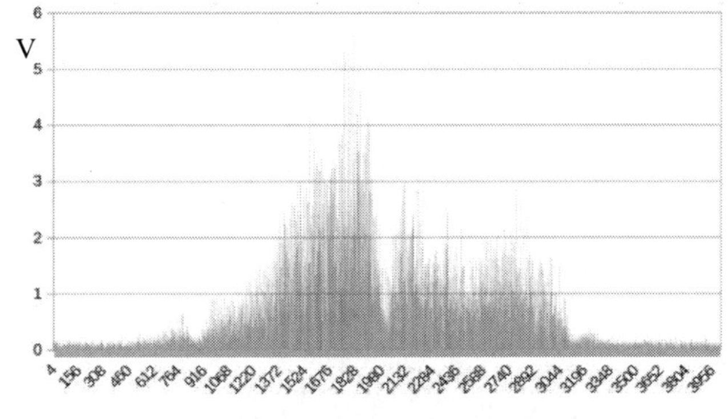

Figure 3. DFT of a signal with low SNR showing non-uniformity in symmetry (test 20210327103909-2G0202e) using relative intensity in Volts on the vertical scale compared at each frequency bin on the horizontal scale

The following chart (Figure 4) is a 'confidence matrix', which is similar to a well-known confusion matrix, except, where a confusion matrix would have known sources along one axis and the same number of unknown sources along a second, the confidence matrix is designed with known sources in columns and each row containing a new, incoming source. In other words, the confidence matrix grows in length with the number of signals received in the test case.

Column A contains the block number of the rising edge of each signal found. The first time a signal is seen, it is not successfully correlated with a known source, since there are no known sources, as yet. Thus, for block 1413 the correlation is 0.38, where 1.00 is a perfect match and 0.00 indicates no correlation.

The confidence matrix shows no sources present in the test other than the four known sensors, shown in columns B, C, D and E. It also shows strong correlation with alternating pairs of signals arriving from each of four sensors. There are no false positive correlations, nor false negative correlations. The number in each cell represents the confidence in making the matching decision. Thus, all positive correlations are above 0.95 indicating that the decisions are made with greater than 95% confidence. In fact, this confidence matrix is from a test with received signals of low SNR and the average positive correlation for this test is 0.97 with a standard deviation of 0.01.

	A	B	C	D	E	F	G	H	I	J	K	L	M	N	O	P	Q
1	1413	0.381423	0	0	0	0	0	0	0	0	0	0	0	0	0	0	0
2	1421	0.985606	0	0	0	0	0	0	0	0	0	0	0	0	0	0	0
3	1429	0.576645	0	0	0	0	0	0	0	0	0	0	0	0	0	0	0
4	1437	0.569673	0.970146	0	0	0	0	0	0	0	0	0	0	0	0	0	0
5	2138	0.388929	0.549711	0	0	0	0	0	0	0	0	0	0	0	0	0	0
6	2146	0.392907	0.548636	0.980437	0	0	0	0	0	0	0	0	0	0	0	0	0
7	2469	0.514161	0.487836	0.633292	0	0	0	0	0	0	0	0	0	0	0	0	0
8	2478	0.5154	0.488585	0.633106	0.953287	0	0	0	0	0	0	0	0	0	0	0	0
9	4536	0.982116	0.582043	0.387855	0.550378	0	0	0	0	0	0	0	0	0	0	0	0
10	4544	0.984775	0.583317	0.387692	0.550525	0	0	0	0	0	0	0	0	0	0	0	0
11	4554	0.558086	0.961378	0.500233	0.525264	0	0	0	0	0	0	0	0	0	0	0	0
12	4563	0.559648	0.975531	0.500785	0.527218	0	0	0	0	0	0	0	0	0	0	0	0
13	5262	0.392161	0.547333	0.980971	0.665639	0	0	0	0	0	0	0	0	0	0	0	0
14	5270	0.388699	0.547698	0.978809	0.663464	0	0	0	0	0	0	0	0	0	0	0	0
15	5593	0.519952	0.492553	0.632407	0.953818	0	0	0	0	0	0	0	0	0	0	0	0
16	5602	0.52003	0.491187	0.629693	0.954135	0	0	0	0	0	0	0	0	0	0	0	0

Figure 4. Confidence Matrix highlighting positive correlations made each pass between new and known sources, where column A contains the number of the block received; that is, the pass

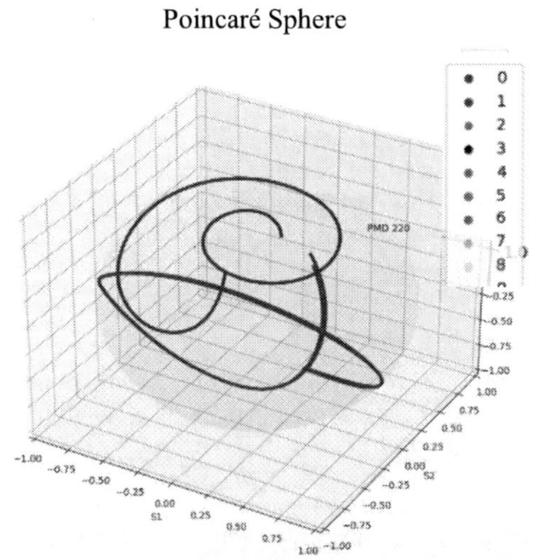

Figure 5. Fingerprints for two devices with low SNR are shown in red and blue curves on the surface of a sphere

This statistic is important when illustrating prototype performance for signals with low SNR. The ability to maintain an average correlation with a confidence factor of 0.97 under low SNR conditions indicates that the fingerprints of wireless edge devices will remain strong even when communications begin to fail.

Polarization measurements from the prototype may be plotted on a spherical coordinate system, called a Poincaré Sphere. Each frequency bin of the DFT contributes a unit vector ending with a single point location on the sphere's surface. In research conducted at the University of Notre Dame, the polarization of a signal has been found to be frequency dependent, leading to a curve, like those shown in Figure 5, as each frequency bin of the DFT is traversed [7].

The fingerprint for a fixed, wireless device may be plotted on a sphere's surface for purposes of visualization, although not necessary for the purpose of correlation. Fingerprints for two separate sensors in the aforementioned chart are color-coded to indicate each device; one, red, and the other, blue. Each point of a fingerprint represents a frequency bin of the DFT. Thus, over the bandwidth of the received signal, a curve meanders around the spherical globe.

Eight tests were run with signals of low SNR. All tests yielded results similar to the test shown above-- there were no false negatives and no false positives.

IV. ELECTRICAL INTERFERENCE

A. Setup

Another set of tests was conducted for conditions involving electrically noisy environments. In these tests, noise-producing equipment was placed near the sensors, one at a time. A table-top rotating fan and a box fan were each used to introduce noise into the environment, one at a time.

The tests involving fans present interesting cases for this technology, since they introduce both electrical interference from the fan motor and motion interference from the rotation of the fan blades within the multi-path.

Both fans were placed, one at a time, on the same counter top as the sensors for this test. This places a fan in close enough proximity to couple electrically with the wireless signals and introduce rotating reflectors in the multi-path environment. This test involved both Bluetooth and Wi-Fi signals, but only the Wi-Fi signals are discussed in this document for simplicity. It suffices to say that no difference was found in the two cases.

B. Results

The DFT of a Wi-Fi signal in this test case appears just as one would expect, with a single main lobe containing a center null. This is the same shape in the frequency response as one would find in a sufficiently strong Wi-Fi signal for good data demodulation. The main lobe is surrounded by two small side lobes, introduced by the finite nature of the DFT. The resulting signal spectrum is shown in Figure 6.

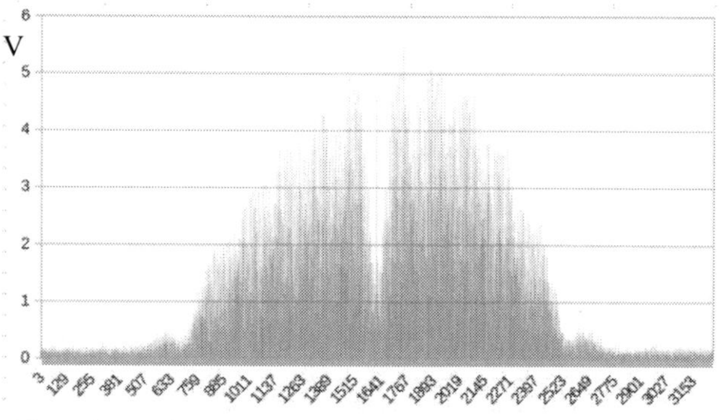

Figure 6. DFT showing relative strength in Volts on the vertical axis and frequency bins on the horizontal axis for a Wi-Fi signal in a test case with a small fan nearby (test I201-F2462-R20-G20-SC16-BS2048-1b)

There were no false positives and no false negatives found in this test case. The average confidence in positive correlations is 98.6% with a standard deviation of 0.01.

As may be seen in Figure 7, which compares a case with no interfering devices, in part A, to the introduced fan, in part B, the noise floor is considerably higher with the fan. Even so, the electrical noise is largely non-polarized and, thus, is for the most part invisible to the algorithms used for fingerprinting. Part C of the figure will be discussed below.

V. Microwave Oven Interference

A. Setup

A test involving interference from a microwave oven is often considered one of the hardest tests to pass in wireless studies. The microwave produces high power signals exactly in the range of frequencies often encountered in the upper ranges of Wi-Fi 2.4 GHz channels. In this test case, we employ channel 11, which is often in the center of such interference.

A microwave oven located near the sensors was turned on for the duration of the test. The result is a series of closely timed pulses which vacillated in amplitude overlaying the sensor signals.

B. Results

Figure 7 shows normal signal amplitude in the time domain in part A, a snapshot of the elevated noise floor from a fan motor in part B, and also a snapshot of microwave background radiation as seen by the receiving antenna on one of the prototypes in part C.

The unusual pulses from the microwave have an effect similar to lowering the received signal SNR by introducing a floor resulting from the presence of the interference. As in the previous tests, the interfering microwave pulses do not seem to significantly influence either the frequency content of individual signals, nor the polarization. Instead, they result in the appearance of a raised noise-plus-interference floor that is not as stable as an environment with no interference.

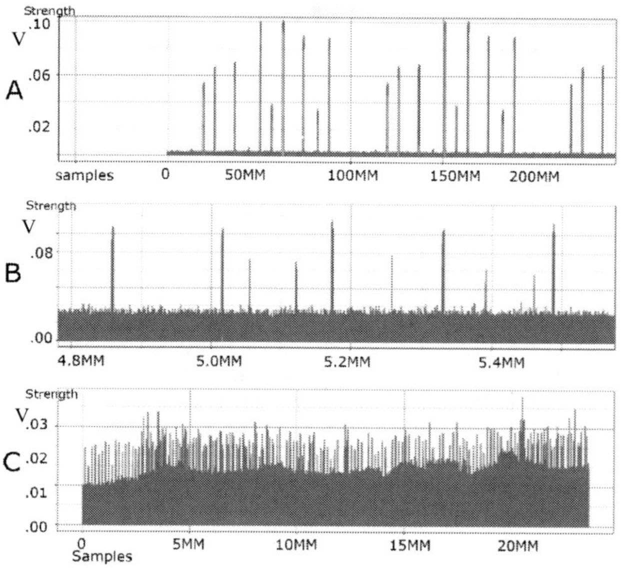

Figure 7. Time domain views of (A) normal sensor activity, (B) fan motor raising the noise floor, and (C) pulses from a microwave raising the noise-interference floor

Taking a closer look at the phenomena, one can see in Figure 8 that the signal spectrum appears as a well-balanced, fairly clean communications signal. Here, we see a main lobe with a null at the center, framed with small side lobes and only a very small amount of deterioration in the right half of the main lobe beginning to form.

Certainly, however, the microwave signal is a major interfering signal and it is clearly seen the in Figure 7 (C) and clearly it lowers the ratio of signal-to-interference-plus-noise of the incoming signals. An examination of the relative intensity (the vertical axis) shows the signal at only half the level of the average intensity of the spectrum in Figure 7.

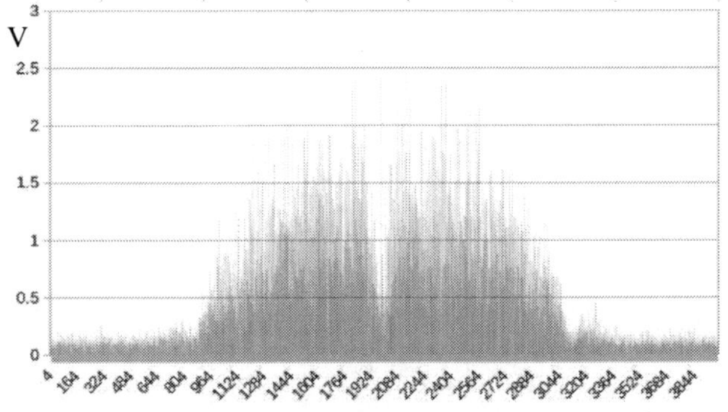

Figure 8. A Discrete Fourier Transform of a signal subject to background microwave interference

If one analyzes a very short period of time, it is possible to see that the background radiation is actually a series of pulses. This may be seen in Figure 9, where a handful of signals fall amidst a continuing series of low amplitude pulses. These do not contain data, of course, but rather are pulses of interfering energy.

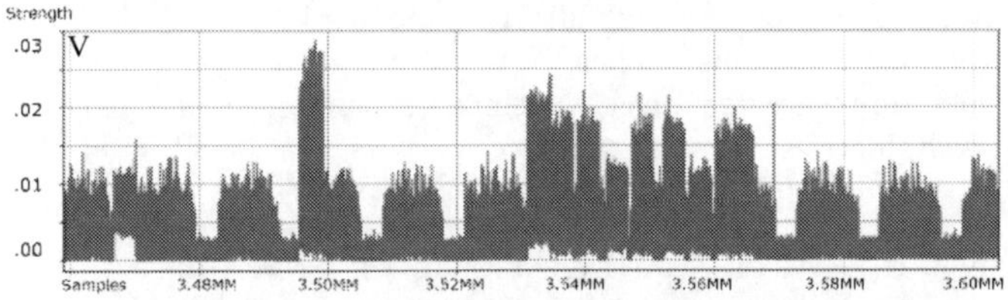

Figure 9. Microwave interference expanded in time shows a series of energy pulses

One might expect that microwave interference would also interfere with the polarization characteristics of the received signals from sensors. However, it was found that the pulses had little effect on the polarization calculation. The average confidence in positive correlation across the test file is 98.0% with a standard deviation of 0.03. Thus, the fingerprints for the identified signals appear to be stable. Fingerprints of the first two devices may be seen in Figure 10. A close examination reveals that the red curve moves very slightly, captured in this image showing the current fingerprint and the previous fingerprint it replaces. Overall, however, the fingerprints for both devices remained fairly stable throughout the test. As in the previous tests, there were no false positives and no false negatives found in this test.

VI. CONCLUSION

In conclusion, the polarization methodology employed for fingerprinting RF signals from wireless edge devices revealed no false positives and no false negatives in 12 tests directed toward studying low SNR and electrical interference from fans and a microwave oven. The confidence of the positive correlations ranged from 97% to 99%, indicating the methodology is resilient to both conditions of low signal strength and electrical interference. Thus, it may be concluded that the fingerprinting of wireless signals using polarization characteristics is quite robust under conditions of low SNRs and electrical interference. In future work, it is recommended that similar tests be performed to study the effects of motion in the multipath on the methodology.

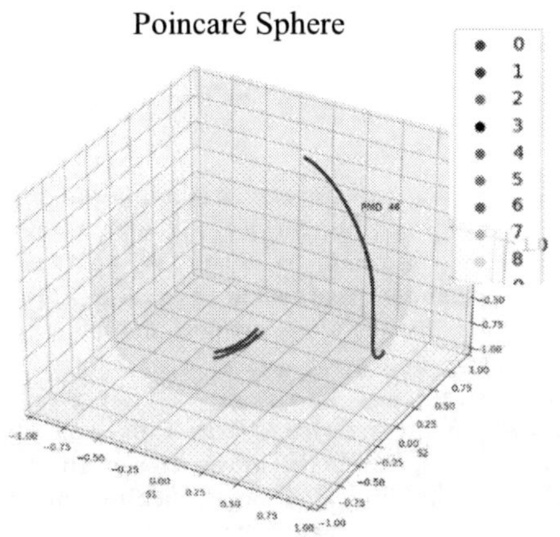

Figure 10. Polarization-based RF fingerprints for two wireless edge devices subject to microwave interference

REFERENCES

[1] 2019 Global ICS & IIoT Risk Report, published by CyberX, a MicroSoft Azure company, 2019, [retrieved: October, 2021]. Available from https://bit.ly/37wsnix

[2] B. Alotaibi and K. Elleithy, "Rogue access point detection: taxonomy, challenges, and future directions," Wireless Personal Communications, June 11, 2016, pp. 1261-1290, DOI: 10.1007/s11277-016-3390-x.

[3] R. P. Heller, T. G. Pratt, J. Loof and E. Jesse, "RF biometric for wireless devices," Proceedings of the Future Technologies Conference (FTC) 2018. FTC 2018. Advances in Intelligent Systems and Computing, vol 881. Springer Nature Switzerland AG, Cham., October 2018. https://doi.org/10.1007/978-3-030-02683-7_65

[4] P. Heller, "Wireless frequency data manipulation for embedded databases use in cybersecurity applications," International Conference on Digital Communications, ICDT, April 18, 2021, pp. 36-42, ISBN: 978-1-61208-835-8.

[5] J. Petrich, VHF-UHF-microwave SDR transceiver on the air, American Radio Relay League Northwestern Division Convention, SEA-PAC 2017, June 3, 2017. [retrieved: October, 2021] Available from: https://seapac.org/seminars/2017/SEA-PAC2017-uhf-sdr-transceiver.pdf

[6] P. Heller, "Radio frequency fingerprinting with polarizaton mode dispersion," a tutorial, Nexcom, Porto, Portugal, April 18, 2021. Available from: https://youtu.be/zE2whBIoaAI.

[7] T. G. Pratt and R. D. Kossler, "Input-to-output instantaneous polarizaton characterization," IEEE Transactions on Antennas and Propogation, Vol. 67, No. 3, pp. 1804-1818, March 2019.

Explainable AI

Introduction to Artificial Intelligence and Explainability

Anne Coull
Objective Insight
Sydney, Australia
Email: anne.objectiveinsight@gmail.com

Abstract— Artificial Intelligence (AI) applies algorithms to make decisions or support human decision-making. AI has the ability to transform every industry sector. While AI cannot yet reason abstractly about real-world situations or interact socially, it is responsible for transforming the online consumer industry, facilitating biometric access to mobile phones, and for bringing science-fiction into reality with driverless cars. Explainability is a major barrier to acceptance and utilisation of AI. This is most apparent in more conservative industry sectors, such as banking and finance, health and security, where the penetration of AI is nominal. Engendering greater user acceptance of AI requires an understanding of its stakeholders, who they are, and what they need to understand. Analysis of the current machine learning models identifies three main groups in the context of explainability: Those models that are transparent and easy to understand from their logical processes; Those models that can be adjusted to take a more human-logical approach that explains itself; and those models that are so complex they need to be explained post-hoc by interpreting their behaviour. Human-centred performance measures for explainability will facilitate continuous improvement and corresponding increased acceptability of AI models.

Keywords- ***Artificial intelligence; machine learning, explainability, stakeholder; acceptance; transparent; model; post-hoc; human-centred explanation; measure.***

I. INTRODUCTION

Artificial Intelligence (AI) utilises algorithms to make decisions or support human decision making by analysing huge data sets, finding patterns, and proposing courses of action, and they do this at scales beyond human capability [7][8]. AI has the ability to transform every industry sector by imitating and augmenting human intelligence and removing inconsistencies in human decision making [8][9][17]. While AI is responsible for the providing biometric access to mobile phones through face recognition, and for turning science-fiction into reality with driverless cars [8][17].

Explainability is a major barrier to acceptance and utilisation of AI [1][20]. "The current generation of AI systems offer tremendous benefits, but their effectiveness is constrained by the machine's inability to explain its decisions and actions" [6]. This is most apparent in more conservative industry sectors, such as banking and finance, health and security, where the penetration of AI is nominal. Explainable AI will be essential if industry leaders, professional specialists and other AI stakeholders are to understand, appropriately trust, and effectively manage this upcoming generation of artificially intelligent partners.

Section II provides an introduction to Artificial Intelligence and Machine Learning. Section III looks at some of the areas where AI has been successfully applied, and analyses why AI is not being utilized more broadly. Section IV investigates user acceptance and Section V discusses different methods for making AI and ML explainable, and approaches for interpreting ML models and generating greater user acceptance amongst the AI stakeholders.

II. ARTTIFICIAL INTELLIGENCE AND MACHINE LEARNING

Machine Learning is one tool in Artificial Intelligence that is largely responsible for its rise. The terms Artificial Intelligence (AI) and Machine Learning (ML) are used interchangeably in literature. In 1959, Arthur Samuel defined Machine Learning as the "Field of study that gives computers the ability to learn without being programmed." Mathematical models are utilized to "train" the AI system based on large volumes of training data so that when it is presented with an input it has not seen before, it can make its own assessment and provide a predictive response [19].

More recently, in 1998, Tom Mitchel [19] described AI as the well-posed learning problem, which outlines how computer systems learn: "A computer program is said to *learn* from experience **E** with respect to some task **T** and some performance measure **M**, if its performance on **T**, as measured by **P**, improves with experience **E**." [19]

A computer or system is said to have artificial intelligence when it has the ability to process large amounts of data, reason, and identify patterns that a human could or could not discern, at a scale unattainable by humans [1].

The science fiction stories of AI self-learning to a degree that its intelligence enables it to operate completely autonomously, while exciting, have little to do with reality. The general AI capability of these autonomous computers would necessitate them have strong capabilities in multiple intelligences and to co-ordinate these concurrently. Narrow AI, where machines are good at one capability, is now part of every-day life, and is highly lucrative for consumer internet where online advertising is targeted to those consumers more likely to click [18]. More recently the self-driving car has progressed to the point of prototypes demonstrating the conflicting decisions required by an autonomous vehicle.

III. AI POTENTIAL VERSUS REALITY

A. *AI Capabilities*

AI can transform every major industry [17]. Many fields, particularly those with huge volumes of reliable data, are already benefiting from the support ML offers to decision making and the inferring of relations far beyond human cognitive capability [1].

Supervised learning is the most common form of Machine Learning, or AI that can perform simple A input to B output mappings [18]:

TABLE I. SUPERVISED LEARING APPLICATIONS [18]

Table Column Head		
Input	***AI***	***Output***
Email	SPAM filtering	SPAM
Audio	Speech recognition	Text transcript
English	Machine translation	Chinese
Ad, user info	Online advertising	Click?
User's face	Facial recognition	Unlock the iphone
Applicants financial info	Loan application risk forecasting	Will you repay the loan
Scene in front of car, lidar reading	Self-driving car	Positions of other cars
Image of a product (eg. A phone	Visual inspection	Identify manufacturing defects

- If the type of input is email and the output required is 'is it SPAM or not?' then the AI performs SPAM filtering, or
- If the input is an audio recording, and the output required is a text transcript then the AI is speech recognition.
- If the required input is English and output another language, Chinese, French, then this is machine translation.
- The most successful form of this type pf Machine Learning is online advertising, where all the large online advertising platforms have a piece of AI that inputs a piece of information about the ad, and some information about the user, and they try to determine the likelihood that you will click. By showing the ads the user is most likely to click on, this has become very lucrative.
- Similarly, facial recognition is used as a form of biometric access control for unlocking mobile phones.
- For a self-driving car, one of the key pieces of AI is one that takes in an image of the surroundings along with other positional input from a radar, and outputs the position of other cars and makes a decision to avoid the other cars.
- Or, in manufacturing, AI is being used to Identify manufacturing defects by taking a picture of the product being manufactured and using AI to perform visual inspection and identify any defects such as scratches [18].

This simple form of Machine learning has taken off in the last few years with the availability of large volumes of digitized data, and has proven very valuable [18].

B. *Why is AI not used more broadly*

ML / AI have proven useful when applied to critical areas of health care, fraud detection, and criminal justice. In healthcare, AI accelerates diagnosis and recommends treatments [22] more consistently than doctors [9]. In criminal justice it facilitates greater consistency in sentencing [22] by reducing the effects of cognitive bias [9].

Deep neural networks (DNN) have been particularly successful due to their ability to efficiently find an answer by extrapolating highly complex learning algorithms with millions of parameters [1]. The complexity of DNNs makes it difficult for a human to understand the path that was taken by the machine to get to the answer presented [1][8] and this raises questions around the trustworthiness of these AI-based systems [22]. AI has made incredible inroads into the software industry but has failed to penetrate more broadly for three key reasons: Availability of huge volumes of data to train the machine learning, ability for AI to generalise across different data sources, and the lack of acceptance by those affected.

To achieve high levels of performance at, speech and image recognition, machine learning approaches require vast quantities of training data [12] [20]. Each training data element includes an example, and a translation of what that training example means. For example, Speech recognition models require 50,000 hours of data and transcripts of that audio. Generating this training data is a significant undertaking with the data itself becoming a valuable differentiating asset. [17][20]. The areas that have extracted great benefit from AI are those with access to that data, such as Google, Facebook, and Apple.

In fields such as health, where the data volumes relate directly to the disease occurrence, the variance in data can drive variance in results. The AI may perform to human level when presented with diseases for which there is a high volume of data, but is ineffective at identifying less-common diseases. From a lung scan, for example, the AI may recognise pneumonia, peristalsis, lung cancer, or pulmonary thrombosis, but it may not recognise tuberculosis, for example.

Generalisability fails when a researcher uses data from only a few data sources. They may work closely with radiologist from the local hospital, for example. They test their machine learning, refine their algorithms based on this limited data input and may get human-level results, but as soon as they take their model to a new context, to another hospital with a different radiologist, their AI algorithm doesn't perform so well. Here lies the gap between research and the real-world. In the health sector, different radiologists have different techniques for scanning patients. The ML algorithm may perform as well as a human with scans from a small sample set radiologists, but misdiagnose when presented with scans from another radiologist [20].

The medical practitioner will not trust the AI to diagnose her patient if she cannot rely on it to perform consistently under different circumstances [20], nor can she be confident of the AI system's diagnosis if there is no explanation for why the AI thinks there might be cancer present. This lack of transparency is fueling the gap between the research community and industry sectors, and our scans continue to be diagnosed by a human [1][16].

There has been resistance to AI in more risk averse industry sectors such as banking, finances, security and health where lack of trust in how these AI models work, along with heavy oversight by regulators, is impeding inhibiting the uptake of AI [1]. Results and metrics from AI systems may be impressive, but explainability will continue to be a barrier to AI adoption in practical implementations [1]. As Michael I Jordan explains: "We will need well-thought-out interactions of humans and computers to solve our most pressing problems" [8].

IV. User Acceptance

Machine learning models are opaque, non-intuitive, and difficult for people to understand [5][6] and as they expand into transportation, medicine, manufacturing and defence, no-one wants to be in the position of thinking the machine is wrong, and not understanding why [2]. Explanations of AI system's reasoning is paramount for users to collaborate and trust them [16].

Acceptance requires Change Management and Explainability [20]: an understanding of how the AI model works, and how it will impact those around it.

We, as researchers and IT professionals need to face into the fact that jobs will be lost through the implementation of AI. AI can automate any one-minute task, and many jobs are made up of a sequence of one-minute tasks [17].

"Explainable AI refers to models that take action to clarify their internal functions so that a human can understand the basis of their decision making" [1]. In order to be understood, an AI model needs to be transparent, interpretable, comprehensible and intelligible by the human audience [4][13].

Elements of Explainability include:

- Trustworthiness: confidence that the model will act as intended when facing a given problem [1].
- Causality: explainable models might should ease the task of finding relationships that could be tested for a stronger causal link between the involved variables [1].
- Transferability: clarity of the boundaries that affect a model provide insight to its limitations, and to other problems. Can the model be applied in different contexts [1]?
- Informativeness: The ML model is only solving part of the problem: The problem being solved by the ML model is only a subset of the problem being addressed by its human user [1].
- Confidence: ML models need to demonstrate stability and reliability [1].
- Fairness: ML models can have built in biases. Explainability facilitates an ethical analysis of the model by exposing these biases [1].
- Accessibility & Interactivity: Explainability opens the door, in certain situations, for users to interact with the model and to be more involved in the processes of improving and developing the ML model [1].
- Privacy awareness: To satisfy GDPR and other regulatory privacy legislations, there is a need to demonstrate to customers how their data is being used [13]. Explainability highlights what data has been captured by the ML model enabling potential privacy breaches to be prevented [1].
- Cybersecurity: Engineers regularly make trade-offs between functionality and cybersecurity. As they design functionality into systems, invariably they introduce cyber vulnerabilities, knowingly and unknowingly [21]. Explainability can make cyber vulnerabilities transparent during the model development so these can be addressed or mitigative controls implemented prior to release.

Change management, along with the increased understanding given by explainability facilitates acceptance by stakeholders of the ML model.

V. Explainable Artificial Intelligence

A. *Classic vs Explainable AI:*

1) *Classic AI*

Classic AI provides the response to the question or task requested, with a confidence level in terms of a probability. It provides no details as to how it reached this outcome, merely the result it came up with. The user has no comprehension of how or why the model produced this response nor the conditions under which this response could be questionable or invalid.

2) *Explainable AI*

Explainable AI provides the same recommendation that the model produced but in a more understandable form, in plain English, along with the reasoning for why and how the model determined this outcome.

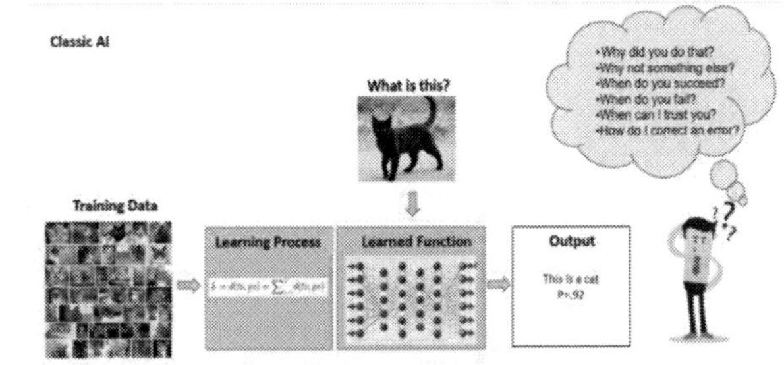

Figure 1. Classic AI [5][6]

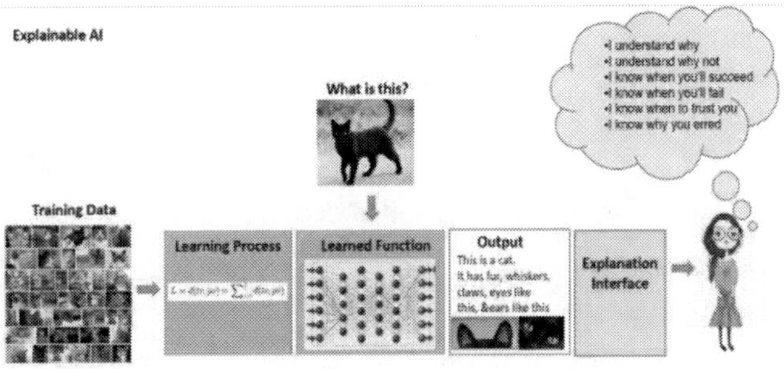

Figure 2. Explainable AI [5][6]

In the example provided, the differentiators were ear shape, eye type, and whiskers, along with other attributes associated with a four-legged furred animal. In addition, explainable AI presents this information through an interface comprehensible by humans.

B. Explainability connects research to reality

1. Explainability facilitates impartiality in decision-making by making any bias generated from the training set transparent so this can be corrected [1].

2. Explainability facilitates robustness by highlighting conflicting outcomes that could destabilise the predictions and make them unreliable [1].

3. Explainability can verify that only meaningful variables drive the output, providing assurance that the model's reasoning is solid and reliable [1].

Explainability requires that algorithms demonstrating accuracy in the research laboratory also perform well in practice and provides explicit evidence for this. This will raise the confidence and trustworthiness of the claims made about the system [22].

"XAI will create a suite of machine learning techniques that enables human users to understand, appropriately trust, and effectively manage the emerging generation of artificially intelligent partners" [5][6].

C. Explainable to Whom: AI Stakeholders

The key to making an intelligent system explainable, is to understand the needs and comprehension styles of the different human stakeholders for that system [1][16].

Different audiences have different requirements. The domain experts, medical practitioners, legal judges, and the decision makers relying on the AI's recommendations will want to understand what problem the model is solving and why the model gives the answers it does. They will need to gain confidence that the model it is stable and reliable, and behaves as expected in every situation. Government regulators external to the organisation, and internal compliance will be interested in the model's ability to meet legislative compliance obligations, data privacy appetite, and cyber security objectives. Internal technology risk will want to understand vulnerabilities and data breach risks the model introduces, and how these can be mitigated. Managers, executives, and board members who may have personal liability responsibilities will need to verify that their risk and compliance exposure is being contained, and that the system is robust and reliable. They may also be interested to understand the opportunities the ML model provides and whether it is transferable to enable new business opportunities.

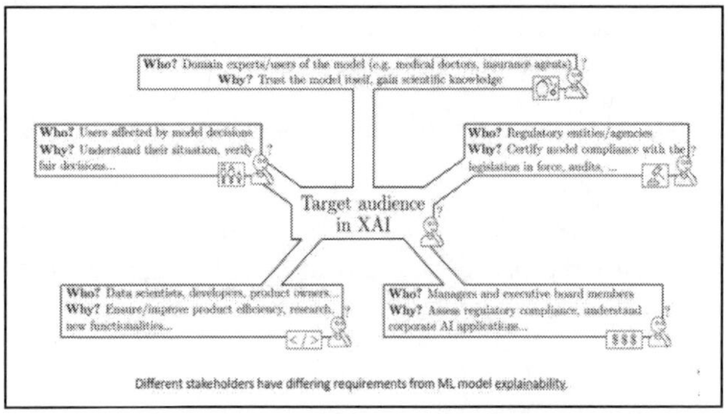

Figure 3. Stakeholders of Explainable AI [1]

Researchers, data scientists, and developers will be interested to understand how the learning model works, the training data that was used, causality between its data elements, what its boundaries and limitations are, and how this model can be applied in different contexts. The users will want to understand how the ML model benefits them and the way they work. They will want to understand the decisioning processes and how closely this aligns to their own. They may be interested in being actively involved in developing and improving the model, but they will most certainly will want to understand how this model will impact their job, their patients and/or clients [1].

D. Explainability Approaches

Machine Learning model explainability is categorized based on how easy it is to understand in its raw state:

1. Transparent interpretable models are easy for humans to understand, by reading the modelling logic;
2. Deep Explanations adjust a more complex model to incorporate explainability, and
3. Post-hoc explanations of opaque models that do not modify the model, but treat it as a black-box [1][6][20].

1) Transparent Interpretable Models

Transparent Models use simple computation structures, such as "if-then rules" within an interpretable architecture. These include:

- Logical / linear regression
- Decision trees
- K-Nearest Neighbours (KNN)
- Rule-based Learners
- General Additive Models
- Bayesian Models [1][16]

In situations where these models become extremely complex, dense, and difficult to decipher, they can be pruned or approximated with a simpler version. This involves identifying and the removing dependent support vectors and eliminating redundant parameters [16].

Bayesian Rule Lists (BRL), developed by Latham et al, provides 85-90% predictive accuracy. These models are structured as sparse decision lists consisting of a series of if… then… statements where the *if* statements list a set of features, and the *then* statements correspond to the predicted outcome. These are simple to follow and easy to understand. This list is built from the training data set: a comprehensive data set generates a comprehensive list of options and predictable outcomes. The example illustrated in Figure IV is based on the data set from the Titanic, and predicts survivability based on gender, adult-hood, and class. Given their high performance and ease of interpretability, BRLs are a preferred model for developing explainable AI [15].

if male **and** adult **then** *survival probability* 21% (19%–23%)
else if 3rd class **then** *survival probability* 44% (38%–51%)
else if 1st class **then** *survival probability* 96% (92%–99%)
else *survival probability* 88% (82%–94%)

Figure 4. Decision list for the Titanic survivors. In parentheses is the 95% credible interval for the survival probability [15].

2) Deep Explanations

Deep Explanations involve adjusting the model itself so that is learns in a more human-logical way and can more easily explain the steps it took to reach its decision [5][6].

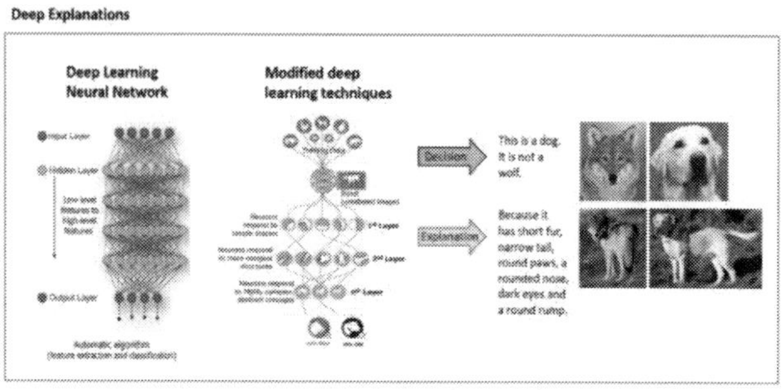

Figure 5. Deep Explanations [5][6]

3) Opaque Model Induction

The guidance from literature for classification of post-hoc explanatory models varies, but a logical method for aligning these complex ML models is to segregate them into:

- Explanation by simplification
- Feature relevance explanation
- Local Explanations
- Visual explanation, and
- Architecture modification [1].

These explanatory models deduce the decisioning of opaque ML by analysing the input to output alignments.

E. Human-centred Explanation Interface

The ultimate purpose of explainability is to enable humans to make informed decisions with valuable input from the AI system. The human-centred explanation interface translates the AI explanations, and presents them as:

- Statements in natural language that describe the elements, analytics, and context that support a choice;
- Visualisations that directly highlight portions of the raw data that support a choice and allow viewers to form their own understanding;
- Specific Cases, examples and/ or scenarios that support the choice the model made;
- Reasons for Rejection of alternative choices that argue against less preferred answers based on analytics, cases, and data [6].

F. *Explainable AI in Human Decision-making*

AI explainability, provided to humans through a suitable interface, will improve the uptake of AI by increasing trust and confidence in the responses the AI provides. Humans will own the decision process, with explainable AI becoming a tool commonly applied to enhance informed decision making [5][6].

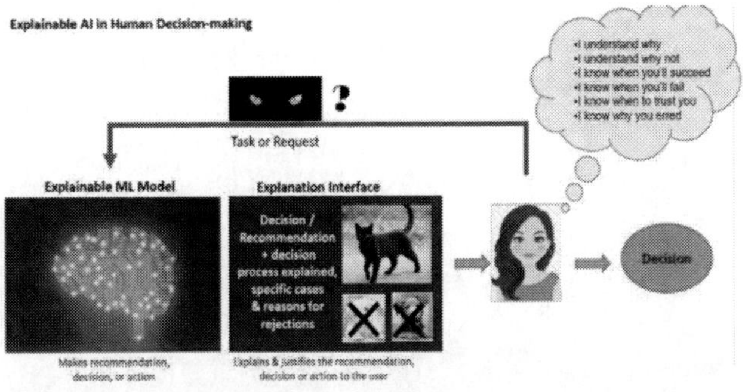

Figure 6. Explainable AI in human decision making [5][6]

The user will raise the request to the AI system, the system will provide a recommendation, along with the explanation for its recommendation, via an easy-to-understand Explanation Interface. The human can choose to take the additional information provided by the AI system into account when they make their decision, or not.

G. *Measuring Explainability Effectiveness*

To ensure explainability of AI improves over time, its effectiveness needs to be measured. Gunning proposed the following human-centric measures:

TABLE II. MEASURING EXPLAINABILITY EFFECTIVENESS

Explainability Effectiveness	
Metric	***Measure***
Model Understanding	Does the user understand the overall model & individual decisions, its strengths & weakness, how predictable is the models decisioning, and are there work-arounds for known weaknesses.
User Satisfaction	Based on explanation clarity & helpfulness as measured by the user
Trustworthiness	Is the model trustworthy and appropriate for future use
Task & Decisioning Performance	Does the AI explanation improve the user's decision, Does the user understand the AI decisioning?
Self-correctability and improvement	Does the model identifying & correct its errors? Does it undergo continuous training?

VI. CONCLUSION

"Life is by definition unpredictable. It is impossible for programmers to anticipate every problematic or surprising situation that might arise, which means existing ML systems remain susceptible to failures as they encounter the irregularities and unpredictability of real-world circumstances." Hava Siegelmann, DARPA L2M program manager [3].

It is not adequate for an AI system to merely perform its task and provide the answers. As Machine Learning and Artificial Intelligence evolve, their ability to enhance human capabilities in every industry will grow. Yet, their uptake will continue to rely on humans. AI systems will need to be able to explain themselves if humans are to trust them, understand them, and work *with* them on critical, life-affecting decisions and tasks.

REFERENCES

[1] A. Arrieta et al., "Explainable Artificial Intelligence (XAI): Concepts, Taxonomies, Opportunities and Challenges toward Responsible AI", available from: ResearchGate arXiv:1910.10045v1 [cs.AI] 22 Oct 2019, accessed March 2021.

[2] A. Bleicher, "Demystifying the Black Box That Is AI: Humans are increasingly entrusting our security, health and safety to "black box" intelligent machines", Scientific American, August 2017, available from: https://www.scientificamerican.com/article/ demystifying-the-black-box-that-is-ai/, accessed September 2021.

[3] DARPA, Researchers Selected to Develop Novel Approaches to Lifelong Machine Learning, DARPA, May 7, 2018, available from: http://ein.iconnect007.com/index.php/article/110412/researchers-selected-to-develop-novel-approaches-to-lifelong-machine-learning/110415/?skin=ein, accessed September 2021.

[4] R. Guidotti et al., "A survey of methods for explaining black box models", ACM Computing Surveys, 51 (5) (2018), pp. 93:1-93:42, accessed September 2021.

[5] D. Gunning, "Explainable Artificial Intelligence (XAI), DARPA/120, National Security Archive", 2017, available from: https://ia803105.us.archive.org/17/items/5794867-National-Security-Archive-David-Gunning-DARPA/5794867-National-Security-Archive-David-Gunning-DARPA.pdf, accessed September 2021.

[6] D. Gunning, "Explainable artificial intelligence (XAI)", Technical Report, Defense Advanced Research Projects Agency (DARPA) (2017), accessed March 2021.

[7] M. I. Jordan, "Artificial Intelligence—The Revolution Hasn't Happened Yet." Harvard Data Science Review, 1(1) 2019. Available from: https://doi.org/10.1162/99608f92.f06c6e61, accessed March 2021.

[8] M. I. Jordan, "Stop calling everything Artificial Intelligence", IEEE Spectrum March 2021, available from: https://spectrum.ieee.org/stop-calling-everything-ai-machinelearning-pioneer-says, accessed March 2021.

[9] D. Kahneman, "Thinking, fast and slow." Penguin Press, ISBN: 9780141033570, 2 July 2012.

[10] A. Korchi et al., "Machine Learning and Deep Learning Revolutionize Artificial Intelligence", International Journal of Scientific & Engineering Research Volume 10, Issue 9, September-2019 1536 ISSN 2229-5518, accessed September 2021.

[11] T. Kulesza et al., "Principles of Explanatory Debugging to Personalize Interactive Machine Learning". IUI 2015, Proceedings of the 20th International Conference on Intelligent User Interfaces, pp. 126-137, 2015.

[12] B. Lake et al., "Human-level concept learning through probabilistic program induction", 2015 Available from:

https://www.cs.cmu.edu/~rsalakhu/papers/LakeEtAl2015Science.pdf, accessed September 2021.

[13] G. Lawton, "The future of trust must be built on data transparency", techtarget.com, Mar 2021, available from: https://searchcio.techtarget.com/feature/The-future-of-trust-must-be-built-on-data-transparency?track=NL-1808&ad=938015&asrc=EM_NLN_151269842&utm_medium=EM&utm_source=NLN&utm_campaign=20210310_The+future+of+trust+must+be+built+on+data+transparency, accessed September 2021.

[14] G. Lawton, "4 explainable AI techniques for machine learning models", techtarget.com, April 2020, available from: https://searchenterpriseai.techtarget.com/feature/How-to-achieve-explainability-in-AI-models, accessed March 2021.

[15] B. Letham et al., "Interpretable classifiers using rules and Bayesian analysis: Building a better stroke prediction model". IUI 2015, Proceedings of the 20th International Conference on Intelligent User Interfaces (pp. 126-137).

[16] Y. Ming, "A survey on visualization for explainable classifiers", 2017, available from: https://cse.hkust.edu.hk/~huamin/explainable_AI_yao.pdf, accessed September 2021.

[17] A. Ng, "The state of Artificial Intelligence, MIT Technology Review", EmTech September 2017. Available from: https://www.youtube.com/watch?v=NKpuX_yzdYs, accessed September 2021.

[18] A. Ng, "Artificial Intelligence for everyone (part 1) – complete tutorial", March 2019, available from: https://www.youtube.com/watch?v=zOI6Oll1Zrg, accessed September 2021.

[19] A. Ng, "CS229 – Machine Learning: Lecture 1 – the motivation and applications of machine learning", Stanford Engineering Everywhere, Stanford University. April 2020. Available from: https://see.stanford.edu/Course/CS229/47, accessed September 2021.

[20] A. Ng, "Bridging AIs proof-of-concept to production gap", Stanford University Human-Centred Artificial Intelligence Seminar, September 2020, available from: https://www.youtube.com/watch?v=tsPuVAMaADY, accessed September 2021.

[21] D. Snyder et al., "Improving the Cybersecurity of U.S. Air Force Military Systems Throughout their Life Cycles", Library of Congress Control Number: 2015952790, ISBN: 978-0-8330-8900-7, Published by the RAND Corporation, Santa Monica, Calif. 2015

[22] D. Spiegelhalter, "Should We Trust Algorithms?". Harvard Data Science Review, 2(1). 2020, available from, https://doi.org/10.1162/99608f92.cb91a35a, accessed March 2021.

[23] 3brown1blue, "Neural Networks: from the ground up", 2017, available from: https://www.youtube.com/watch?v=aircAruvnKk, accessed September 2021.

Application Services in Space Information Networks

Anders Fongen
Norwegian Defence University College, Cyber Defence Academy (FHS/CIS)
Lillehammer, Norway
Email: anders@fongen.no

***Abstract*—As Low Earth Orbit satellites (LEO) are evolving from "radio mirrors" to "network entities" it is reasonable to foresee a development of satellite networks which not only forwards network traffic, but engage in middleware operations, discovery services and even collaborate applications. However, efforts already investigating "data centers in space" do so without taking into regard the special properties of orbiting spacecrafts and their relation to the demographic characteristics on the ground below them. In this position paper, an outline of a distributed system hosted in a Space Information Network (SIN) will be presented. Of special interest is the cyclic properties of the link topology and the predictability of the workload offered by its client on the surface below. Beside the general operating principle, a selection of discovery and application services will be used to demonstrate the feasibility of the principles, as well as to identify remaining problems and research topics.**

***Keywords*—LEO satellites; space information networks; AaaS in space**

I. INTRODUCTION

A number of Geosynchronous Equatorial Orbit (GEO), High Eliptical Orbit (HEO) and Low Earth Orbit (LEO) satellites together with high altitude aircrafts (balloons, drones) may form a distributed system sometimes called a Space Information Network (SIN). Although most often proposed for the provision of communication services only, some efforts also investigate the SIN as "cloud computing in space".

The advantages offered by a SIN should not only be global coverage, but also faster Round Trip Time (RTT). In theory, a satellite at 300 km altitude can offer an RTT of only 2ms, far better than any surface based path to a data center. Shorter RTT enables new applications for synchronous collaboration and remote control.

The main challenges with the AaaS (Application as a Service) principle in a SIN is the transfer of state during handover operations. For low-orbit spacecrafts, handover takes place at short intervals and must be subject to scalability analysis since a potentially high number of client sessions are kept in the spacecrafts.

The rest of the paper is organized as follows: In Section II, the distinct properties of a SIN, compared to other distributed systems are presented. In Section III, a small modeling effort is shown together with a plot considering population density during orbital period. Related research is briefly discussed in Section IV. A more technological perspective on a number of basic elements are discussed in Section V followed by a presentation of three example application services in Section VI. Finally, a summary and suggested future research problems are given in Section VII.

II. PROPERTIES OF A SIN

A SIN has properties distinct from an ordinary distributed mobile system. Unlike a mobile system, where the users move around a more or less stationary infrastructure, a SIN system will consist of a mobile infrastructure and stationary (as seen from space) users. Besides, the mobility patterns of the SIN infrastructure are highly predictable, and cyclic. At any time in the future, the position of the spacecraft, the topology of the inter-satellite links and the relative position of the ground stations are known, as well as the demographic characteristics of the population at the surface below.

Demographic characteristics refer to population density, age distribution, language, etc, as well as other preferences learned through earlier pass or from other satellites. The characteristics can be predicted to estimate type and volume of service requests for which the satellites can prepare in advance.

The workload estimation may also be used to schedule delay tolerant communication and computational activities to periods of low activity. The population pattern of the earth leaves short, but frequent periods of no human activity below (except for expeditioners and unmanned sensors) where background activities like synchronization and replication can take place. Ground stations can be used for intermittent high-speed communication with the terrestrial network and should be located in locations with low population density. Also, inter-satellite communication for background activities can take place in the polar regions, where the longitude distance between the satellites is short.

III. POPULATION DENSITY ESTIMATIONS

For the purpose of studying the varying population density on the ground below a satellite during its orbital period, a Python program was made which models the orbit and correlates the satellite position with demographic data available for download [1].

The downloaded data is easily accessed and incorporated into the program. Each grid element limited by longitude great circles and latitude small circles is represented with a value indicating the number of people per square km.

The modeled orbits are all assumed to be circular with 90 minutes orbit cycle o, and with inclination angles ϕ of 60, 70 and 80 degrees, respectively. From the length of the arc a, which is expressed as a function of time t:

$$a = (t/o) \bmod 1 * 2\pi \tag{1}$$

The corresponding longitude lo and latitude la is calculated as a function of a and ϕ:

$$la = \arcsin(\sin(\phi) * \sin(a)) \quad (2)$$

$$lo = \arccos(\cos(a)/\cos(la)) \quad (3)$$

A graphical representation of the result is shown in Figure 1, with the horizontal axis showing time in minutes and the vertical axis the corresponding population density. Different fill patterns represent the different orbit inclination angles as indicated in the legends. As expected, the plot shows that there are short bursts of high population density below with idle periods in between. Please observe that there seems to be one high peak for every 90 minutes cycle, with only modest traffic in between.

The plot is far from accurate in its details, but indicates the opportunity for the satellite to spend its communication resources on maintenance and updating tasks between busy periods.

Since higher inclination angles means relatively more time over polar regions the results were expected to show bigger variations than what is indicated in the figure. But the most important question remains as: How can these idle periods be used for communication and computation tasks not related to client requests, and to prepare the spacecraft for the next populated area on its itinerary?

IV. Related Research

Most efforts on SIN have envisioned the structure as a provider of communication services only, where the communication endpoints are located on the earth's surface. Existing infrastructure like the Iridium system has been in operation for three decades and proves the feasibility of a LEO system for global telephone service. More recent initiatives like the Starlink infrastructure are currently being deployed on a very large scale for the provision of global Internet access [2].

Other projects have proposed "cloud computing" in space by deploying data centers in larger satellites with volume and energy resources sufficient for their operation. Other smaller satellites may carry units for "fog computing" in a distributed fashion in order to provide replicated services through communication paths with fewer hops [3] [4].

The resource management in satellites with great variations in its workload can be predicted, but machine learning approaches may also contribute to a management scheme which better adapts to unpredictable variations. Zhou et al. offer their results on a study based on neural networks in [5].

In order to improve the communication capacity of SIN units, lots of research has gone into the development of antennas for spatial multiplexing (space-division multiple access, SDMA), beamforming, non-orthogonal multiple access, optical communication links etc. [6] [7].

The proposals made in this position paper will not deal with technical details in the communication technology, but rather view the SIN as a distributed system which borrows its methods and solutions from the field of distributed computing. The author is not aware of other efforts to investigate this perspective to the extent necessary for a SIN offering application services.

V. Technological aspects of SIN services

Services offered by a SIN will have properties different from ordinary distributed systems. A technological discussion on how to support these properties follows in subsequent paragraphs.

A. State Transfer Between SIN units

For any location on earth, a LEO satellite will pass from one horizon to the other in a matter of minutes. Frequent handover to a trailing satellite every few minutes is necessary in order to provide a ground terminal with continuous service. For the provision of communication services only, this is a solved problem. For application services, however, a handover requires a state transfer of possibly complex and large data structures, e.g.:

- Web session objects, with open connections to files and databases
- Cached contents in Domain Name Service (DNS) proxies
- Shared document collections expected to be available and up to date
- Ongoing chat and media-rich conferences

Some of these data structures will be bound to a client session and their content subject to client actions. Others, like cached content from discovery protocols, are dependent on the collective actions of the client community. This kind of information can also be speculatively pre-fetched, based on expected client requests derived from the correlation of orbital parameters and demographic data.

State bound to client sessions cannot be pre-fetched, but must be transferred from leading satellites, i.e. the previous satellites (front and front-west, since the earth is rotating counter clockwise), and passed on to trailing satellites (back and back-east). Communication between satellites in the same orbital plane may effectively use optical links for high speed communication since their relative positions are fixed, while links to satellites in the neighbouring orbital plane would need adjustable beams as their relative position changes with the latitude position. The optical links will not compete with ground links for transmission capacity.

One can visualize the collection of client states being "fixed" in the sky above the client's position while the satellites move and continuously relay the state objects in the opposite direction. Some session objects will be passed to trailing satellites in the same orbital plane, others to the orbital plane to the east, depending on the hand-over operation (of which the sending satellite is assumed to be informed of).

The handling of shared storage (document collections and databases) which should be available for ground terminals takes the form of a replication problem where availability, consistency and ordering semantics must be taken into account. The timeliness of updates is also of interest, since the predictable patterns of user request allows some updates to

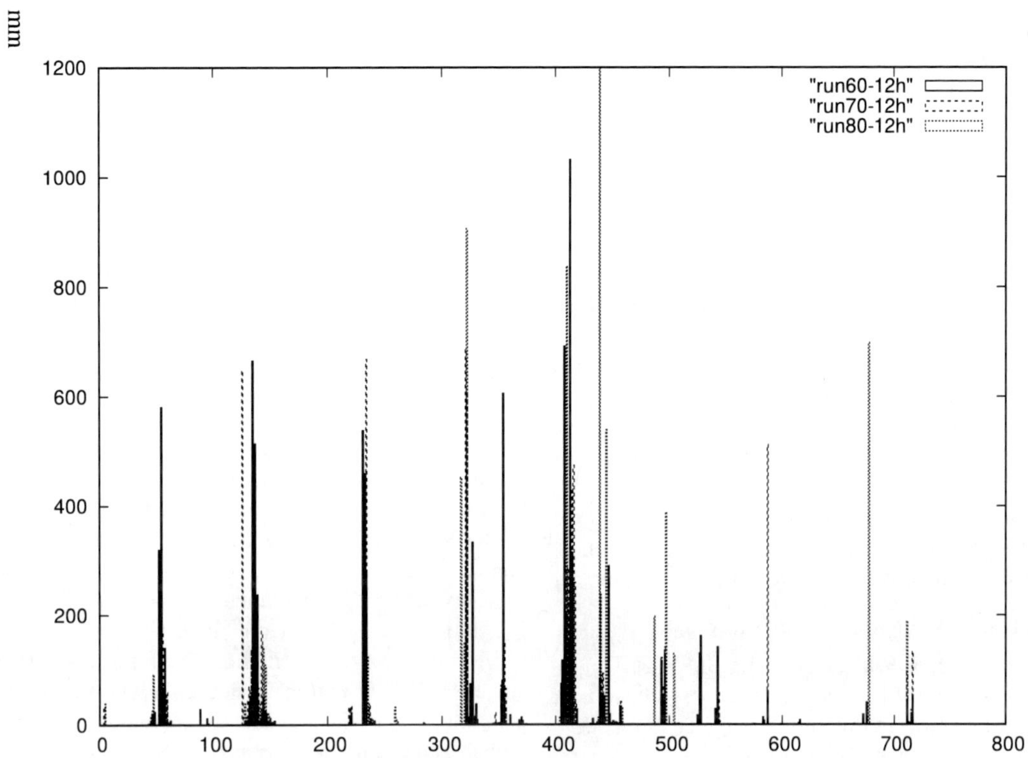

Figure 1. Population density below a satellite during 12 hour orbit

be postponed until more communication and computational resources are in supply.

Only objects with *serializable* properties (in the sense used in the Java programming language) may be passed on between spacecrafts. Objects representing local OS resources like sockets, files and mutexes will not. This limitation will impose the same system design restrictions as what are found in traditional mobile and distributed systems.

B. Delay Tolerant Services

A significant fraction of client requests is expected to be forwarded to other resources, possibly terrestrial. Due to response time requirements, the requests and the resulting reply need to be given high priority. Other requests can be regarded as delay tolerant, and the forwarding operation may be postponed to a later instant where resources have better availability, e.g. when the satellite is within range of a ground station. Requests falling into this category can be:

- E-mail operations, both inbox update and sending (subject to message priority)
- Certain type of sensor readings, e.g., environmental observations
- Software updates
- Transfer of large files
- BitTorrent applications
- Cache refreshes
- Speculative (proactive) replication

C. IP address structure

The satellites will expose their network endpoint for client connections, but it is not advisable to give each satellite a unique IP address. With separate Internet Protocol (IP) addresses, handover operations would require complicated arrangements for maintaining existing flows and connections. A more appealing approach is to give all satellites the same IP address for their service endpoint, since clients on the surface will never address more than one of them. An IP address that is preserved across handover will allow a transparent transfer of User Datagram Protocol (UDP) flows from one satellite to the next. Transmission Control Protocol (TCP) connections may also in theory be transferred, but would require a modified TCP protocol stack.

Satellites will need to invoke services in other satellites through their inter-satellite links. The interfaces used for this purpose must have unique IP addresses within a private/non-connected subnet, since these interfaces should not be reachable from endpoints elsewhere, e.g., in the Internet.

For the forwarding of IP datagrams between satellites, the inter-satellite link interfaces could be used for IP-based routing, but a more flexible solution would be to leave forwarding actions to the link layer, e.g., by employing Multiprotocol Label Switching (MPLS). The connection between a terrestrial client and a spacecraft should be handled likewise by a link-layer tunnel which also take care of keeping the handover operation transparent at the IP layer.

D. Speculative caching

As a satellite enters a populated region, the expected workload offered by terrestrial clients is estimated from a range of data sources: The demographic data of the region, the set of requests from earlier passes, the requests received from immediate leading spacecrafts etc. These data sources can be subject to statistical or machine-learned algorithms in order to determine the content of on-board data storage that will provide the best and fastest response to the requests from that region.

This content may be loaded from leading satellites or from ground stations. For this reason, the location of ground stations become a significant factor for the caching scheme. Even existing data objects may be loaded if the master copy is updated.

The cached data objects may be updated through client requests, and the replication of updates to other storage units must observe the decided consistency and ordering semantics.

VI. Outline of Example Applications

The following paragraphs will discuss the SIN's ability to support a small selection of simple applications, chosen in order also to identify architectural limitations. The selection includes both discovery service, streaming service and storage service.

A. Discovery Service - DNS

Domain Name Services (DNS) is of utmost importance for the daily transactions taking place on the Internet. The performance of the DNS service may well form a bottleneck in these transactions since most of them require the DNS service invocation to complete prior to the actual application service. The SIN-based DNS service will act as a DNS proxy and pass on requests through the communication service if they cannot be resolved by the local cache.

The chosen strategies should aim to maximize the cache-hit rate, which is an easily measured number. Due to the diversity of requests during the complete orbital period, a single body of cached DNS entries of reasonable size is not expected to produce an acceptable hit rate. Due to the predictability of requests during the orbital period, ground stations may receive request statistics from recently passed areas and upload a selection of cache entries based on previously received statistics. Ground stations need to be interconnected in order to obtain this, and cache entry selection may well be subject to machine-learning algorithms.

This approach exploits the great variations in request traffic during the orbital period, and the ground stations should be located in less populated areas in order not to compete with traffic from ground terminals.

B. Conversational Service - SIP

As was mentioned in the introduction, a LEO spacecraft can offer a shorter RTT than most terrestrial paths, but requires that clients are served by the same spacecraft or by a short path of spacecrafts. This poses an interesting research problem, since client handover should happen in a synchronous manner to keep the path short.

A Voice-over-IP (VoIP) service depends on the Service Description Protocol/Session Initiation Protocol (SDP/SIP) protocols for signalling, but not for media traffic, which is typically handled by the Realtime Transport Protocol (RTP) protocol. The latency requirements will not be applied to the signalling phase, which can progress and finish in a relaxed manner, but the media transfer phase should benefit from the low latency offered by the SIN to enable applications like music rehearsals, remote control with video feedback etc.

A SIP server can be implemented in each satellite and will locate and connect VoIP users even on other parts for the SIN, as well as those connected to terrestrial SIP servers. SIP servers do not normally facilitate media traffic, but leave that to realtime-centric protocols like RTP. The perceived quality of the VoIP service relies more on the sound quality than the connection latency, and the properties of the IP communication services of the SIN becomes the most important factor.

Multi-part VoIP sessions identify the need for multicast services in the SIN. IP multicast is not a candidate technology, since the SIN is not an IP network. The link layer tunnelling technology used for the SIN infrastructure must be able to establish and maintain a forest of multicast trees in the presence of frequent handovers and relaying to endpoints in the IP-based terrestrial network. Multi-part VoIP has been researched in RFC4353, RFC4579 and, most detailed, in RFC5850 [8]. The latter identifies mechanisms for multicast endpoints, based on IP multicast protocols. Arrangements for multicast through L2 tunnels must be developed and implemented in the VoIP User Agent for the end systems directly connected to the SIP.

C. Storage Service - Content Delivery Network

Since the vast majority of web transactions are protected by the `https` protocol, traditional web caches do not offer any reduction in latency or traffic volume. Content Delivery Networks (CDN), however, works fine over https and offers improved web performance. Can a CDN be deployed in a SIN?

A CDN combines DNS and Hypertext Transfer Protocol (HTTP) services to provide content from the replica located closest to the client. One replica may be contained in the satellite above, and the DNS provided by the SIN will refer the client to its IP address if the content is to be found there.

Contrary to terrestrial CDN services, the CDN provided by the SIN will not benefit from the storage of localized information, since the satellite traverses the entire earth's surface. Ground stations may assist the satellites in loading information for the surface area ahead in its path, information which may be discarded at a later instant. The content of any CDN instance is therefore subject to speculative/proactive replication from ground stations based on demographic properties ahead, and possibly from leading satellites in the same orbital plane.

As earlier stated, the SIN satellites may share the same IP address. It simplifies the client configuration, and ongoing sessions (TCP connections etc.) with SIN services are not interrupted during a handover to another satellite. The CDN design is also simplified since the service will always be found on the same IP address. On the other hand, it is infeasible to give guarantees that the actual CDN instance under invocation contains the actual information object. This problem cannot be solved by the DNS service, and a form of request forwarding must be implemented in order to forward requests to supplementary CDN servers.

VII. Conclusion

The architecture principles of a service-oriented satellite network is the focus of this position paper. The contribution in the proposal is to take the cyclic properties of the orbit and a map of the population density into regard for the scheduling of traffic with ground stations and other satellites. A number of example services are discussed in more detail.

The conclusion from the initial analysis is that several established protocols will need modification in the User Agent software in the terrestrial clients, and that certain service qualities need to be chosen by the client user, e.g., the priority of mail messages. This is somewhat similar to the required modifications found in Delay Tolerant Systems.

Trust management has not been addressed in this article, which is an obvious requirements for the protection of data and separation of activities. Trust Management is being investigated and the results are subject for publishing in a future paper.

The satellite platform will need a Service Provider Interface in order for independent service providers to implement services in the satellites.

Other future research activities in this field of interest include machine-learning for workload prediction, optimization of replication activities, resource management and scalability analysis.

References

[1] "Gridded population of the world v.4.11," https://sedac.ciesin.columbia.edu/data/collection/gpw-v4/sets/browse, [Online; accessed 30-Aug-2021].

[2] "Starlink web site," https://www.starlink.com/, [Online; accessed 30-Aug-2021].

[3] S. Briatore, N. Garzaniti, and A. Golkar, "Towards the internet for space: Bringing cloud computing to space systems," in *36th International Communications Satellite Systems Conference (ICSSC 2018)*, 2018, pp. 1–5.

[4] S. Cao *et al.*, "Space-based cloud-fog computing architecture and its applications," in *2019 IEEE World Congress on Services (SERVICES)*, vol. 2642-939X, 2019, pp. 166–171.

[5] H. He, D. Zhou, M. Sheng, and J. Li, "Mission structure learning-based resource allocation in space information networks," in *ICC 2021 - IEEE International Conference on Communications*, 2021, pp. 1–6.

[6] X. Zhang, L. Zhu, T. Li, Y. Xia, and W. Zhuang, "Multiple-user transmission in space information networks: Architecture and key techniques," *IEEE Wireless Communications*, vol. 26, no. 2, pp. 17–23, 2019.

[7] Y. Su *et al.*, "Broadband leo satellite communications: Architectures and key technologies," *IEEE Wireless Communications*, vol. 26, no. 2, pp. 55–61, 2019.

[8] D. Petrie, J. Rosenberg, A. Johnston, R. Sparks, and R. Mahy, "A Call Control and Multi-Party Usage Framework for the Session Initiation Protocol (SIP)," https://rfc-editor.org/rfc/rfc5850.txt, May 2010, [Online; accessed 30-Aug-2021].

Optimal Scheduling with a Reliable Data Transfer Framework for Drone Inspections of Infrastructures

Golizheh Mehrooz and Peter Schneider-Kamp

Dept. of Mathematics & Computer Science
University of Southern Denmark
Odense, Denmark
email: mehrooz@imada.sdu.dk email: petersk@imada.sdu.dk

***Abstract*—Unmanned Aerial Vehicles (UAVs) or drones have gained a lot of interest due to their advantages for inspecting infrastructures. However, they have a limited flight time. In order to solve this problem, we designed a cloud server and analyzed a reliable communication link between the cloud server and the drones. Furthermore, we have proposed an optimal scheduling algorithm to assign an energy-efficient trajectory for the Internet of Drones applications of infrastructure inspection. An optimal scheduling algorithm based on extended OR-Tools as a travelling salesman problem solver is hosted as a Docker container in the cloud server. We implemented a framework and validated the quality aspect of the optimal scheduling algorithm along with the communication link between the cloud and the drones. The overall architecture of the designed platform is illustrated along with the static analysis of the communication link and scheduling algorithm.**

Keywords*—*UAV, Cloud server, ROS, Scheduling, Rosbridge.

I. INTRODUCTION

Drones, also called Unmanned Aerial Vehicles (UAVs), are defined as small aircraft, which are operated without a human pilot [1]. With the development of new technologies, drones have received an increasing amount of attention in various areas for automatizing labor-intensive tasks [2]. Likewise, new European Union regulations for drone inspections have eased the process of obtaining permission for inspecting the special case of linear infrastructures such as power pylons. These regulations require the drone to stay within close range to the linear infrastructure [3] [4]. Therefore, finding optimal routing and scheduling algorithms that minimize the flight time drones spend away from the immediate vicinity of the linear infrastructure [4] represents a highly relevant task. In this regards, designing a cloud-based platform, which includes a Python package for the optimal routing and scheduling solution for inspection drones, will improve the inspection speed, cost, accuracy, and safety.

For this reason, a considerable amount of research has been conducted in order to transfer data between the drone and the cloud server. In these scenarios, the data collected should be transferred to the cloud server, where they can later be aggregated and analyzed using specialized data processing algorithms [5]. In the work presented in this paper, we propose a novel Internet of Drones (IoD) data transfer framework for cloud-based applications. Data includes either navigational data for controlling drones or the images to be analyzed in the cloud by using customized machine learning algorithms to detect and explain outliers [6]. To transfer these data between the cloud and the drones, we utilize a reliable communication link named *Rosbridge* [7]. We analyze the communication delay by considering various data sizes. The main contributions of the work presented in this paper are as follows:

1) An optimal scheduling algorithm based on extended OR-Tools [8] as a Traveling Salesman Problem (TSP) solver for inspection drones along the linear infrastructure.
2) A system design and architecture framework for transferring data such as navigational data or the images from the drone to the cloud server and vice versa.
3) An analysis of *Rosbridge* for transferring various data sizes between the cloud and the drones.

Figure 1 illustrates the overall system architecture and design corresponding to contribution (2). As can be seen in the figure, the proposed framework has two layers. The first layer is the cloud server. The cloud server is based on containerizing applications by using Docker. The design further is divided into a frontend (i.e., OpenLayers) and a backend (i.e., Linear infrastructure Mission Control (LiMiC)).

LiMiC is implemented as a python package for solving the routing and scheduling problem. OpenLayers is used as an open-source frontend technology for designing a web interface to monitor and control drones. The Docker platform is used to accelerate the development process and scale applications with ease. The image processing service, which is also designed as a Docker container, hosts customized machine learning algorithms for analyzing the images along the infrastructure. Kubernetes is designed for managing the container applications. In addition, we use databases for storing data in the cloud server.

The second layer in Figure 1 (2) shows the Robot Operating System (ROS)/ROS2 as a drone control unit. This layer hosts ROS/ROS2 as a high-level software for the drone system. The communication link between the cloud server and the drone system is *Rosbridge* while the communication link between the users and the cloud server is Hyper Text Transfer Protocol (HTTP).

The paper unfolds as follows. In Section II, we summarize the background of the scheduling and IoD applications for

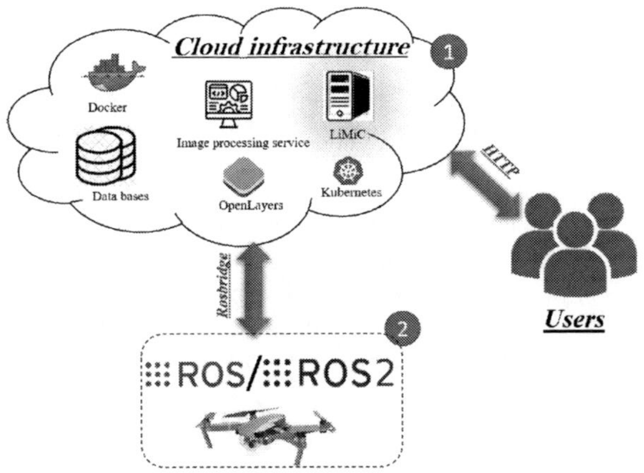

Figure 1. Overall system structure

drones inspection of linear infrastructure. In Section III, we explain the optimal multi-drone scheduling problem by using the extended OR-Tool. We measured the time of multi-drones scheduling in Fyn, Denmark. In Section IV, we analyze *Rosbridge* as a communication protocol for IoD applications. Sections V concludes this paper and presents directions for future research.

II. Related work

In this section, we explore the background of the communication link between the cloud server and the drone. We also investigate the optimal routing and scheduling algorithms for IoD applications.

A. Data Transfer framework for IoD applications

A variety of research and publications have been undertaken on different IoD applications for establishing a communication link between drones and the cloud server. In this regard, the widely used IoD protocols are *Rosbridge* [4], and HTTP [9].

The HTTP protocol is a popular communication protocol for Internet of Things (IoT) applications. It provides a request/reply mechanism for transferring data. HTTP implements four methods: GET, POST, PUT, and DELETE. In [10], the authors integrated drone resources as a web service into the cloud. In this scenario, the drone becomes part of the cloud server and can be accessed ubiquitously [10]. The authors have used RESTful HTTP components in their system architecture. They have used the HTTP GET method with the resource URI to retrieve the current energy level. In the work presented in this paper, we have also used HTTP protocol for communicating between the backend, e.g., LiMiC [4], and the web interface which is hosted in the cloud. The HTTP GET method in this paper is used to update the drone telemetry data on the web interface.

Rosbridge is another increasingly popular communication protocol. It provides a communication interface to application programs without venturing into the specialized world of robotics engineers [11]. *Rosbridge* acts as a middleware abstraction layer to access the applications programs that are not themselves robotics. A cloud-based web application that uses *Rosbridge* has gained a lot of interest for providing real-time flight data monitoring and management for Drones [12].

In [7], the authors designed and implemented a web interface for controlling and monitoring drone flight. They have used *Rosbridge* as a communication link between the cloud and the drone. They have analyzed the communication delay in their framework. However, they have not measured the communication delay for transferring large data such as images. Additionally, they have not considered the scheduling problem for multi-drones. In the work presented in this paper, we extended the previous work [4] [7] by considering the scheduling problem (extending LiMiC) and analyzing the delay time for transferring large data such as images.

B. Optimal Routing and Scheduling algorithm

The state of art of drone routing and scheduling mainly involves the TSP [13] and the Vehicle Routing Problem (VRP) [14]. TSP is the classic routing problem, in which there is just one vehicle, while the VRP is the generalization of TSP with multiple vehicles [8]. In VRP, each customer is served by exactly one vehicle [15]. Each vehicle starts the path from the start position, performs the task, and returns to the start position.

In [15], the authors considered the occurrences of failures that make drones unable to continue the flight. They have found that the amount of lost demand depends on the location where drones fail, such as failure at the beginning of the path or on the way back to the start position. In the work presented in this paper, inspection drones should not return to the start position. Furthermore, we have not considered the drone failures scenario because in the case of infrastructure inspection, if one drone fails it does not cause a significant disturbance of the overall inspection mission. The main reason is that, in real drone flight for inspections, they usually fly within a small distance from each other. Therefore, in the case of failure, another drone close to that location can cover the inspection task.

The Drone Scheduling Problem (DSP) aims to design a group of flight tours for the drones. In [16], the authors explain DSP to solve the problem of inspecting as many vessels as possible in a short time. In this regard, they have prioritized highly weighted vessels to be inspected first [16]. In the case of power pylons inspection, the main important parameter is the time due to the battery constraint on the drone. Therefore, our main goal in this work is to find the optimal scheduling solution in a short time for a group of drones.

III. Optimal Scheduling with Extended TSP solver

There are well-known developed solutions for the TSP that can solve a multitude of path planning problems. The goal of these algorithms is to find the shortest route (less costly path) for a salesman who needs to visit customers at different locations and return to the starting location.

OR-Tools [8] is an open-source software for solving the optimization problem for vehicle scheduling. In order to use

OR-Tools, we need to create data. The data include the number of drones and the distance matrix detailing the distance between any two locations under consideration, as well as the start and the end location for the route. In this paper, as we are not interested in the drone returning to the start location, we modify the distance matrix to 'trick' the solver. This comprises adding an extra row to the matrix with 0 values. This assumption does not contribute any additional cost to the path. For the case of power line inspections, the distance matrix is an array, in which i, j entry is the distance from pylon A to pylon B. The distance from pylon A to pylon B is calculated based on an extended A* algorithm as explained in [4]. In order to create a distance matrix without undue waste of computational time, we use the fact that the distance from pylon A to pylon B is the same as the distance from pylon B to pylon A. Therefore, we have a symmetric distance matrix as it is shown in Figure 2. Here, the pairs marked in red have a reverse-ordered counterpart, which implies that we can skip the calculation of these pairs.

	A	B	C	D
A	AA	AB	AC	AD
B	BA	BB	BC	BD
C	CA	CB	CC	CD
D	DA	DB	DC	DD

Figure 2. Symmetric matrix with repeated pairs marked

OR-Tools offers two general approaches for scheduling problems such as the *first solution strategies* and the *meta-heuristic strategies*. The *first solution strategies* are designed to find a single path between all points. This approach is a fast method for finding the optimal route. The *meta-heuristic strategies* are slower than the *first solution strategies* in general but more reliable at finding the optimal route. The advantage of using the *meta-heuristic strategies* is that, its potential to avoid local minima, which the *first strategies* often end up in.

We have measured the scheduling time for 10 power pylons in Denmark by using the above approaches for a single drone. The scheduling using the *first solution strategies* takes **0.45** seconds while the scheduling time using the *meta-heuristic strategies* takes **2.49** seconds. We have also performed multi-drone scheduling by using the *meta-heuristic strategies*. We considered 5-10 power pylons on Fyn (Denmark). Figure 3 illustrates the results.

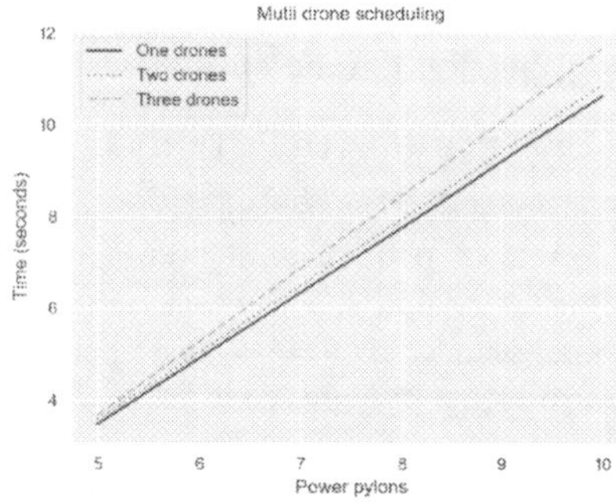

Figure 3. Multi-drone scheduling in Fyn (Denmark)

As can be observed in this figure, there is a linear relationship between the time and number of the power pylons. By increasing the number of power pylons calculation, time is also increased to a similar degree. However, there is a slight difference of scheduling times to be noted for different numbers of drones. We can, thus, conclude that the calculation time increases linearly with the number of power pylons. The reason is, unsurprisingly, that data matrix for solving the scheduling problem for 10 power pylons has more rows and columns compared with the data matrix with 5 power pylons.

IV. Data Transfer Framework

In this section, we demonstrate a framework for transferring large data such as images from the drone to the cloud and vice versa. We have also analyzed the communication delay for transferring data of various sizes between the cloud and the drones. Figure 4 illustrates the overall drone-cloud based framework corresponding to Figure 1.

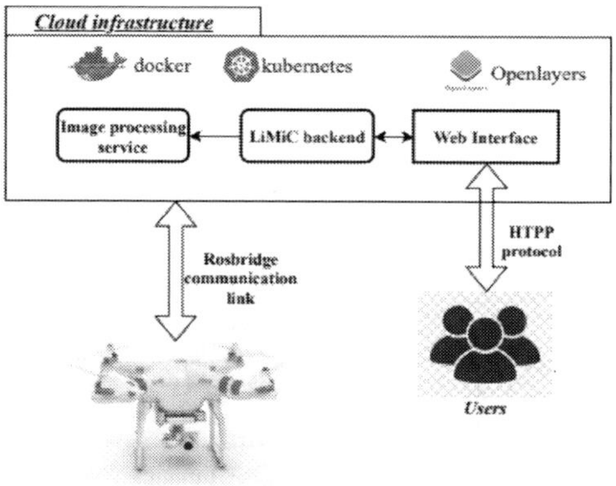

Figure 4. Overall system communication framework

As can be seen from this figure, we have used various technologies such as Docker [7] for containerizing applications, Kubernetes [7] for scaling and managing container applications, and OpenLayers [4] for designing the web interface. We have also implemented different services such as an image processing service, LiMiC, and the web interface. The image processing service is designed for applying machine learning algorithms on the images. It is implemented as a Docker container. LiMiC is designed as a backend service for solving optimal routing and scheduling problems. The web interface is implemented as a frontend service for controlling and monitoring drone flight.

The communication link between the cloud server and the drones is provided by *Rosbridge*, while the communication link between the cloud server and users uses HTTP. In this regard, as an example, the user sends the HTTP GET request to the server to get the drone's battery status. In this paper, we have measured the *Rosbridge* communication delay for various data sizes such as images. Figure 5 demonstrates the results.

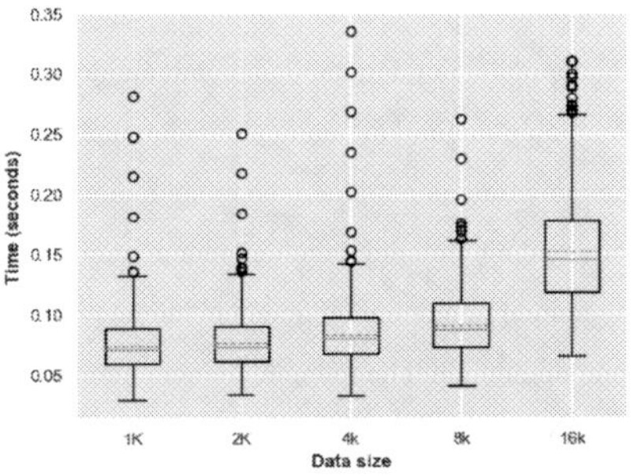

(a) Small data size

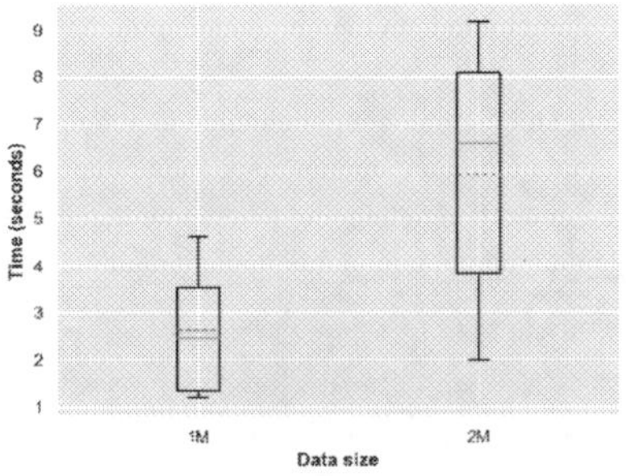

(b) Large data size

Figure 5. Data transferring delay time

As clearly can be seen in Figure 5(a), the average time for transferring data in the range of 1KByte to 8Kbyte range from 0.07 to 0.09 seconds. Therefore, there is only a slightly and statistically likely insignificant difference for transferring data in this ranges. However, the time for transferring 16KByte data is close to double the time for transferring 8KByte.

Figure 5(b) illustrates the data transfer delay for large data sizes, particularly 1MByte and 2MByte. As can be seen in this figure, there is a significant increase in the delay for transferring 1MByte data compared 2Mbyte data from **2.5** seconds to **6** seconds on average. Generally, we can conclude that the communication delay time over the *Rosbridge* protocol for small data sizes is within the range of **0.05** seconds to **0.10** seconds, however, for large data size, it is increased to more than double from **2.5** seconds to **6** seconds on average. We have not been able to fully explain this statistically significant non-linear increase in delay time. However, wireless network communication performance can also be considered as an important factor for this non-linear significant increase in this data range.

V. Conclusion

This paper proposed an algorithm for optimal scheduling and a communication link between the drones and the cloud server for IoD applications of linear infrastructure inspection. *Rosbridge* is designed as a communication link between the cloud server and the ROS. We analyzed the *Rosbridge* communication delay time by measuring the transfer time and delays for different data sizes.

The cloud server has been designed based on containerizing applications by using Docker and includes LiMiC. The LiMiC has been extended for solving the optimal routing and scheduling problem. We have implemented an optimal scheduling algorithm with the extended OR-Tools algorithm as a TSP solver for inspection drones along linear infrastructures. We have investigated two general approaches for scheduling such as the *first strategies* and the *meta-heuristic strategies.* We have also analyzed multi-drones scheduling times with *meta-heuristic strategies*.

Future work could be to implement Data Distribution Service (DDS) in ROS2 for providing the communication link between the cloud server and the drones. Furthermore, we could consider using secure channel such as HTTPS instead of simple HTTP.

Acknowledgement

The research leading to these results has received funding from the Innovation Fund Denmark Grand Solutions grant 8057-00038A Drones4Energy project.

References

[1] F. Li, S. Zlatanova, M. Koopman, X. Bai, and A. Diakité, "Universal path planning for an indoor drone," *Automation in Construction*, vol. 95, pp. 275 – 283, 2018.

[2] E. Es Yurek and H. C. Ozmutlu, "A decomposition-based iterative optimization algorithm for traveling salesman problem with drone," *Transportation Research Part C: Emerging Technologies*, vol. 91, pp. 249 – 262, 2018.

[3] Energy world, "Utilities in europe to use long-distance drones to inspect transmission liness," Available: https://energy.economictimes.indiatimes.com/news/power/utilities-in-europe-to-use-long-distance-drones-to-inspect-transmission-lines/65007676?redirect=1, 10 2021.

[4] G. Mehrooz and P. Schneider-Kamp, "Optimal path planning for drone inspections of linear infrastructures." in *GISTAM*, 2020, pp. 326–336.

[5] R. Montella, M. Ruggieri, and S. Kosta, "A fast, secure, reliable, and resilient data transfer framework for pervasive iot applications," in *IEEE INFOCOM 2018 - IEEE Conference on Computer Communications Workshops (INFOCOM WKSHPS)*, 2018, pp. 710–715.

[6] J. H. Sejr and A. Schneider-Kamp, "Explainable outlier detection: What, for whom and why?" *Machine Learning with Applications*, 2021.

[7] G. Mehrooz and P. Schneider-Kamp, "Web application for planning, monitoring, and controlling autonomous inspection drones," in *Mediterranean Conference on Embedded Computing (MECO)*, 2021, pp. 1–6.

[8] Google OR-Tools, "Traveling sale man problem," Available: https://developers.google.com/optimization/routing/tsp.

[9] B. Mah, "An empirical model of http network traffic," in *Proceedings of INFOCOM '97*, 1997, pp. 592–600.

[10] S. Mahmoud, N. Mohamed, and J. Al-Jaroodi, "Integrating uavs into the cloud using the concept of the web of things," *Journal of Robotics*, vol. 2015, June 2015.

[11] C. Crick, G. Jay, S. Osentoski, and O. C. Jenkins, "Ros and rosbridge: Roboticists out of the loop," in *2012 7th ACM/IEEE International Conference on Human-Robot Interaction (HRI)*, 2012, pp. 493–494.

[12] S. Sarkar, M. W. Totaro, and K. Elgazzar, "Leveraging the cloud to achieve near real-time processing for drone-generated data," in *2019 IEEE Women in Engineering (WIE) Forum USA East*, 2019, pp. 1–6.

[13] R. Rasmussen, "Tsp in spreadsheets—a fast and flexible tool," *Omega*, no. 1, pp. 51 – 63, 2011.

[14] C. Prins, "A simple and effective evolutionary algorithm for the vehicle routing problem," *Computers and Operations Research*, vol. 31, no. 12, pp. 1985–2002, 2004.

[15] M. Torabbeigi, G. Lim, and S. J. Kim, "Drone delivery schedule optimization considering the reliability of drones," in *International Conference on Unmanned Aircraft Systems*, 06 2018, pp. 1048–1053.

[16] J. Xia, K. Wang, and S. Wang, "Drone scheduling to monitor vessels in emission control areas," *Transportation Research Part B: Methodological*, vol. 119, pp. 174–196, 2019.